MINISTRY AND SPIRITUALITY

.

Henri J. M. Nouwen

·

MINISTRY AND SPIRITUALITY

Creative Ministry

The Wounded Healer

Reaching Out

·

A Dayspring Edition

CONTINUUM · NEW YORK

1996
The Continuum Publishing Company
370 Lexington Avenue
New York, NY 10017

Printed in the United States of America.

Library of Congress Catalog Card Number: 96-084430
ISBN: 0-8264-0910-5

Contents

■

PREFACE

THE THREE BOOKS brought together in this volume, *Creative Ministry,*
The Wounded Healer, and *Reaching Out,* were written between 1969 and
1974. This was a time of transition for me, during which I came to the
definite decision to move from the Netherlands to the United States. For a
long time, I had been convinced that it was my vocation to live and work
as a priest of the Diocese of Utrecht in Holland and that my times of study
and teaching in the United States were a preparation for my ministry there.
Only after much traveling back and forth, long debates, and many inner
struggles did I come to the conclusion that I could fulfill my vocation better
in the United States than in Holland.

In retrospect I realize that much that happened to me during those years
helped me to articulate the spirituality which is expressed in these books,
especially in *The Wounded Healer* and *Reaching Out.* I experienced an intense
loneliness, often felt like a stranger in a strange land, yearned for friendships,
wondered about the meaning of my vocation, questioned long-held beliefs,
and searched for a sense of belonging. All these inner stirrings forced me
to develop a new spirituality that would allow me to live this time of
transition in a creative way and to make it an occasion for spiritual growth.

My psychological and theological formation, as well as my opportunity
to teach in Europe and the United States, made it possible for me to develop
a somewhat systematic approach to the very personal problems I was dealing
with. I discovered the truth of Carl Rogers's conviction that what is most
personal is most universal.

I am deeply grateful for the many encouraging responses to these three
books that I have received over the past twenty-five years. These responses
helped me to trust that what I am living day by day is not just important
for me but also of potential value to others. I gradually came to a new
understanding of the call of Jesus to lay down my life for my friends. Maybe
all my education was finally meant to give expression to the human search
for a true home, a search that was intimately my own.

Although these three books clearly reflect the spirit of the late sixties and early seventies when they were written, as well as my own male-dominated language at that time, I realize that the main concerns they raise are still very much with me today. The search for a spirituality based on a deep communion with God, a nurturing community with our fellow travelers and a creative ministry to the poor is already central in these books and remains so today.

I am deeply grateful to Susan Brown for critically reading these texts and making the language more inclusive and expansive without changing its original intent.

It fills me with great joy that, many years after this difficult time of transition, the books that are its fruits can still be a source of comfort and inner healing.

I very much hope that this beautiful edition will minister to many friends and fellow travelers.

Henri J. M. Nouwen
1996

CREATIVE
MINISTRY

∎

To Seward, Helen,
and Anne Hiltner
in memory of
James Seward Hiltner

Jesus said to Simon Peter:

When you were young
you put on your own belt
and walked where you liked;
but when you grow old
you will stretch out your hands
and somebody else will put a belt round you
and take you where you would rather not go.

(John 21:18)

ACKNOWLEDGMENTS

∎

THIS BOOK WOULD never have been started without the stimulation of the summer school students of the University of Notre Dame, who by their enthusiasm encouraged me to write and keep writing during six hot weeks, and who convinced me that spirituality can be discussed with a sense of humor. This book would never have been finished, however, without the honest and straightforward criticism of the Chicago priests, which made me rethink different issues and rewrite different chapters.

I owe much to the members of the Moreau Community for their hospitality, expressed not only by offering a quiet room in which to write but also by supportive friendship when writing did not seem very easy. I am especially thankful to Louis Putz for making me feel at home, to Jim Buckley for his constant help, and to Bob Antonelli for his personal interest, which made me beat the deadlines.

I also want to express my deep appreciation to Charles Sheedy and Jim Burtchaell for their invitation to give the lectures, to Jack Egan and Don McNeill for their valuable suggestion for corrections, and to Betty Bartelme for her skillful help during the final stages of the manuscript.

I am very thankful to Rita Gorkowski and Carolyn Dalsgaard, who spent many hours typing and retyping the manuscript, and to Jeff Sobosan, who was so generous as to interrupt his own writing to reshape quite a few of my crooked sentences.

The Frank J. Lewis Foundation, sponsor of the pastoral theology program at the University of Notre Dame, offered the financial support for the preparation of this text.

I have dedicated this book to Seward Hiltner, teacher and friend, who introduced me into the field of pastoral theology; to his wife, Helen, and daughter, Anne, who taught me much through their friendship and trust; and to his son, James Seward, who made me realize that the length of life is less important than the intensity and sincerity with which it is lived.

CONTENTS

■

INTRODUCTION

·

Beyond Professionalism

THE MAIN CONCERN of this book is the relationship between professionalism and spirituality in the ministry. Since many very concrete experiences
and events made my interest in this relationship grow, I would like to start
with one of the cases that will illustrate the theme that runs through the
following chapters.

One day during the past year a parish priest presented to a small group
of pastors, of which I was a member, a report of his hospital visit to a
twenty-six-year-old married woman who suffered from the fatal Hodgkin's
disease. The priest, a very intelligent pastor, was quite aware of the fact that
this young woman would never leave the hospital and that she probably
would die within the coming year. He brought the report of his pastoral
visit to the group because he wanted to consult his fellow ministers about
how to be of real help to his parishioner in the months ahead.

He described the young woman as a very happy, open person with a
good sense of humor and full of energy. He wrote down parts of his conversation with her, word for word as far as he could remember, and concluded
with the honest confession that he had felt extremely nervous during the
visit and very uneasy and dissatisfied as he had left her alone on the ward.

When we studied this pastoral visit more closely the conversation between
the priest and his sick parishioner gave the impression of a long and painful
attempt to avoid the reality that a very attractive young woman was soon
going to die. They talked about the nurses, the food, the pains, the possibility of getting some sleep, and a great deal about how things would be later
when she would be home again. It was obvious that the pastor himself was
hardly aware of his avoiding the real issue; but in reading his own report
over and over again, he discovered what really had taken place, and during

17

the discussion with his colleagues it was possible for him to become aware that he probably could have been of more help to this woman if he had known a little more about pastoral care for a dying patient.

But then, somewhat surprisingly, one of the group members asked the priest, "Say—I wonder if you are really aware of the fact that *you* are going to die, too, perhaps not within a year but in any case pretty soon." Suddenly, all the discussions about skillful pastoral care stopped and there was a long silence. Then the priest said: "Perhaps not—perhaps I am more afraid to talk about death than my parishioner is, and perhaps I do not want her to remind me of my own mortality. . . ."

This response gave a dramatic shift to our "professional" discussion and made us more and more aware of the fact that those of us who want to be real ministers to dying patients can never be so when we have not been able to face our own deaths and relate in a Christian way to death's undeniable reality. And it did not take long to realize that the question about ministry was intimately related to the question about the spiritual life of the minister.

This is only one of the many examples that have made me ask if spiritual guidance and professional formation in the ministry are not so closely related that any separation will, in the long run, do harm to both aspects of the daily life of the man or woman who wants to be of Christian service to others.

Perhaps we have to say that one of the main reasons for the many frustrations, pains, and disappointments in the lives of numerous Christian ministers is rooted in the still-growing separation between professionalism and spirituality. However, this separation is quite understandable if we look at the development of theological education during the last decade.

First of all, many seminaries have given up the routine of the spiritual exercises that structured the daily lives of the students who wanted to prepare themselves for the ministry. Daily hours of meditation, recitations of long prayers, and regular services were often forced upon students as an essential condition for the saintly life at which they were asked to aim. Often it was suggested that only through this prayer life could one protect oneself from the many dangers of the great world, and that no minister would succeed in the long run if he or she were not faithful to what generations of ministers had found to be a support in their busy lives.

But, when times changed and the lives of ministers developed in new ways, it became less and less obvious how the many hours of piety were related to the daily concerns of parish life. Ministers began to feel that prayer was more and more experienced as an escape into the safety of the interior life and a way of avoiding the burning issues that should stir the Christian conscience and be a challenge to engage in creative action. They would say:

"Let us not close our eyes in order to indulge in nice and gratifying thoughts about God and God's mysteries, but let us keep them open to the growing needs of the world around us. Why spend our time in rather dull and fruitless hours of meditation and contemplation when we could use our time better to train ourselves in the necessary skills and techniques that help us to be of real service to our brothers and sisters?" It is no wonder that chapels became less popular places to visit and spiritual directors had fewer clients, and that, instead, much more attention was paid to supervised pastoral training in hospitals, prisons, parishes, and special city projects.

But there is another story, too, usually told by those ministers who for many years have been deeply immersed in the activities, worries, and concerns of the daily life of their congregations or neighborhoods. The multiformity of their work, the different forms of activities they became involved in, the great variety of persons they met, and the broad range of problems they touched finally made them wonder how they could live a unified life under such conditions and how their own most personal integrity could be maintained in the middle of so many contrasting stimuli. Many of these ministers have given so much of themselves in their daily, often very demanding, pastoral activities that they feel empty, exhausted, tired, and quite often disappointed.

This fatigue strikes so hard because thanks are rarely expressed, progress is seldom obvious, and results not often visible. Even when one knows how to be a good counselor and how to respond meaningfully to the needs of individuals and groups, even when one is fully prepared to be an agent of social change, the most burning question remains: "What moves me to do all this; where do I gain the strength to find unity in all my diverse activities; how can I obtain the strength that helps me to be like Paul, who, in the middle of all his adventures, kept himself one through his unshakable faith in Christ?"

Going back to regular prayers? Spending more time with the reading of the Scriptures? More meditation and hours of silence? Days of recollection? Retreats? Many have tried these but felt lost. It seemed as if they were saying: "If I cannot find God in the middle of my work—where my concerns and worries, pains and joys are—it does not make sense to try to find God's Spirit in the hours set free at the periphery of my life. If my spiritual life cannot grow and deepen in the midst of my ministry, how will it ever grow on the edges?"

The question that seems to come up more and more in the circles of those who want to dedicate their lives to the Christian ministry is the one that lies beyond professionalism. There is hardly a doubt any longer that being a minister calls for careful preparation, not only in terms of the knowledge and understanding of God's Word but also in terms of the ministerial relationships through which God's Word comes to human beings. Just as doctors, psychologists, psychiatrists, and social workers need special skills to be of real help to others, so priests or ministers will never be able to fulfill their tasks in a responsible way without the necessary training in the core functions of ministry, such as preaching, teaching, caring, organizing, and celebrating. Pastoral training centers have provided many priests and ministers with the necessary professional preparation and offered them many ways to make their work more satisfying, meaningful, and effective.

But although the main concern of ministers over the last years has been to find a place in the row of various helping professions, the question that is brought to their minds with an increasing urgency is: "What is there beyond professionalism—is ministry just another specialty in the many helping professions?" This question comes to the foreground again at a time when young students are questioning the value of the complicated distinctions between academic disciplines and are trying to come to terms with what is central and unifying in their lives.

During the last few years I have become overwhelmingly impressed by the fact that priests, ministers, and theological students who asked for supervision in their pastoral work were asking questions that went far beyond their professional concerns. In the beginning the emphasis quite often was on the best technique, the most appropriate method, the most effective approach: "How do I preach to a church congregation in a language that will make me understood? How can I be of help to a husband and wife struggling with marriage conflicts? How do I assist a dying patient? How do I behave when my community requires me to protest against the housing situation, wants me to work to alleviate poverty, or fight segregation and social injustice? Should I remain nonviolent at all cost, or is there a time when violence might be the only ethical response?"

These questions are extremely important and call for intelligent discussions, careful research, and, often, long training under competent supervision.

But these questions are not the last ones and not the most decisive. Sometimes it even seems that underneath all these concerns is the question about the spirituality of the man or woman who raises them. Many students and trainees are struggling with their own sense of being. Long before they can ask themselves how to preach the Gospel to others, they find themselves struggling with confusing questions: "Who is God to me? Does Jesus Christ really motivate my life? How do I think about my own life and death? What do I really have to do with my neighbors? Is it my desire, task, or vocation to intervene in anyone's life at all? Should I speak about love when I question in my own heart that love is a possibility? Why read, talk, and teach about prayer when I have never really experienced much of anything that deserves this title?"

These questions are not phrased in this very explicit way, but during the discussion of sermons, pastoral visits to sick people, religion classes, or any other ministerial task, I found that these questions are, knowingly or unknowingly, at the base of many frustrations for today's ministers. And even if it is perhaps possible for doctors to cure patients even when the doctors hardly believe in the value of life, Christian ministers will never be able to be ministers if their own most personal faith and insight into life do not form the core of their pastoral work.

So, ministry and spirituality never can be separated. Ministry is not an eight-to-five job but primarily a way of life, which is for others to see and understand so that liberation can become a possibility.

There is today a great hunger for a spirituality that is a new experience of God in our own lives. This experience is essential for every minister but cannot be found outside the limits of ministry. It must be possible to find the seeds of this new spirituality right in the center of the Christian service. Prayer is not a preparation for work or an indispensable condition for effective ministry. Prayer is life; prayer and ministry are the same and can never be divorced. If they are, the minister becomes a fixer-upper and the priesthood nothing more than another way to soften the many pains of daily life.

If the desire for silence, for moments of contemplation and meditation, is not born out of our concern for this world, we will soon become bored, not understanding why we have to be subjected to so many pious exercises. If God does not become more and more living to those who minister to the people of God every day, God will not be found in the desert, the convent, or the silent hours either. If professionalism is to be prevented from degenerating into a form of clerical manipulation, it has to be founded on the deep-rooted spiritual lives of ministers as their spirituality develops out of their constant care for those they work with.

This is the main thrust of the following chapters. I hope to be able to show through the analysis of the five main functions of the ministry—teaching, preaching, individual pastoral care, organizing, and celebrating—the seeds of a spirituality for every man and woman who wants to be of service.

It will become clear that every Christian is a minister. The ordained ministry can be considered as a focus since ordained ministers give the most visible shape to the different forms of Christian service. Therefore, the words "minister" and "priest" are often used in the following chapters. But what is true for ministers and priests in the formal sense is true for every man and woman who wants to live in the light of the Gospel of Jesus Christ. Therefore, in essence, this book is about the lifestyle of every Christian.

1

BEYOND THE TRANSFERENCE
OF KNOWLEDGE

■

Teaching

From a Violent to a
Redemptive Way of Learning

Introduction

THERE WAS A TIME when God sent angels from heaven with an urgent message for us on earth. And they are still coming. A few months ago a Vietnamese Buddhist monk came to Holland, and one day he walked into the house where I lived. He was a thin, slender man whom you would be afraid to touch. But his clear, fearless eyes radiated an insight so deeply impregnated with affection that the only thing you could hope for was understanding. While he looked straight into my eyes he said: "There was a man on a horse galloping swiftly along the road. An old farmer standing in the fields, seeing him pass by, called out, 'Hey, rider, where are you going?' The rider turned around and shouted back, 'Don't ask me, just ask my horse!'"

The monk looked at me and said: "That is your condition. You are no longer master over your own destiny. You have lost control over the great powers that pull you forward toward an unknown direction. You have become a passive victim of an ongoing movement which you do not understand." It seemed as if he carved his message on my skin like a tattoo and then asked me to let it be seen wherever I go.

When we look at the situation of those who teach and those who are taught, the same question comes to mind: Do teachers and students really know where their horses are going?

Students are men and women who are supposed to be in the exceptional situation that allows them to reflect on themselves and their society under the guidance of competent teachers. They have set aside a certain amount of time in their lives to look explicitly at their own condition and at the condition of the world in which they live in the hope of being better able to understand and act accordingly.

But when we realize that today a "school" is no longer a "schola," which means free time, but has become a highly complex industry that prepares students for an even more complex society, we might become receptive to the words of the Vietnamese Buddhist monk. If teaching means providing people with enough academic weapons to outdo others, to make more money, to have better careers, and more esteem in their neighborhoods, we had better start asking ourselves if there is any word from God that supports this approach.

The most universal and most appreciated role of the Christian ministry through the ages has been teaching. Wherever Christians went to be of service, they always considered teaching as one of their primary tasks because of their conviction that increasing insight in human beings and our world is the way to new freedom and new ways of life. And although Christian churches frequently failed to live up to this conviction, even prevented the free growth of science and limited the fearless search for new fields of knowledge, they have always read in the Gospel a call to develop human potentialities to the fullest through ongoing education.

The ministry of teaching has never limited itself, therefore, to the teaching of religion. Education is not primarily ministry because of what is taught but because of the nature of the educational process itself. Perhaps we have paid too much attention to the content of teaching without realizing that the teaching relationship is the most important factor in the ministry of teaching.

In this perspective, I raise the question: What do those who call themselves teachers or students really claim to be when they look at themselves in the light of the Gospel of Jesus Christ? In order to respond meaningfully to this question, I would like to describe two basic models of teaching—the violent model and the redemptive model—and then explicate the main resistances against learning.

By speaking in models, I will never do justice to individual teachers. I am not trying to. I only hope to map out basic structures that can help us to discover where we ourselves are and in which direction we want to go.

I. Teaching as a Violent Process

If we look at the overall educational situation today it seems as if students are constantly confronted with the complicated problems of their world and almost daily presented with new skills, methods, and techniques to get these problems under control. In fields like medicine, sociology, psychology, chemistry, biology, economics, and even theology, there is an amazing preoccupation with manipulative devices and the degree to which they satisfy immediate needs, relate to urgent problems, and keep an acceptable balance in the style of our lives. "Getting things under control" is what keeps most teachers and students busy, and a successful teacher is often the individual who creates the conviction that students have the necessary tools to tame the dangerous lions they are going to face as soon as they leave the training field.

As long as teaching takes place in this context it is doomed to be a violent process and evoke a vicious cycle of action and reaction in which students face their world as new territory that has to be conquered but is filled with enemies unwilling to be overruled by strangers. The teacher who enters this arena is forced to enter into a process which by its nature is competitive, unilateral, and alienating. In short: violent.

Let us have a closer look at these three characteristics of teaching as a violent process.

1. Competitive

Competition has become one of the most pervasive and also destructive aspects of modern education. The way students look at their fellow students and their teachers, the way they expect their grades and degrees, the way they prepare their exams and take them, the way they apply to college and graduate school, and even the way they spend their free time; all these areas and many more are impregnated by an all-embracing sense of rivalry. You only have to walk during the last week of a semester on a college campus to pick up the mysterious A-B-C-D-and-F language that seems to be on everyone's lips. The sadness of all this becomes clear when you see that students are only happy with high grades when they are sure that their fellow students have lower grades. It is obvious that in a system that encourages this ongoing competition, knowledge no longer is a gift that should be shared but a property that should be defended.

Students who are aware of the fact that all their accomplishments, not only academic but athletic and social accomplishments as well, will be compared with those of others, and who realize that their grades will decide their further schooling, their future jobs, and even their military status, understandably can easily become victims of a paralyzing fear.

This fear makes many students oversensitive to the reactions of their friends and teachers. This fear makes them extremely self-conscious, highly defensive in their relationships with others, constantly concerned about the possibility of failure, and very hesitant to take any risks or do anything unexpected. Often this fear becomes the unaccepted ruler over everything they write, say, or even think. Through this fear, competition has become the great preventive in students' free development of their total personalities.

To show how deeply this competition has permeated the educational system, I would like to take a closer look at one of the teaching methods, which at first glance seems to be least competitive, the classroom discussion.

When you enter a college classroom you will see that discussions have become an important part of modern education. The presupposition is that students learn more through discussion than through the absorption of ready-made information.

But is this always true? Quite often a closer analysis of an ongoing discussion shows that what in fact is happening is a sort of intellectual battle from which people tend to return more closed-minded than when they entered it. Students sitting around the table, asking questions of their teacher, or phrasing their ideas and opinions before each other, are often more like soldiers charging with rifles than like friends shaking hands.

Quite often the process goes like this: A student enters into the discussion without knowing much about the subject to be discussed, but with both a desire to know more about it and a fear of showing his ignorance. As soon as someone states an opinion, the most common reaction is not the internal question: "How can I understand *her* opinion better?" but "What is *my* opinion?" So, too, does silence often mean an occasion more to prepare an answer than to enter the train of thought of the other. And once two, three, or more opinions are stated the primary concern becomes defense of the chosen position, even when it is hardly worth defending.

And so we see how after a while people try to convince themselves and others of ideas that in the beginning they hardly wanted to consider as their own—ideas that were only meant as hesitant attempts to participate in an exchange of thoughts. And how could it be different when teachers are looked upon as those who are going to tell students, sooner or later, how much they are worth and when fellow students are rivals in the big fight for academic survival? Who wants to be weak and vulnerable in such a situation? More important, who can really learn in this way?

2. Unilateral

The second characteristic of the violent form of teaching is that it is, in the final analysis, a unilateral process. Even the many discussion methods, which suggest that people learn from each other, can quite often be easily unmasked as simply more acceptable ways to get a definitive message across or to sell a so-called indispensable product. And when different forms of discussion prove to be not much more than cheap methods of advertisement, it is not so surprising that many students become quickly irritated by them, complain that they do not learn from them, and prefer straight lectures—which at least dispense with reading another book.

This all goes to say that underneath many methods of teaching is still the prevailing supposition that someone is competent and someone else is not and that the whole game is to try to make the one just as or nearly as competent as the other. When this ideal is realized, the teacher is no longer considered as a teacher and the student as a student, and both can depart with not much more accomplished than the ability to tell stories about each other as an entertainment in their later years.

In this context teachers are strong: They know and should know. Students, however, are weak: They do not know and should want to know. The whole movement, therefore, is from teacher to student, from the strong to the weak, from one who knows to one who does not yet know. It is basically a unilateral process.

3. Alienating

Finally, the violent process of teaching is alienating because the eyes of the students are directed outwards, away from themselves and their direct relationships into the future, where the real things are supposed to happen. School, then, comes to be seen as only a preparation for later life, for the "real" life. One day the classroom will at last be left behind, the books will be closed, the teacher forgotten, and life can begin. School is just an indoor training, a dry swim, a quasi life. It is not surprising, therefore, that many students are bored and tired during class, are killing time by anxiously waiting until the bell rings and they can start doing as they please. Nor is it so strange that many say they have nothing or little to do with what happens at school and must go by blind faith that one day they will be thankful for the knowledge they received.

It is not so strange, then, that many teachers are looked upon as belonging to a world that is not the world of the students and that a hidden hostility often grows from this, expressing itself in a total lack of thankfulness towards those who have given much of their time, energy, and concern to prepare students for society.

This whole process is alienating because neither students nor teachers have been able to express their own individuality or use their regular relationships with each other as a primary source of learning. They have been pulled away from their own experiences; they are staring into the horizon expecting something to appear there, while at the same time they have become blind to what is happening right in front of them.

When many people spend about twenty years in school, it can be asked how valuable their lives have been if they should die at the end of those twenty years. Do those years serve only as a preparation for another twenty years, which, in their turn, have to make possible a final twenty years of retirement? But when people do not really live here and now, why should they look forward to living somewhere else later? This is the core of alienation, a reality that is all too visible in the lives of many students and teachers.

We have now described the violent process of teaching as one that is competitive, unilateral, and alienating. While it might never be found in its total naked destructiveness, it should, nonetheless, be clear that elements of it can be detected in many of our contemporary educational methods.

Now we are ready to look at an alternative model, which I have called "redemptive." I would hope that the foregoing elaboration has created the desire to hear more about it.

II. *Teaching as a Redemptive Process*

If it is true that in many instances we have become the passive victims of an educational process whose impact on us we can hardly appreciate, it is imperative that we ask what exactly has happened to us. As my first general impression, I suspect that we too often have lost contact with the source of our own existence and have become strangers in our own houses. We tend to run around trying to solve the problems of our world while anxiously avoiding confrontation with that reality wherein our problems find their deepest roots: our selves. In many ways we are like the busy people who walk up to a precious flower and say: "What for God's sake are you doing here? Can't you get busy some way?" and then find themselves unable to understand the flower's response: "I am sorry, but I am just here to be beautiful."

How can we also come to this wisdom of the flower that being is more important than doing? How can we come to a creative contact with the grounding of our own lives? Only through a teacher who can lead us to the source of our existence by showing us who we are and, thereby, what we are to do.

But where are these teachers? Some people think we have lost our real teachers and live in a time without wise guides. But is that really so? Or should we say that there are no teachers because there are no students? Teachers can only become teachers when there are students who allow them to be their teachers, and students can only become students when there are teachers who allow them to be their students. Only through this mutual acceptance can they enter into a teacher-student relationship that can be described as redemptive. In contrast to the violent form of teaching—which is competitive, unilateral, and alienating—therefore, the redemptive form of teaching can be described as evocative, bilateral, and actualizing. Let us examine these characteristics more closely.

1. Evocative

The first characteristic of a redemptive teacher-student relationship is that each tries to evoke in the other her or his respective potentials and make them available. When students really want to have teachers they have to give them the freedom to become teachers by offering their own life experiences as a source of insight and understanding. Only the students who allow access to their own life experiences can evoke in someone the possibility of becoming a real teacher. In this sense teachers depend completely on students, who have to give trust, confidence, and friendship, who have to share their weaknesses and strengths, their desires and needs.

Do not conclude too quickly that this is unrealistic. There are, in fact, classrooms in which discussions become evocative forms of learning, and students are able to offer their own experiences to their teachers and fellow students in order to facilitate a deeper understanding. In such cases, instead of the famous "Yes-but" dialogue, you will hear "Tell me more" or "That reminds me of" or "To that I could add something." Competition is absent and the teacher no longer is the fearful judge but the one to whom is given the opportunity to be teacher and the one who can invite students to become more and more accessible to learning.

Perhaps teachers cannot be true teachers unless they are also to a certain degree friends. In other words, when Jesus said to his disciples: "I shall no longer call you servants . . . I call you friends" (Jn 15:15), he became in truth their real teacher because all fear was overcome and real learning could begin.

2. Bilateral

The second characteristic of a redemptive teaching relationship is that it is bilateral. This means that not only do the students have to learn from their teachers but, conversely, the teachers have to learn from their students. When teachers are not willing to become students and to allow their students to be their teachers, they will never be able to make their teaching a redemptive process. Teachers and students are together searching for what is true, meaningful, and valid, and they should give each other the chance to play each other's roles.

Few teachers, however, feel free enough to allow their students to know more than they, let alone to leave their students free enough that they can learn from them. They tend to think that they lose respect and esteem when they allow their students to guide them and, in so doing, fail to realize that it is exactly this freedom that will create the relationship by which they will be able to redeem their students from their fears and give them the freedom to grow. In this process, moreover, it is not so much teachers' intellectual superiority that counts as it is their maturity in facing the unknown and their willingness to leave unanswerable questions unanswered.

If teaching is a bilateral process, it is an essentially open-ended process. Discussion, therefore, is no longer a method to get a well-prepared opinion across to students but an exchange of experiences and ideas whose outcome is not determined. In this way, discussion might well lead to new and surprising perspectives and insights.

When teachers and students are willing to be influenced by each other, learning can become a creative process that can hardly be boring or tiring. It is only through a relationship of this sort that deep learning can take place.

3. *Actualizing*

This brings us to the third aspect of teaching as a redemptive process. It is not alienating but actualizing. This is to say if learning is in some way to be a preparation for the future, it can only be so when the future becomes present in the teaching relationship here and now. To build a better world, the beginnings of that world must be visible in daily life. There is no reason to expect much to happen in the future if the signs of hope are not made visible in the present. We cannot speak about ways to bring about peace and freedom if we cannot draw from our own experiences of peace and freedom here and now. We cannot commit ourselves to work for justice and love in tomorrow's society if we cannot discover their seeds in the relationships we engage in today. A nonviolent world cannot be born out of a violent teaching process any more than justice can be born out of jealousy, mildness out of cruelty, or love out of hate. But when schools are places where community can be experienced, where people can live together without fear of each other, and where learning can be based on a creative exchange of experiences and ideas, then there is a chance that those who come from them will have an increasing desire to bring about in the world what they experienced during their years of formation.

In this sense, schools are not training camps to prepare people to enter into a violent society but places where redemptive forms of society can be experimented with and offered to the modern world as alternative styles of life. Teaching then can become a way of creating a new lifestyle, in which people are able to relate to each other in a basically nonviolent way. And the teachers themselves, in trying to live this way, will discover that learning is a way of life that goes far beyond the classroom situation, that it creates new relationships which do not finish when students leave, that it is a process which asks for continuation and is not limited by grades and degrees, and that it is a challenge to an ongoing renewal of one's style of life.

We have now described the redemptive process of teaching as evocative, bilateral, and actualizing. This ideal obviously never will be fully realized. But if we are able to realize at least the beginnings of it in our own situations, we might be encouraged to take the reins into our hands and lead the horse away from violence in the direction of increasing freedom.

Nonetheless, we would indeed be fooling ourselves if we thought the choice for a redemptive form of teaching was obvious. If this were the case, all the words written thus far would have been superfluous. The choice is not obvious, because we are faced with a deep-seated human resistance against learning. It is toward this resistance that we must now turn in order to better understand it and thereby to be able to remove it.

III. Resistance Against Learning

Learning is meant to lead to a redemptive insight into the condition of humanity and our world. But do we always desire insight? Bernard Lonergan writes:

> Just as insight can be desired, so too, it can be unwanted. Beside the love of light, there can be a love of darkness. If prepossessions and prejudices notoriously vitiate theoretical investigations, much more easily can elementary passions bias understanding in practical and personal matters. To exclude an insight is also to exclude the further questions that would arise from it and the complementary insights that would carry it towards a rounded and balanced viewpoint. To lack that fuller view results in behavior that generates misunderstanding both in ourselves and in others. To suffer such incomprehension favours a withdrawal from the outer drama of human living into the inner drama of phantasy.[1]

Lonergan calls such an aberration of understanding a "scotosis," derived from the Greek word *skotos,* which means darkness, and the resultant blind spot a "scotoma." By introducing these terms, he has helped us to come to a better understanding of the massive resistance against learning. For it is exactly this scotosis that prevents us from really dealing with those factors that are crucial today. By this scotosis, this exclusion of painful insights, we prevent our own experience from becoming part of the learning process and become like unengaged spectators in the procession of life.

I am trying to say very simple and obvious things here. But if it is true that the most obvious things can easily become the most threatening things to us, then perhaps they also can become the easiest subjects of scotosis.

Scotosis means long and fierce discussions about justice and equality while we hate our teachers or ignore the needs of our fellow students. Scotosis means endless academic quarrels in a world filled with atrocities and much talk about hunger by people suffering from overweight. Scotosis allows church people to indulge in comfortable discussions about the Kingdom of God while they should know that God is with the poor, the sick, the hungry, and the dying. In Lonergan's words: "Scotosis means an aberration which prevents the emergence into consciousness of perspectives that would give rise to unwanted insights."[2] It is indeed startling to discover how we keep ourselves free from those unwanted insights.

Why is this scotosis so difficult to heal? What keeps us blind to the obvious? If we could find some answers to these questions, we could begin, at least in part, to understand why there is such a powerful resistance to learning and why it is so difficult for teaching to become a redemptive process.

I would like to suggest three reasons that keep us from learning and at the same time might explain many of our teacher-student scotomas: (1) a wrong supposition, (2) false pressure, and (3) horror of self-encounter.

1. A wrong supposition

Many teachers as well as many students still operate under the faulty supposition that it is better to give than to receive. Teachers want to give something to students—an idea, an opinion, a specific skill, advice, or any other thing they think students are waiting for—and students, in turn, value their teachers according to what they have to give.

It is difficult to recognize the meaning of Jesus' saying: "There is more happiness in giving than in receiving" (Acts 20:35), because it is difficult to confess that perhaps the greatest service we can offer to others is to receive and to allow *others* the happiness of giving. For much of the happiness in our lives is derived from the fact that we can give and that our friends have been willing to receive our gifts, to make them a part of their lives, and to allow themselves to become dependent on us through them. We feel happy when we see the picture we gave our friends displayed most advantageously on a wall of their living room. The question is: Would we have given them the freedom to put it in the attic?

A gift only becomes a gift when it is received; and nothing we have to give—wealth, talents, competence, or just beauty—will ever be recognized as a true gift until someone opens his or her hands or heart to accept them.

This all suggests that if we want others to grow—that is to discover their potential and capacities, to experience that they have something to live and work for—we should first of all be able to recognize their gifts and be willing to receive them. For people only become fully human when they are received and accepted. In this way, many students could be better students than they are if there were someone who could make them recognize their capacities and could accept these as a real gift. Students grow during those moments in which they discover they have offered something new to their teachers, making them feel not threatened but, rather, thankful. And teachers could be much better teachers if students were willing to draw the best out of them and show their acceptance by thankfulness and creative work. Too many people cling to their own talents and leave them untouched because they are afraid nobody is really interested. They then regress into their own fantasies and suffer from a growing loss of self-esteem.

As long as we keep living with the wrong supposition that giving is our first task, our scotosis cannot be healed, and the most creative insights will stay out of our consciousness.

2. False pressure

A second reason that prevents our scotosis from healing is that we are taught in the deadly network of a modern educational process, which makes us believe we are better and more competent when we have better grades, higher degrees, and more academic rewards. A great many hours are spent by both teachers and students trying to keep up with the physically and mentally exhausting routine of academic life. We have put such a high value on degrees and certificates that we are willing to trust ourselves blindly to someone with an M.D. or a Ph.D. who, a few months earlier, when she was still struggling for her exams, we were more inclined to identify as one of those irresponsible, rebellious students.

This false pressure of society, which forces us to pay undue attention to the formal recognition of our intellectual accomplishments, tends to pull us away from our more personal needs and to prevent us from coming to insights into our own experiences that can form the basis of a creative life project.

3. Horror of self-encounter

The final and most powerful resistance against learning, however, is much deeper and more profound. It is the resistance against a conversion that calls for a "kenotic" self-encounter. We will only be able to be creatively receptive and break through the imprisonment of academic conformity when we can squarely face our fundamental human condition and fully experience it as the foundation of all learning in which both students and teachers are involved. It is the experience that teacher and student are both sharing the same reality—that is, they are both naked, powerless, destined to die, and, in the final analysis, totally alone and unable to save each other or anyone else. It is the embarrassing discovery of solidarity in weakness and of a desperate need to be liberated from slavery. It is the confession that they both live in a world filled with unrealities and that they allow themselves to be driven by the most trivial desires and the most distasteful ambitions.

Only if students and teachers are willing to face this painful reality can they free themselves for real learning. For only in the depths of our loneliness, when we have nothing to lose anymore and do not cling any longer to life as to an inalienable property, can we become sensitive to what really is happening in our world and able to approach it without fear.

This conversion, which is not a sudden event but an ongoing process, is the most important prerequisite for arriving at redemptive insights and removing our many blind spots.

So we have seen how a wrong supposition, false pressure, and horror of self-encounter make it extremely difficult to heal our scotosis, to take away our resistance against learning, and to make a redemptive form of teaching a real possibility.

Conclusion

The core idea of this chapter has been that ultimately we can only come from a violent form of teaching to a redemptive form of teaching through a conversion that pervades our total personalities and breaks the power of our resistance against learning.

Jesus can be called Teacher in the fullest sense of the word precisely because he did not cling to his prerogatives but became one of the many who have to learn. His life makes it clear to us that we do not need weapons, that we do not need to hide ourselves or play competitive games with each other. Only when we are not afraid to show our weaknesses and allow ourselves to be touched by the tender hand of the Teacher will we be able to be real students. For if education is meant to challenge the world, it is Jesus himself who challenges teachers as well as students to give up their defenses and to become available for real growth. In order to come to this conversion, which is the healing of our scotomas, we might be thrown from our horses and be blind for a while, but in the end we will be brought to an entirely new insight, which might well bring about a new humanity in a new world.

2

BEYOND THE RETELLING
OF THE STORY

·

Preaching

Insight and Availability

Introduction

IN 1857 Anthony Trollope wrote in *Barchester Towers*: "There is, perhaps, no greater hardship at present inflicted on mankind in civilised and free countries, than the necessity of listening to sermons."[1] I would not be surprised to find many people today who are willing to agree with him.

It is, therefore, the more amazing that there are still so many preachers who want to preach and so many people who are willing to listen. Why is this so? Perhaps because people today, just as much as a century ago, have a lasting desire to come to such an insight into their own condition and the condition of their world that they can be free to follow Jesus Christ: that is, to live their lives just as authentically as he lived his. The purpose of preaching is none other than to help people to come to this basic insight.

Insight is more than intellectual understanding—it is knowledge through and through, knowledge to which the whole person can say yes. It is an understanding that pervades a person from head to heart, from top to toe, from brain to guts. When we can come to this totally permeating knowledge, we will be able to really listen to the Word of God and to follow the light that has entered into our darkness. In this way, one of the most crucial purposes of preaching is to remove these real and all-too-visible obstacles that cause us to listen without understanding.

Not too long ago during Sunday Mass in a Dutch church, a friend of mine gave a sermon on which he had spent at least three days of preparation.

After the service I saw a seventeen-year-old boy sitting in the last pew. Since I had helped my friend with his sermon, I was curious to find out how people felt about it. So I walked over to the boy and said: "Say, how did you like that sermon?" He looked at me as if I could not have asked a sillier question, brushed his hair away from his eyes, and said: "Sir, I never listen to sermons. That is when I take my nap." Thrown somewhat off balance by his response, I looked around to find someone who could give me a little more support. When I saw a man, in his thirties, walking out of the church with his wife and children, I stopped him, saying: "Mister, can I ask you a question? What did you think about the sermon today?" He immediately responded: "Well—that priest certainly looked like a nice young man—but I think he still has a lot to learn. All that talk about Camillo Torres and Martin Luther King—and that we all should help to change the church— You know, sir? I wish they would let *me* get up on that pulpit and say something. Sometimes my hands are just itching and I am about to stand up and say something back—but my wife feels that I say enough at home and should at least be quiet in church."

The boy's indifference and the man's irritation are two reactions to preaching that prevent many people from listening to those ministers and priests who are trying their best to reach the hundreds still willing to visit their churches on Sunday. If insight is the purpose of preaching, and if indifference and irritation are two of the main obstacles that confront it, we find ourselves right in the middle of the problem of preaching.

Preaching belongs to the heart of the Christian ministry. Historians, systematic theologians, and especially biblical scholars—all have many contributions to offer for a better understanding of this crucial ministerial task. It would, however, be extremely presumptuous even to try to touch the many aspects of preaching. Therefore, I would like to limit myself to just one question: "What kind of preacher can help take away those obstacles that prevent the Word of God from falling on fertile ground?"

This is really a question about the spirituality of preachers. But before we can realistically approach it, we must first take a close look at two of the main difficulties in preaching: One is in the message itself, the other is in the messenger. Therefore, I would like to divide this chapter into three parts: (1) the problem of the message, (2) the problem of the messenger, and (3) the preacher who can lead to insight.

I. The Problem of the Message

In order to bring any kind of message to people there has to be at least the willingness to accept the message. This willingness means some desire to listen, some question that asks for an answer, or some general feeling of uncertainty that needs clarification or understanding. But whenever an answer is given when there is no question, support is offered when there is no need, or an idea is provided when there is no desire to know, the only possible effect can be irritation or plain indifference.

It is no secret that those who address themselves to people in church find quite often that the number of people present is in inverse proportion to the eagerness to listen. And when teachers and lecturers express a certain jealousy in regard to the many people who come under the influence of a preacher, they tend to forget that few audiences are so little motivated to listen as a church congregation. What causes this lack of motivation? I suspect there are two aspects of the message that can explain at least part of this phenomenon: (1) redundancy and (2) fearfulness.

1. Redundancy of the message

If we say that preaching means announcing the Good News, it is important to realize that for most people there is absolutely no news in the sermon. Very few people listen to a sermon with the expectation of hearing something they did not already know. They have heard about Jesus—his disciples, his savings, his miracles, his death and resurrection—at home, in kindergarten, in grade school, in high school, and in college so often and in so many ways and forms that the last thing they expect to come from a pulpit is any news. And the core of the Gospel—"You must love the Lord your God with all your heart, with all your soul, and with all your mind and you must love your neighbor as yourself"—has been repeated so often and so persistently that it has lost, for the majority of people, even the slightest possibility of evoking a response. They have heard it from the time of their earliest childhood and will continue to hear it until they are dead—unless, of course, they become so bored on the way that they refuse to place themselves any longer in a situation in which they will be exposed to this redundant information.

It is fascinating to see how people sit up straight, eyes wide open, when preachers start a sermon with a little secular story by way of appetizer but immediately turn on their sleeping signs and curl up in a more comfortable position when the famous line comes: "And this, my brothers and sisters, is exactly what Jesus meant when he said . . ." From then on most preachers are alone, relying only on the volume of their voices or the idiosyncrasies of their movements to keep in contact. It is indeed sad to say that the name of Jesus for many people has lost most of its mobilizing power. Too often the situation is like the one in the Catholic school where the teacher asked:

"Children, who invented the steam engine?" Everyone was silent until finally a little boy sitting in the back of the class raised his finger and said in a dull voice and with watery eyes: "I guess it is Jesus again."

When a message has become so redundant that it has completely lost the ability to evoke any kind of creative response it can hardly be considered a message any longer. And if you feel you cannot avoid being present physically at its presentation you at least can close your eyes and mind to it.

2. Fear of the Truth

But redundancy is only one aspect of the message that prevents people from listening. And even though it may be realistic to admit that there is hardly any news in the sermon for most people, the core message of the Gospel nonetheless contains a Truth that no one has yet fully made true. And real listening means nothing less than the constant willingness to confess that you have not yet realized what you profess to believe. Who likes to hear, for example, that the last will be first, if he happens to be first? And who wants to hear that those who are poor, who mourn, who are hungry, thirsty, and persecuted are called happy, when she is wealthy, self-content, well-fed, praised for her good wines, and admired by all her friends? Who wants to hear that he has to love his enemies and pray for those who persecute him when he calls his boss an S.O.B. and his own son a good-for-nothing tramp.

The message might be the same all through life and might be repeated over and over again in different words and styles, but those who will let it really come through allow themselves, at the same time, the possibility of coming to an insight that might well have consequences for their style of life, which they are not eager to hear. The truth, after all, is radical: It goes to the roots of our lives in such a way that few are those who want it and the freedom it brings. There is, in fact, such an outright fear of facing the Truth in all its directness and simplicity that irritation and anger seem to be a more common human response than a humble confession that one also belongs to the group Jesus criticized.

In this way, many breakfast discussions on Sunday are, for example, nothing less than clear-cut attempts to undo any possible effects of the threatening Truth. When someone says, "I wish I could get up there and tell those priests how life is when you're married and have three kids," he or she is often expressing what is in fact a deep-seated resistance to confess that the Gospel is also speaking to a person with a family. And just as indifference can make us unavailable to the word of the Gospel, irritation can bar the way for new and liberating insights.

Redundancy of the message and fear of the Truth seem to be the two basic reasons why preachers have such difficulty in coming close to their audiences. This is perhaps even more the case when those who are present scarcely feel free to walk out. Many still feel bound to some authority from heaven, from Rome, or from the church leadership who has convinced them that if they are unwilling to suffer one hour a week, they will surely suffer a great deal more when all their weeks have passed. As a result, preachers are again facing an extremely hard task: To proclaim the Good News, which for many is neither new nor good.

Before we can ask what kind of preacher will be able to break through this deep-seated human resistance against the message, we have to be honest enough to confess that it is not just the message but also the messenger who often keeps listeners away from painful but liberating insights. Let us, therefore, now examine the problem of the messenger.

II. The Problem of the Messenger

Many preachers increase the resistance against listening instead of decreasing it by the way they tend to get their eternal message across. A critical analysis of many sermons would show that if Isaiah was correct when he said: "Listen and listen, but never understand! Look and look, but never perceive!" (Is 6:9), many preachers do not help to allow a few exceptions to his prophecy. It would prove useful, then, to have a closer look at a few ways of preaching that might make us better understand the problem of the messenger. In this regard I suggest that the two main reasons why preachers often create more antagonism than sympathy are: (1) the assumption of nonexistent feelings and (2) the preoccupation with a theological point of view.

1. Assumption of nonexistent feelings

A large number of sermons start by making untested suppositions. Without any hesitance, many preachers impose feelings, ideas, questions, and problems on their hearers that are often completely unknown to the majority, if not to all of them. Some preachers make their hearers ask themselves why their chasubles are red on Pentecost, why the last Sunday of the liturgical year is not in December, why Lent lasts forty days, why All Souls' Day is immediately after All Saints' Day—questions about which people could not care less and which are usually left-over problems from the priest's own education for the ministry.

Sometimes whole sermons are built on clerical feelings that are quite alien to laypeople. I remember one sermon that began as follows:

> Today we all congregate together to celebrate the ascension of our Lord Jesus Christ. Only a few weeks ago our hearts were still filled with joy because of the resurrection of our Lord, and now already we feel with the Apostles the sadness about his leaving us. But let us not despair, because Jesus does not leave us alone but is going to send us the Holy Spirit within a few days. And not only for the Apostles but also for this community gathered around his altar the Spirit will bring new life and new hope—

It came as no surprise to find that everyone was mentally absent by the time the preacher finished his introduction. I counted about thirty people scattered in the big church. None seemed to remember how happy they had been at Easter or to realize how sad they were on Ascension Day. There was no congregation, no celebration, no community, certainly no despair or desire to have the Holy Spirit come soon. Just a few isolated individuals who had kept in mind that Ascension Day was a day of obligation and were faithful enough to go to Mass.

Even more irritating than this, however, are preachers who somehow seem to know exactly how everybody feels. A good example is the following introduction:

> Brothers and Sisters in Christ,
>
> In a time in which we all have become part of the big American rat race, in which we are forced to be victims of our watches and slaves of our agendas, in which we are running from one committee meeting to another, we have become deaf to the voice of God, who speaks in silence and reveals himself in the quiet moments of prayer.

Well, this certainly tells us a lot about the preacher—but what about the grandmother who spent a good part of the week solving crossword puzzles, what about the boy who just came back from the baseball field, and his teacher who spent her free Saturday reading Dostoyevsky, and what about the housewife who enjoyed a nice afternoon with her kids at the city zoo?

Someone in the congregation might say yes to the preacher, but most will feel just as far from his words as they feel from the so-called rat race. They might not be aware of this, but in one way or another—by a protective numbness or an outright expression of hostility—they will show that they are not really with him.

2. Preoccupation with a theological point of view

A second and even more difficult problem to overcome is the preoccupation with a theological point of view. Some preachers become so excited about a recent book they have read or a new viewpoint they have heard that they feel compelled to have others share their enthusiasm. They quickly and, as it often happens, disappointingly find out, however, that Karl Rahner, Harvey Cox, or Edward Schillebeeckx do not appeal as much, if at all, to their hearers as they do to themselves. The main reason is not that these theological ideas are not valid or meaningful but rather that not only those who preach but also those who listen have their own "theologies." Let me explain this with a story.

A theology student was asked to give a sermon about the Kingdom of God. He carefully studied the Scriptures and read the latest literature on the subject. But when he thought he had a clear idea about the Kingdom of God and was ready to present his sermon, it was suggested that he first visit four families living in the parish where he was going to preach and ask them what they thought about the Kingdom of God.

So he went first to a meteorologist, a scholarly man who had read many books and had discovered that making predictions is a pretty tricky business. And the meteorologist said: "The Kingdom of God is the fulfillment of God's promises, and humanity has to refrain from unhealthy curiosity about exactly how this will happen."

Then the student went to a storekeeper, whose business had been a failure and whose wife had been sick for many years. And the storekeeper said: "The Kingdom of God is heaven—where I finally will receive my reward for enduring my hard, bothersome life."

From the storekeeper he went to a wealthy farmer, who had a strong wife and two beautiful and healthy children. And the farmer said: "The Kingdom of God is a beautiful garden, where we all will continue the happy life we started in this world."

Finally, the student came to the house of a laborer, who had learned a good trade and was proud that he was able to earn his money with his own hands. And the laborer said: "The Kingdom of God was a smart invention of the Church to keep the illiterate happy and the poor content, but since I can take care of myself and have a good job I have no need anymore for a kingdom to come."

When the theology student came home from these visits and read his sermon again, he realized that his ideas were close to those of the meteorologist, who was used to living with uncertainties, but that the storekeeper looking for a reward, the farmer hoping for the continuation of his happiness, and the laborer who saw the Kingdom in the works of his own hands would not understand him. And when he read the Scriptures again he discovered that there was a place for all four of these parishioners in the Kingdom of God.[2]

Perhaps the greatest temptation of preachers is to think that only they have a theology and to believe that the best thing to do is to convert all those who listen to their way of thinking. In this way, however, preachers fail to realize that in a very real sense they have not loved their neighbors as themselves, since they have not taken their neighbors' views and experiences just as seriously as their own. When this is true, in fact, many of those who listen will become indifferent or irritated without exactly knowing why. And preachers who spend a great deal of time studying books and preparing their sermons will themselves become more and more disillusioned as they start feeling that nobody wants to listen to the Word of God. All the while, however, these preachers have forgotten that God's Word does not have to be exactly the same as their own. When preachers address themselves to nonexistent feelings and are anxiously preoccupied with their own theology, they tend to increase instead of decrease the already existing resistance against the message.

At this point one might well be inclined to ask how preachers can overcome this problem. From the outset, however, we have to say that the question itself is misdirected, for there is no tool, no technique, no special skill which can solve this problem. But perhaps there is a "spirituality"—a way of living—that can give hope to ministers who want to bring their people to a liberating insight which can make them free to follow Christ. Let us, therefore, now examine the kind of preacher who can help others come to this insight.

III. The Preacher Who Can Lead to Insight

The task of every preacher is to assist people in their ongoing struggle of becoming. And this is accomplished primarily by speaking about Jesus Christ, who lived his life with an increasing willingness to face his own condition and the condition of the world in which he found himself in such a way that we are encouraged to follow him; that is, to live our lives with the same authenticity even if they lead us to tears, sweat, and, possibly, violent death.

Every preacher is called upon to take away the obstacles that prevent this painful process of becoming fully human. This is a difficult task since there seems to be a profound resistance against change, at least when it concerns our basic outlook on life. Once we have a more or less satisfying standpoint, we tend to cling to it, since it always seems better to have at least a poor standpoint than to have none at all. In this sense we are basically very conservative. We are constantly tempted to deny our most precious human ability—which is to shift standpoints—and yield easily to our tendency to settle for the comfortable routine. In many ways we are resistant to the call of him who says that when you are young you can put on your own belt and walk where you like, but when you grow old you will stretch out your hands and somebody else will put a belt round you and take you where you would rather not go (Jn 21:18). In complete contrast to our idea that adult-hood means the ability to take care of oneself, Jesus describes it as a growing willingness to stretch out one's hands and be guided by others.

It is no wonder, then, that preachers who hope to remove the obstacles of this process of growth and to have their people become free to surrender themselves and let others gird them are considered people with great courage.

The two aspects of preaching that seem to be most essential for preachers to facilitate this ongoing process of becoming are: (1) the capacity for dialogue and (2) availability.

1. The capacity for dialogue
When I use the word "dialogue" I do not think about dialogue homilies in which everyone can say what he or she wants, nor about a public discussion or any other specific technique to make people participate. No, nothing of that sort is meant by the word "dialogue." I simply mean a way of relating to men and women so that they are able to respond to what is said with their own life experience. In this way dialogue is not a technique but an attitude of preachers who are willing to enter into a relationship in which partners can really influence each other. In a true dialogue preachers cannot stay on the outside. They cannot remain untouchable and invulnerable. They have to be totally and most personally involved. This can be a completely internal process in which there is no verbal exchange, but it requires the risk of real engagement in the relationship between the one who speaks and those who listen. Only then can we talk about a real dialogue.

When this dialogue takes place, those who listen will come to the recognition of who they really are since the words of the preacher will find a sounding board in their own hearts and find anchor places in their personal life experiences. And when they allow the preacher's words to come so close as to become their flesh and blood, they can say: "What you say loudly, I whispered in the dark; what you pronounce so clearly, I had some suspicion about; what you put in the foreground, I felt in the back of my mind; what you hold so firmly in your hand always slipped away through my fingers. Yes, I find myself in your words because your words come from the depths of human experience and, therefore, are not just yours but also mine, and your insights do not just belong to you but are mine as well."

When those who listen to a preacher can say this, there is a real dialogue. And if they were a little more spontaneous than most of us are, they would say, "Yes, brother (or sister), you said it. Yes. Amen. Alleluia." Only then are we able to recognize real dialogue and affirm our real selves and come to the confession not only of our deficiencies and mistakes but also of ourselves as people in desperate need of the Word of God, which has the power to make us free. But when we are not able to understand what is going on within ourselves, when we do not know what we really want, feel, or do, then words that come from above cannot penetrate into the center of our beings. When emotions, ideas, and aspirations are cluttered together in an impermeable dirty crust, no dew can bring forth fruits and no clouds can "rain on the just."

But whenever anxious and impenetrable people are approached by one who expresses solidarity with them and offers insight and understanding as a source of recognition and clarification, then their confusion can be taken away and paths that may lead to light can become visible. Then the meteorologist, the storekeeper, the farmer, and the laborer will realize that the person up there is simply taking away the veil that prevented them from seeing not the preacher's but their own viewpoints. Then they will recognize that the preacher is speaking about them and that the Word of God is for all.

A beautiful example of this dialogue is the sermon given by William Sloane Coffin, Jr., in Battell Chapel in New Haven, Connecticut, on April 10, 1970, during the days of the Black Panther trial. He started this sermon with the following words:

> Most of us who are here today are in deep distress. The Panther trial is polarising not only our Yale–New Haven community and increasingly the entire nation; it is also polarising ourselves. The innermost feelings of many of us are now so sharply divided that they are destroying our

capacity to think and act with anything approaching conviction and compassion.[3]

That is dialogue, and because many in Coffin's audience could say yes, they recognized their own paralysis, and this recognition created their first desire to move again and do something. The words that followed were so extremely effective because Coffin's hearers were ready for them. It is no surprise that this sermon was an important contribution to the creative response to the fearful situation in New Haven.

But again, dialogue is not a technique or a special skill you can learn in school but a way of life. Nobody can imitate William Sloane Coffin or any other effective preacher. In the final analysis, dialogue can only become actual through a willingness on the part of the preacher to be available to the congregation in a very basic sense. And so, I would finally like to examine this availability as the core of the spirituality of preachers.

2. Availability

Availability is the primary condition for every dialogue that is to lead to a redemptive insight. Preachers who are not willing to make their understanding of their own faith and doubt, anxiety and hope, fear and joy available as a source of recognition for others can never expect to remove the many obstacles which prevent the Word of God from bearing fruit.

But it is here that we touch precisely upon the spirituality of preachers themselves. In order to be available to others, one has to be available to oneself first of all. And we know how extremely difficult it is to be available to ourselves, to have our own experiences at our disposal. We know how selective our self-understanding really is. If we are optimists, we are apt to remember those events of the day that tend to reinforce our positive outlook on life. If we are pessimists, we might say to ourselves: "Again, another day that proves I am no good." But where are the realists, who are able to allow all their experiences to be theirs and to accept their happiness as well as their sadness, their hate as well as their love, as really belonging to their own human experiences? When one does not have all one's experiences at one's disposal one tends to make only those available to others that fit best the image one wants to have of oneself and the world. And this is exactly what we call closed-mindedness. It is blindness to an essential part of one's own reality.

Preachers who want to be real leaders are those who are able to put the full range of their life experiences—experiences in prayer, in conversation, and in their lonely hours—at the disposal of those who ask them to be their preachers. Pastoral care does not mean running around nervously trying to redeem people, to save them at the last moment, or to put them on the right track with a good idea, an intelligent remark, or practical advice. No! All human beings are redeemed once and for all. Pastoral care means in the final analysis offering your own life experience to your brothers and sisters and, as Paul Simon sings, to lay yourself down like a bridge over troubled water.

I am not saying that you should talk about yourself, your personal worries, your family, your youth, your illnesses, or your hang-ups. Those things have nothing to do with availability. Talking about them is only playing a narcissistic game. No, I mean that preachers are called to experience life to such a depth that the meteorologist, the storekeeper, the farmer, and the laborer will all one day or another realize that they are touching places where their listeners' lives also really vibrate, and in this way preachers allow their listeners to become free to let the Word of God do its redemptive work. Because, as Carl Rogers says: "What is most personal is most general."[4] Thomas Oden explains this when he writes: "Repeatedly I have found, to my astonishment, that the feelings which have seemed to me most private, most personal, and therefore the feelings I least expect to be understood by others, when clearly expressed, resonate deeply and consistently with their own experience. This has led me to believe that what I experience in the most unique and personal way, if brought to clear expression, is precisely what others are most deeply experiencing in analogous ways."[5]

When people listen to preachers who are really available to themselves and, therefore, able to offer their own life experiences as sources of recognition, they no longer have to be afraid to face their own condition and that of their world because the ones who stand in front of them are living witnesses that insight makes us free and does not create new anxieties. Only then can indifference and irritation be removed, only then can the Word of God, which has been repeated so often but understood so little, find fertile ground and be rooted in the human soul.

So we have seen how, through availability, a real dialogue can take place which can lead to new insight. This is to say that the Word of God, which is a sign of contradiction and a sword piercing the human heart, can only reach people when it has become the flesh and blood of those who preach it.

Conclusion

I have used a lot of words to say a very simple thing: Preachers are those who are willing to give their lives for their people. The Word of God is always coming into the world, though it is often met with indifference and irritation. Those who preach are called upon to remove these obstacles and lead their listeners to a true insight that can set them free.

If preachers want not to increase the resistance against the Word but to decrease it, they have to be willing to lay themselves down and make their own suffering and their own hope available to others so that they too can find their own, often difficult way. Nobody can ever claim to be a real preacher in this sense. Only Jesus could, since only he entered into a full dialogue with those he loved by laying down his life in total availability. But out of all those who witnessed his death and saw the blood and water come from his pierced side, only a few were willing to cast off their indifference and irritation and come to the liberating insight: "In truth this man was the son of God" (Mt 27:54).

Every time real preaching occurs the crucifixion is realized again: for no preacher can bring anyone to the light without having entered the darkness of the Cross. Perhaps Anthony Trollope was right when he said that the necessity of listening to sermons is the greatest hardship inflicted on humankind in civilized and free countries. But if we want our countries to become really free and civilized, let us hope that there always will be people to endure the hardship of preaching and lead their listeners through their own darkness to the Light of God.

3

BEYOND THE
SKILLFUL RESPONSE

■

Individual Pastoral Care

Competence and Contemplation

Introduction

IN ORDER TO DEAL concretely and specifically with the relationship between individual pastoral care and the spirituality of ministers, I would like
to start this chapter with the story of Michael Smith, a pastoral trainee in
Stone Memorial Hospital. The head of the section where Michael was working told him that one of the patients, Mr. Kern, had cancer and was in very
critical condition, and that a visit might be worthwhile.

Michael, dressed in a white coat like the medical interns but with a name
tag identifying him as a chaplain, entered Mr. Kern's room for a pastoral
visit. There the following conversation took place:

MR. KERN: You're a new one. I don't believe I've seen you among the doctors.
MICHAEL: You haven't, I'm sure, though I have been meaning to call on you
    sooner. I should have been here sooner than this. I am one of the chaplains,
    Chaplain Smith.
MR. KERN: How do you do.
MICHAEL: I just want to say hello to you. I want to let you know that we're
    around and that we'll be happy to help in any way we can. The chaplain's
    office answers on extension 2765, and, in case you are interested, there are
    services here on Sunday—several ecumenical and one Mass for Catholics.
MR. KERN: I am Jewish.

MICHAEL: Oh, fine. In that event you may be interested to know that though he is not here daily, a rabbi makes regular visits here at Stone Memorial. Could I call him for you?

MR. KERN: Please do not. I would prefer not to bother him—or anyone.

MICHAEL: If you wish—How ill have you been?

MR. KERN: Enough to die, but I don't! And all this doctoring has done and does no good—a continual torture. But I do not care to talk. Will you please excuse me?

MICHAEL: I'm sure that I have come in at a very inopportune time, and I hope that I have not disturbed or upset you. Still, I would like to drop in from time to time, if for no other reason than to say hello, just to see how things are with you.

MR. KERN: You would indeed be doing me a very great favor—and would be respecting my wishes perfectly, as I have told the doctors—if you and everyone else would leave me entirely alone. My own family, except for my wife, does not come to see me. I have told my daughter not to come. I don't want her to see me in this condition. Yet people insist. Even a dying animal—a dying animal—can crawl off by itself to die. I repeat: You will be doing me a favor if you leave—and do not return.

Back at his room Michael wrote: "I feel discouraged, even guilty. It was almost as if I had been kicked in the stomach."[1]

This painful visit and the even more painful reflection on it raise three questions that have been raised over and over again in respect to individual pastoral care.

1. Who are you, Michael, to visit Mr. Kern?
2. What kind of relationship do you expect to have with this patient?
3. What do you think you can do for him?

These three questions refer to the pastoral identity, the pastoral relationship, and the pastoral approach. In recent years many ministers and priests have been involved in special training programs in order to become more adept at serving the individual needs of their fellow human beings. Under the guidance of competent supervisors and with the help of new insights in psychodynamics and especially psychotherapy, many have been working hard to make their ministry relevant to men and women struggling with the meaning of their lives and their deaths. But while concentrating on their own identities, or the relationships they have with people, and the help they can offer, many ministers and priests begin to realize the far-reaching implications for their own most personal lives. It is these implications for the spirituality of ministers that I would like to discuss here.

We will divide this chapter into three parts: spirituality and pastoral identity, spirituality and the pastoral relationship, and spirituality and the pastoral approach.

I. Spirituality and Pastoral Identity

The first question Michael Smith had to face was: Who am I? He was not a doctor on the hospital staff who was expected to cure Mr. Kern of his cancer; he was not a psychologist trained to help Mr. Kern cope with his anxieties; he was not a social worker able to see just how far the relationship with his wife and daughters could be of any support to Mr. Kern. What, then, was his specialty, his own unique contribution, his most personal tool?

The question is a very realistic one in a world that is becoming more and more professionalized and where one specialty after another is developing. There was a time when the minister indeed was doctor, psychologist, social worker, and nurse all at once; the minister was the factotum of the community, the center of knowledge and wisdom. But today many ministers feel that they are amateurs in every field and professionals in none. And in the middle of this confusion they often feel very inadequate, suffer from painfully low self-esteem, and doubt if their theology can be made operational to such a degree that people can be helped in an effective way.

It seems that there are two sides to pastoral identity which demand careful attention: self-affirmation and self-denial.

1. Self-affirmation

After the visit to Mr. Kern, Michael found himself discouraged and guilty. He felt that he had imposed himself on someone who had neither asked for nor wanted his help and that as a pastor he had failed completely.

No minister can ever live a creative, meaningful life when this feeling becomes predominant. Those who think they have no special contribution to make to their brothers and sisters—that they are considered more as decorations than assets to life, more tolerated than needed—will in the long run become depressed, apathetic, dull, and irritable. Or they will simply decide to leave the ministry to enter what they then call a "real" profession.

But where does that leave Mr. Kern and many people like him? In what kind of condition is a man who does not want to see his own children when he is dying, who curses the doctors who try to give him relief, and who asks for a little corner into which he can crawl like an animal and perish, not wanting anyone to know or see that he, too, does not have his life in his own hands. Neither medicine nor psychology, neither psychiatry nor social work can ever respond to the final question of why we come to life, slowly learn to stand on our own feet, attach ourselves to partners, give life to others, and allow them to continue what we started but will not see fulfilled. Those who have not been able to give meaning to their own life cycles and accept them in their terminable reality cannot die as *human beings* but have no other way than the way of animals.

It was quite understandable that the head of the section where Mr. Kern stayed asked Michael to go and visit this patient. She knew that Michael could not cure him, but she also realized, perhaps only vaguely, that there is a tremendous difference between dying and slipping away, between giving your life and forsaking it in a hopeless battle, between reaching out to the light that becomes visible in the hour of death and turning away your head and allowing yourself to be drawn into a pit of despair.

Michael might not have been able to make Mr. Kern's death an act of human surrender; life perspectives usually don't change in an hour. But he should at least realize that he was indeed asked to save Mr. Kern's life— that is, to offer hope, to convert hate into love, to make death an ultimate human gift, and to make it possible for Mr. Kern's wife and children to find strength in that same light they saw in the eyes of their husband and father, who was the first to enter it fully.

When ministers discover that they really can give life to people by enabling them to face their real life conditions without fear, they will at the same time cease looking at themselves as individuals on the periphery of reality. They are then right in the center. Many doctors realize how dangerous it is to operate on a person who has no will to live, many psychologists are humble enough to confess that they cannot give meaning to life and death—even if they might have many insights into the motivations that make people hurt and heal each other. Many sociologists know that no structural changes will make sense as long as it remains unclear where such changes will lead. When people no longer see the meaning of their existence they lose perspective, grasp what is most satisfying to their immediate needs, escape in fantasies, sex, and drugs, and find their lives disintegrating to the point of suicide.

Individual pastoral care is in many ways the care most needed and in fact asked for—at least if we can understand the questions. Pastoral training, therefore, perhaps means first of all the education of pastors so that they might hear questions and become aware of the fact that they are needed more than they realize—that thousands of people are constantly asking Alfie's old question: What is it all about anyhow? Why should we eat and drink, work and play, raise money and children, and fight constantly a never-ending sequence of frustrations? Or to say it with the Yogavasistha: "What happiness can there be in the world where everyone is born to die?"[2]

It is on this level that ministers are called to move. And if they become aware of the real questions which are raised right in front of them, they will see that they indeed can touch the heart of life. Then they can cast off their low self-esteem and discover that by affirming the lives of their neighbors they are in fact affirming their own ministerial identity.

2. Self-denial

But at the moment when one might start feeling self-confident or proud, a few disturbing words of Jesus come to mind: "If anyone wants to be a follower of mine, let him renounce himself . . . for anyone who loses his life for my sake will find it" (Mt 16:24–25). Above all, one remembers the almost unbelievable statement of St. Paul: "Yet it is no longer I, but Christ living in me" (Gal 2:20). Just when ministers might have discovered that they not only have a contribution to give but touch the core of life, just when they are ready to affirm themselves, to feel that they are fulfilling their hopes and realizing their deepest aspirations in life, they are faced with the urgent call to deny themselves, to consider themselves servants, useless laborers who are last in line.

Michael put on a white coat so that, just like the medical interns, he might be accepted as one of the team. But the fact is that Michael does not really belong to the hospital, does not have any status or institutional tool. He is not there to cure Mr. Kern. In many ways he is an outsider, who does not know much about illnesses but only knows about people who happen to be ill. Perhaps his coat is a symbol of his unwillingness to show that he, in fact, has no medical tools or techniques but is allowed to come in from the outside only in order to let Mr. Kern know that although he can do nothing about his cancer he is concerned about the way this patient chooses to live and the way he chooses to die.

Many ministers and priests are extremely concerned to be *in* with the competent people and to have a clear-cut identity. But is it really so important to come to this professional self-fulfillment? The great influence of Freud, Jung, Rogers, and Frankl has raised for many ministers the question: How can I be my real self, personal as well as professional? It seems that the clerical waiting list for sensitivity training has become considerably longer than the one for Trappist guest houses. But is it our vocation to

fulfill our own selves to their ultimate degree and to create situations in
which we can come to what we consider to be the most meaningful, beautiful, and intensive experience?

Thomas Merton, in one of his later works, wrote:

> It becomes overwhelmingly important for us to become detached from
> our everyday conception of ourselves as potential subjects for special
> unique experiences, or as candidates for realisation, attainment and
> fulfillment.[3]

If Mr. Kern would have been able to profit from Michael's visit, it certainly would not have been because Michael knew a great deal or had answers to the questions of life but because he was unarmed and could lose
himself for someone else and thereby give him the freedom to talk—not
only about his cancer, his problems, or his present worries but also about
why he lived the way he did and how he is now facing the task of dying.

We cannot minister to others when we are unwilling to deny ourselves
in order to create the space where God can work. How can we really be of
help to others if we keep concentrating on ourselves? As long as we are
trying to keep our minds on things, we are not really concentrated. Falling
asleep, in fact, means ceasing to try to do so. Only when we can forget
about ourselves for a while can we become really interested in others—that
is, enter into the center of their concerns.

So self-affirmation and self-denial are both a part of the identity of the
minister. Are they contrary to each other? The new understanding of the
Zen Buddhist tradition certainly has made it clear that we feel more at home
with the idea of self-fulfillment than with the idea of self-emptying. Dr. H.
H. M. Fortmann, the Dutch priest-psychologist, wrote while expecting his
own death to come soon:

> The religious problem of the West . . . has to be related to the inflation
> of the Ego. We have lost the awareness that there is a kind of knowledge,
> which can only be reached by a reverent process of making loose and
> empty.[4]

Since the East-West dialogue has become a part of many people's lives,
especially young people's, we have become aware of the fact that there are
two forms of consciousness: one that says, Be yourself so you can be creative, and the other that says, Lose yourself so God can be creative in you.
The former stresses individuality, the latter unification.

Pastoral education during recent years has been under the strong influence of Western behavioral sciences. This explains at least part of the emphasis on self and individual creativity. It also makes quite understandable why the search for professional identity in the ministry has received so much attention. But if we read certain signs of the times correctly, it might well be true that the Wise Men from the East again belong to those who truly worship Christ and that the growing interest in the way of Siddhartha, so beautifully described by Hermann Hesse, is a powerful suggestion for the pastors of the future. If the inflation of pastors' egos prevents their mystical union with God, no Michael can help any Mr. Kern to make death a final act of surrender.

But self-affirmation and self-emptying are not opposites because we simply cannot give away what we do not have. We cannot give ourselves in love when we are not aware of ourselves. We cannot come to intimacy without having found our own identities. Jesus lived thirty years in a simple family. There he became a man who knew who he was and where he wanted to go. Only then was he ready to empty himself and give his life for others. That is the way of all ministry. Through long and often painful formation and training, ministers have to find their places in life, discover their own contributions, and affirm their own selves: not cling to the self and claim it as their own unique property but go out, offer their services to others, and empty themselves so that God can speak through them and call people to new life.

So the identity of the pastor, as it becomes visible in pastoral care, is born from the intangible tension between self-affirmation and self-denial, self-fulfillment and self-emptying, self-realization and self-sacrifice. There are periods in life when the emphasis is more on one than on the other, but in general it seems that as people become more mature they will become less concerned with girding themselves and more willing to stretch out their hands and to follow Jesus, who found his life by losing it.

II. Spirituality and the Pastoral Relationship

The growing emphasis on self-denial in the service of others, besides being crucial for pastoral identity, is also essential to the pastoral relationship. Even if Michael knew quite well what his own role was among the many professionals he was working with, the question remains: What was his relationship with Mr. Kern? Mr. Kern did not ask for him, as was quite obvious from the discussion. And why should Michael knock on the door of a stranger? Simply because the head of the section became concerned about his condition? That the doctor visited is understandable, since Mr. Kern came to the hospital to be treated by doctors. But in allowing himself to be brought to the hospital Mr. Kern was certainly not expecting to be visited by a total stranger who was affiliated with a religious organization completely alien to his life.

Michael was aware of this. He simply said who he was and where he could be reached. He also explained that three religions were represented in the hospital by a minister, a priest, and a rabbi, and that Mr. Kern could ask for their services whenever he wanted. Mr. Kern, however, did not want any service of this kind, and that would have ended the discussion had Michael not shown a little more interest and asked how ill Mr. Kern had been.

There are two concepts that can help us understand a little better the uniqueness of the pastoral relationship: the contract and the covenant.

1. Contract

Many professional relationships between people fail because of an unclear contract. If two people make an appointment with each other, there is a *formal* contract to meet. If one is asking for help and the other giving help, the *informal* contract is that the problem will be the focus of the meeting. But quite often there is a *secret* contract, which does not always become clear. Sometimes a person looks for advice but receives a sermon, or wants to be listened to but gets a pep talk, or hopes for information but does not hear more than "um, hm."

Within a pastoral relationship between two people many different expectations, which are often the cause of great frustrations, can exist. The fact that Michael was so deeply frustrated that he felt "kicked in the stomach" is obviously related to his wrong expectation that Mr. Kern would at least be willing to respond to his desire to be of help. And although Mr. Kern's reaction was exceptional, there are many pastors whose unhappiness about their individual pastoral care is directly related to the unclarity of the contract. I remember a woman saying to a pastor: "My boy does not want to go to church anymore. What should I do?"

The pastor said: "You do not quite know how you should react to this new situation, do you?"

The woman said: "Yes, that is what I was trying to say, but what I want to know is what to do."

Here the pastor has started to counsel while the woman wants direct advice. The result, of course, is that the woman goes home unhappy and the pastor feels he did not get anywhere.

People can be helped in many ways: by support, advice, instruction, a correction, a clarification of feelings, or simply listening. But they are never helped if they expect one thing and receive another. And the first responsibility of pastors is to help their parishioners become aware of the kind of help they really want and to let them know if they are able to give it.

As long as the secret contract remains secret there is an increased chance that unnecessary disappointments will result. The temptation of many pastors is to become too preoccupied with just one model of personal relationship: pastoral counseling. That model suggests a process in which pastor and parishioner meet in such a way that the parishioner can clarify feelings and mobilize energies to find his or her own way. Often this requires many well-structured meetings, special skills on the part of the pastor, and special attitudes on the part of the parishioner. But this kind of contract is rather rare in a regular parish. More usual are the many short and casual contacts and conversations in the context of which much or little can happen, according to the sensitivity of the pastor.

Some pastors say that they are always busy but have the feeling of never accomplishing anything. This may, of course, be simply the result of poor planning. But when pastors have really found their own identities, they discover at the same time that it is exactly their task to relate to many people in many different ways. It is, in fact, these alternatives of relating that enable pastors to exercise a ministry that has many forms and many possibilities.

Within this perspective the desire to have one specialty and to limit oneself to a single way of relating is more an escape than a virtue. It is true that this multiformity of the ministry can create great frustration, but this frustration might belong to the essence of the ministry and point to a way of relating that goes beyond the contractual way of the other professions. Let us therefore now look at the concept of the covenant as an important corrective of the contractual view of the pastoral relationship.

2. Covenant

The word "contract," predominantly an economic term, has come to stand for a powerful concept in the field of human relationships. The distinctions between formal, informal, and secret contracts have helped very much to clarify many failures in professional relationships between people. It is easy to see, therefore, how these distinctions have likewise helped many pastors to better understand the different problems as well as possibilities in their relationships with people.

But just as self-affirmation is not the only aspect of pastoral identity, so contract is not the last word about the pastoral relationship. Just as Michael went to see Mr. Kern even though he was not invited, many ministers and priests knock on doors, ring bells, and walk into houses where nobody is waiting for them. No doctor would think of going from one house to another to ask if there is anybody ill enough to need her help. No psychologist would call on people to find out if there are emotional problems that will give him a chance to exercise his expertise. But the pastor takes initiatives and can even be considered as an aggressive practitioner who wants "to proclaim the message and, welcome or unwelcome, insist on it" (2 Tm 4:2).

The fact that the word "contract" cannot really express the pastoral relationship indicates that if pastors like to consider their relationships with individuals professional relationships; their profession is of a different kind from all the other helping professions. And here the biblical term "covenant" adds a critical note to the contractual view of the pastoral relationship. Yahweh established not a contract with the people but a covenant. A contract finishes when one of the partners does not adhere to his or her promises. Once a patient no longer pays her doctor, the doctor is free to prefer another patient instead; so, too, when a man does not keep his appointments with a psychologist, the psychologist in turn does not feel obligated to visit him and ask him why he did not come. There is indeed an understandable cynicism in the joke that calls a psychiatrist one who is willing to be your friend for twenty-five dollars [or hundred and twenty five in the nineties!] an hour.

But Yahweh says: "Can a woman forget her baby at the breast, feel no pity for the child she has borne? Even if these were to forget, I shall not forget you" (Is 49:15). And the one who understands this covenant responds: "Though my father and mother forsake me, Yahweh will gather me up" (Ps 27:10). In the final analysis, it is not the professional contract but the Divine Covenant that is the basis of a pastoral relationship. In the covenant there is no condition put on faithfulness. It is the unconditional commitment to be of service.

This is perhaps the greatest challenge to everyone who wants to make God's covenant visible in this world: for who does not expect a return for good services? Perhaps we do not ask for money after a pastoral conversation, perhaps we do not even expect a small gift at Christmas or a word of thanks, but can we really detach ourselves from our subtle condition of change? A very good friend of mine, a priest who decided to become a bartender in Amsterdam, said one day: "I don't want to be called pastor because I have seen too many so-called pastors who are spiritual prostitutes, selling their love under the condition of change. If my relationship with someone is affected by the subtle pressure that she should stop drinking so much, get away from drugs, be less promiscuous, cut his long hair, go to court, to church, or the city hall, I am still not really with him or her but with my own preoccupations, value systems, and expectations, and have made of myself a prostitute and degraded my sister or brother into a victim of my spiritual manipulations."

Many ministers complain that nobody says thanks to them, that hours spent with people don't bring about any change, that after many years of teaching, preaching, counseling, organizing, and celebrating people are still apathetic, the church still authoritarian, and society still corrupt. But if our gratification has to come from visible change, we have made God into a corporate executive and ourselves into sales managers.

Michael received no thanks for his honest desire to be of help, but even after Mr. Kern's remark "I do not care to talk," he said, "Still, I would like to drop in from time to time, if for no other reason than to say hello, just to see how things are with you." That reaction does not make sense if we look for gratification, though we can perhaps discover in Michael's awkward and unhandy approach something of God's faithfulness, which by its incomprehensibility can evoke irritation as well as sympathy.

So we have seen that the pastoral relationship can never be completely understood within the logic of a professional contract. Every woman or man asks for thanks, hopes for success, and expects change to come about— ministers as much as anyone else. God, however, offered us not a contract but a covenant, and God challenges those who want to make this covenant visible in this world never to make human success a criterion of their love.

III. Spirituality and the Pastoral Approach

When the identity of the minister is found in the creative tension between self-affirmation and self-denial and when the nature of the pastoral relationship carries the signs of a professional contract but is ultimately based on the covenant of God with humanity, we are left with the question of the pastoral approach. Can anything specific be said about how ministers or priests should behave when they find themselves in a one-to-one relationship with someone in need of help?

What should Michael have done when he entered Mr. Kern's room? Was it wrong to start talking about the variety of services the hospital had to offer? Should he have acted differently, said something else, or absolutely nothing? Should he have asked how Mr. Kern was doing after he had just heard that Mr. Kern was not at all in the mood to talk? These were probably

Michael's main problems when he came to his supervisor. He might have said: "Okay, I did a miserable job. I even feel guilty about it, but—tell me, what should I have done or said?"

Many ministers and priests today take special training exactly because of their need to be more skillful in their individual pastoral relationships. The increasing number of pastoral training centers is witness to the great desire to find an answer to the "how to do it" question. How to have a good conversation with students? How to help a person in a crisis situation? How to have a meaningful contact with the confused teenager or the rebellious young adult? How to help an embittered dying patient? How to do this and how to do that? Sometimes I have the strange feeling that we are still too preoccupied with the old doctor's problem of how to get the child to swallow the bitter pill. Sweetening the pill, having music play in the background, or providing a distracting puppet show? But the pill has to be swallowed.

Quite often pastors look to the experts of the behavioral sciences to give them answers for their urgent questions. And many psychologists, sociologists, counselors, and sensitivity trainers become rich today by teaching their ways to eager ministers who admire their skills and hope to find in them a solution for their deep-seated feelings of inadequacy.

I do not want to underestimate the tremendous importance of the help the social sciences can offer pastors. One of the main reasons for great hope in the field of pastoral care is precisely the still developing dialogue between pastors, sociologists, social workers, psychologists, and psychiatrists. But I also feel that there is a unique dimension to pastoral care that goes beyond the expertise of the behavioral sciences and even beyond professionalism. It is to that dimension that I would like to pay special attention here. I would like to do this by focusing on a specific aspect of many new forms of pastoral training: the pastoral report.

One of the most important things pastors learn in their training is to write down their experiences. Charles Hall, executive secretary of the Clinical Pastoral Education movement, once said: "What is worth saying is worth writing." If Michael had not written down his painful pastoral visit, he could not have learned much from his experience. But what was there to be learned? I would like to discuss this by using two terms: role definition and contemplation.

1. Role definition
It is no secret that ministers are not accustomed to writing. A good number, of course, boast: "Oh, I could write a book about things that happen in this parish." But very few do. Doctors write their medical reports, psychologists

their test reports, social workers their case reports. But most pastors do not have any document available to help them define their own role. Russel Dicks, one of the pioneers of the clinical training movement, says: "We believe that until the minister develops a method of keeping records of his own with individuals, he has no right to claim a place for himself among the skilled workers in the field of human personality."[5]

By studying the written reports of their pastoral work with individuals, ministers are able to clarify their own experiences. They also have a concrete way of identifying exactly what happened in their pastoral work and a unique chance to think realistically about alternative manners of pastoral behavior. In this way they are able to define what took place and what has to be done.

When Michael looked over the report of his visit to Mr. Kern, he realized that his nervousness had made him cling to concrete information and behave more like an officer of a tourist bureau than a pastor. He also became aware that he could have prevented much pain if before the visit he had asked the doctor or nurse something about Mr. Kern—his religion and his physical and psychological condition. He started wondering whether his white coat, which of course made him look like a doctor, had not created most of the hostility. He was likewise able to think about different ways of relating to an extremely hostile and bitter man, who was unable to face his situation and unable to show his need for human help.

So Michael learned from his experience. But experience is a very ambivalent word. Many priests, who use their years of experience as an argument for their competence, tend to forget that only a few people learn from experience. One carefully reported and critically evaluated event can often teach a person more than years filled with experiences empty of understanding. When, however, we can define where we stand we can also draw a map of where we want to go. Every professional is responsible for his or her own definition. When priests cannot define their role carefully, they will never be able to make it clear to anyone else. Michael started to define his role when he wrote down his experiences. Perhaps his next visit was a little less frustrating as a result.

But if we look upon role definition as the last word in individual pastoral care, then we miss the core of the ministry, which is not skillful practice but reverent contemplation. It would be well, therefore, to finally examine the meaning of contemplation.

2. Contemplation

The great concern of many supervisors such as Russel Dicks has been to help ministers learn the best response to a given stimulus. Michael's responses to

Mr. Kern's stimuli certainly could have been a lot better. Many alternative responses are imaginable. And although it would be naïve to say that ministers should stay away from all special skills, tools, and techniques in human relationships—we might even wish they had a few more!—skillful responses certainly do not constitute the core of the ministry. Those who write down their experiences not only have a chance to define the event and the best response to it but also have an invaluable source of theological contemplation.

When Anton Boisen, the father of the clinical training movement, asked his students to write down their experiences, he thought first of all not about the "how to do it well" question but, rather, about the question, "What can I learn from this person whom I meet as a pastor?" For him the most forgotten source of theology was what he called "the living human document." In *The Exploration of the Inner World* he writes:

> Just as no historian worthy of the name is content to accept on authority
> the simplified statement of some other historian regarding the problem
> under investigation, so I have sought to begin not with the ready made
> formulations contained in books, but with living human documents and
> with actual social conditions in all their complexities.[6]

For a person of faith no meeting is accidental. Mr. Kern and Michael met. And even though Michael was in no way able to help Mr. Kern as he thought he could, perhaps Mr. Kern told Michael something he should never forget: A human being can become so hard, so bitter, and so disappointed in life that the only wish he or she has left is to be allowed to crawl into a corner and die like an animal. Mr. Kern shows in a most naked and terrifying way the condition in which we can find ourselves when we lose faith in the possibility of love.

Michael might have read Kierkegaard, Sartre, Camus, Kafka, and many others who write about anxiety and guilt, loneliness and alienation, sin, and death. But now he stands face to face with a man who says: "You will be doing me a favor if you leave—and do not return." Michael might have said: "Oh, just another stubborn, proud fellow who wants to be left alone"—but then he would not really be contemplating the human condition as it becomes visible in Mr. Kern's despair.

Mr. Kern does much more than refuse to talk. He is a living, human document which can give rise to the most fundamental questions of theology: questions of sin and salvation, guilt and forgiveness, isolation and reconciliation, and, finally, life and death. In his case, however, these questions become more than theoretical—they have immediate implications for the understanding of everyone relating to him: the doctors, whom he can no longer face; his children, whom he refuses to see while dying; his wife, who will live on with a memory of an embittered husband; and Michael, who wanted to help him die but could not.

Pastoral care means much more than pastoral worries. It means a careful and critical contemplation of the human condition. Through this contemplation pastors can take away the veil and make visible to themselves and to others the fact that good and evil are not just words but visible realities in the life of every individual. In this sense, every pastoral contact is a challenge to understand in a new way God's work with humanity and to distinguish with a growing sensitivity the light and the darkness in the human heart.

In this way, contemplation is not just an important aspect of the lives of priests or an indispensable condition for a fruitful ministry. Ministry *is* contemplation. It is the ongoing unveiling of reality and the revelation of God's light as well as our darkness. In this perspective, individual pastoral care can never be limited to the application of any skill or technique since ultimately it is the continuing search for God in the life of the people we want to serve. The paradox of the ministry indeed is that we will find the God we want to give in the lives of the people to whom we want to give God.

And so we have seen that if the pastoral approach does not go beyond the level of skills and techniques ministers are tempted to become manipulators of people. Only when they learn to see their pastoral relationships as a vital source of theological contemplation can they themselves also be ministered to by those for whom they care.

Conclusion

The main purpose of this chapter has been to show the implications of individual pastoral care for the personal lives of ministers themselves. I hope that the central movement from professionalism to spirituality has been clear. In the search for professional identity, ministers move from self-affirmation to self-denial; in the establishment of professional relationships, they move from contract to covenant; and in the professional approach to the individual needs of their sisters and brothers, they move from role definition to contemplation.

If ministers want to be of real help in their contacts with people, they have to be professionals with special information, special training, and special skills. But if they want to break through the chains of our manipulative world, they have to move beyond professionalism and, through self-denial and contemplation, become faithful witnesses of God's covenant.

Only Jesus can be called pastor in this sense. He cared for many people in their most individual needs. He cared for the woman at the well, for Mary Magdalene, for Nicodemus, and for the men traveling to Emmaus who felt their hearts burn when he talked with them. Jesus was certainly skillful in his relationships with people and was not afraid to use his insights into the stirrings of the human heart. But when asked about the source of his knowledge, he said:

> My teaching is not from myself:
> it comes from the one who sent me; . . .
> When someone speaks on his own account,
> he is seeking honour for himself;
> but when he is seeking the honour of the person who sent him,
> then he is true
> and altogether without dishonesty.
>
> *(Jn 7: 16–18)*

Ministers who care for people are called to be skillful but not fixer-uppers, knowledgeable but not dishonest, professional but not manipulative. When they are able to deny themselves, to be faithful, and to understand the meaning of human suffering, then those who are cared for will discover that through the hands of those who want to be of help God's tender love is being shown.

4

BEYOND THE MANIPULATION OF STRUCTURES

■

Organizing

The Christian Agent of Social Change

Introduction

WHEN WE WANT to examine the relationship between organizing and spirituality, we can perhaps start nowhere better than with the many painful questions asked by ministers and priests who have become aware of their vocation to be agents of change.

After many hours, days, and years of teaching, preaching, and individual pastoral care, most ministers suddenly stop and ask themselves:

> Why do I spend so much time in preaching the Word of God while those I really would like to reach are never in my church? Why do I teach children and adults to prepare them for a society that for many does not offer even the possibility of living the life I am trying to advocate? Why do I call people together to celebrate their unity while they are not able to live together in peace but are torn apart by hate, competition, and segregation?
>
> Why do I spend so many hours talking about the individual pains of people, while I leave the society that creates these pains unchanged?

There is a growing frustration in the lives of many ministers and priests because of the awareness that their everyday work does not really touch the structures of life. They feel like people who help the wounded but are unable to stop the war. Their words in the pulpit, the classroom, and the rectory may be a support to many people and give them the courage to face their lives again, but what about the sick society itself, suffering from war, pollution, poverty, crimes, and violence? When there is something basically wrong with the world in which we live, what help are all our words?

Is it our task to help people adapt to a society that is not worth adapting to? What does it mean to talk to a woman who does not have enough bread for her children? No counseling skill will take away her hunger. What does it mean to preach love and understanding in a community where people have no decent houses to live in, no jobs to earn a living, where children have no space to play, and where most people have lost faith in the words of those who announce a better world to come?

More and more priests are haunted by these questions and wonder if the church has not in fact moved away to the periphery of life and, although still caring for people, has failed to change the structures of society itself in order to make a real Christian life possible.

Over the last years this awareness has grown, and many ministers and priests are wondering if it is really possible to become agents of social change, to extend their pastoral care not only to individuals but to social structures as well. New training centers have developed, such as the Ecumenical Institute and the Urban Training Center in Chicago. In such places the first question is not: How can I help this person who has a problem? but: How can I help this society change so that fewer people have problems? The focus is not so much on the pastoral relationship and the pastoral approach but on careful analysis of the social situation, definition of the specific issue at hand, inventory of the sources of the community, and development of a careful strategy to bring about social change.

But do ministers and priests have a task in the complex field of community organization? When that term suggests that it is the task of ministers to take all the responsibility for many specific projects into their own hands, I certainly would say no, but when it indicates the vocation to make people aware of their hidden potentialities, to unify many different self-interests into a common concern, to remove the paralyzing influence of fatalism, and to offer a vision that makes people see their social responsibility and strive beyond the many concrete actions to a Christian community in faith, then ministers might very well consider themselves organizers in a unique way. They can awaken the dormant powers in their milieus. They can break through the chains of pessimism and collective depression and make their people aware that things do not necessarily have to be the way they are.

They can prevent people from falling back in apathy after unexpected disappointments and from using destructive escapism instead of constructive action. They can help create a mentality of hope and confidence, which makes a community flexible and adaptable to new situations and always alert for new possibilities and new perspectives.

In this sense, ministers and priests can be agents of social change without having to be trapped in the pitfalls of a manipulative world. But this requires a spirituality, a way of living that allows us to be very much involved in this world precisely because we are free toward it and do not cling to it with a destructive possessiveness. To describe this spirituality we first have to identify the different dangers to which people are exposed in their social activities. Therefore, I will divide this chapter into two parts: (1) the pitfalls of the organizer and (2) the Christian agent of social change.

I. The Pitfalls of the Organizer

When we ask people about the condition of our world today we quickly become aware that many of them have come to the conclusion that our society is so completely rotten and its structures so totally a failure that the only solution to the problem is a total structural and social change. They are willing to fight for it and do anything possible to make this new society come about. They have become aware that the slogan "Change the world by beginning with yourself" does not work and that, rather, if we truly want to change, then the world in which we live has to change first. They feel that changing people without changing the structures is a waste of time and that real change has to come from the outside, even if violence, cruelty, and execution have to be used to bring it about. This is the attitude of the commissar of the Russian Revolution as described by Arthur Koestler in *The Yogi and the Commissar*. This is also the attitude of those who do everything possible to upset the existing order in the conviction that the new world will be born out of the ashes of the old.

There are probably very few ministers and priests who share this conviction in all its consequences. However, many of them, who have become deeply aware of the overwhelming problems of our society, might nonetheless be inclined to suggest tactics and strategies that are still based on the supposition that humanity will only change if our structures change first.

It seems to me three pitfalls, three dangers, threaten this type of social activism: concretism, power, and pride.

1. The danger of concretism

The danger of concretism is the inclination to make very concrete and specific results the main motivation for continuing social action. It seems that much of the suffering and frustration of people working in ghettos, slums, or underdeveloped areas results from the fact that the changes they hoped to accomplish did not come about. They start their work with great enthusiasm and generous willingness, but after a few years, when they see that the situation is still essentially the same as when they started, they leave disappointed and sometimes bitter, hurt by a loss of self-esteem and feelings of failure and worthlessness. Not a few Peace Corps members, VISTA workers, and Papal Volunteers can witness to this experience.

Quite often the reason for this attitude is that they enter their work with preconceived ideas about how things should be, as if they were saying: "*This* is what these people need"—better houses, better education, better recreational facilities, sewer systems, labor unions, cooperatives, and so on. But these very specific aims might well ruin their effectiveness, make them blind to what people really need, and deaf to what they say. So, often, totally in contrast with their desire, they create hostility in the people they want to help.

I remember once working in a very poor Dutch neighborhood. I visited a family with ten children, who were walking around in rags during the day and sleeping together in three large old beds at night. So I felt the help they needed was obvious. I ordered some clothes and bought a few more beds. But later, when I entered the house unexpectedly, there was a big party going on with beer and cakes. My good friends had sold the beds and most of the clothes in order to invite their friends and neighbors in to celebrate the birthday of their eldest son. Actually, they had enough clothes—though they didn't know how to repair them—and sleeping in separate beds seemed lonely for most of the children.

It is quite obvious that my help was more an expression of what I thought a good life ought to be than what they thought about it. This same kind of mistake is made in many situations. New houses, for example, are given to people without realizing that living in them might not be nearly as important as living close to one's friends.

A good number of population programs have totally failed because well-meaning helpers were handing out their new inventions—pills, IUDs, and other contraceptives—without carefully asking themselves how people feel about having large families, what it means to a husband and wife to have none or only a few children, and how other populations judge the values of life. Quite often sex education has been considered a solution to problems without a careful study of the motivation of people's sexual behavior, and new, expensive programs have been endorsed as if all people think, feel, and act alike. In short, our own preconceived views have caused more hindrance than assistance in our attempts to improve the world and help our sisters and brothers.

2. The danger of power

People who organize are in constant danger of creating small kingdoms for themselves. It is extremely difficult to take initiatives and develop new plans without claiming them as yours. Just as many parents find it hard to let their children choose their own lifestyles, many "organizing priests" want to keep running the show and telling people what to do.

One way of exercising power over people is to become subject to what Dr. John Santos, head of the psychology department at the University of Notre Dame, calls the education-enlightenment hypothesis—that is, the belief that if we tell people what makes good sense to us, it will automatically make good sense to them as well. Many social reformers still think that when you give people the right information and the right instructions they will become so enlightened that they will do exactly what you have in mind. But people do not always feel that those things you consider good for them are so.

Many well-intentioned projects written up by many well-educated people have been ignored and even ridiculed by those who have other values and perspectives. While you think a hundred-dollar bill is worth much, someone else might just light a cigarette with it. Education itself can become a form of power when we think that we are helping people by presenting them with our value system as the ideal way of life. The black power movement was, in part, a reaction against the education-enlightenment hypothesis that made us think that blacks would be much happier if they were allowed to share white people's way of life. But, in fact, this only means that education has become propaganda and that offering help has become part of the power game.

The most subtle desire for power, and the most difficult to overcome, is the desire for thanks. As long as people keep thanking us for what we have done for them, they are, in effect, admitting that they were at least for some time dependent on us. And it is perhaps exactly for this reason that we find in areas where people are living in very poor conditions a certain resistance against explicit thankfulness. Nobody likes to be considered in need of help or unable to be self-sufficient—facts which an expression of thanks often explicitly asserts. It should therefore come as no surprise that men and women who have spent many days helping others seldom hear a word of thanks. Expressed gratitude would only be, in such cases, a reminder of dependency and a threat to self-respect. Not only individuals but even whole countries have thus refused gifts of money and badly needed medicine because they preferred to die with what self-respect they had rather than to live with the feeling that others have to keep them on their feet.

But for those who are aware of the needs of people and want to do something about those needs, it is difficult to live without at least a small kingdom of thankful people who are willing to say that without help they would not be who they are now or do what they do now.

3. The danger of pride

Finally, there is the great temptation of pride. All of us who want to change society are in danger of putting ourselves above it and being more conscious of the weaknesses of others than of the weakness in our own souls. Reformers, who are convinced that things have to become different, are out to convert the world but are tempted at the same time to think that they themselves do not need conversion. Instead of seeing themselves as full members of that same society which needs reform, they might approach it with the fantasy of redeemers who are untouchable and are always right and just.

They might see the cruel segregation between races but be blind to the fact that what they see dramatically happening on the world scene is also happening in themselves when they condemn certain people as being stupid, others as being narrow-minded, and still others as being conceited. They might be highly critical of capitalism and the waste of money but not see that their own style of life would be impossible without the capitalistic society they disparage. They might feel that many people should have a better life and more human respect but at the same time be unable to listen to people, accept their criticism, and believe that they can learn from them. They might always be busy going from one meeting to another and forget that they tend to lose contact with the sources of their own existence and become deaf to the voice that calls from within. They might even be afraid to be alone and face the fact that they themselves are in just as much need of change as the world they want to convert.

The three dangers of every person who is concerned about social change are, therefore, concretism, power, and pride. When Jesus had become aware of his vocation to criticize the society in which he lived, to question its basic supposition, and to work for the Kingdom to come, he knew that he too could become an organizer in the long row of those who had already called themselves Messiahs. And indeed he was tempted to bring about immediate results and change the stones into bread, to take the power and the glory of all the kingdoms of the world, and to prove his invulnerability by throwing himself down from the parapet of the temple and allowing the angels to guard him.

But only through overcoming these temptations could he become a revolutionary who was able to break through the narrowing chains of his world and surpass all political ambitions in order to make visible the Kingdom to come. In this sense, Herbert McCabe is right when he says:

> The likeliest model for the Christian minister—is the revolutionary leader: indeed, the priest should be a revolutionary leader, but one who goes in and through what in today's terms is called a political revolution to a depth which today we call metaphysical or spiritual. This interpretation of the revolution in its ultimate depths *is* the proclamation of the gospel—[1]

We are now ready to ask ourselves what the main traits are of those who want to be Christian agents of social change.

II. The Christian Agent of Social Change

All those who have become aware of the illnesses of the society in which they live and feel a growing need to work for social change are faced with the temptations of concretism, power, and pride. And many have become so deeply impressed by these temptations that they do not see how to avoid them. It almost seems that being an agent for social change and a Christian becomes a contradiction. Many ask themselves: How can I work for a better world without developing hate against those who contradict me, without being tempted to gossip and conspiracy? How can I work for the deprived blacks without sharing their hostile feelings for whites? How can I help the poor without hating those whom I see as their exploiters? How can I criticize the establishment without being conceited, self-righteous, and closed-minded? In short, how can I actively work for a better world and not harm the Christian values that tell me to love my enemies as well as my friends?

Many people who get hurt in this struggle for social reform have indeed been so overwhelmed by this problem that in order to avoid becoming like the commissar who was willing to sacrifice the individual to change the structure, they choose what is in effect the opposite way: the way of the

Yogi. It is not difficult to understand why many people, tired by social action and disappointed with its results, have chosen the inward way. All over the country we see new centers of meditation and concentration in which people try to come to terms with this chaotic world by changing the world from within and making themselves internally free. Quite often they have turned to the East to find a new way. Many have become so deeply convinced that all the conflicts of the world find their origins in the human heart, and that their internal life is just a miniature of the cruel battlefields of the large society, that for them the only real place to start changing the world is in the center of their own inner lives.

Arthur Koestler writes: "The Yogi believes that nothing can be changed by external organization, but everything by the individual attempt from within, and that everyone who thinks otherwise escapes the real problem."[2]

It might be worthwhile to ask if the charismatic movement within the Catholic Church is not in some way an expression of this same attitude. By concentrating on inner conversion and the eradication of evil from the human heart, by stressing personal love and the creation of small communities of prayer, many deeply committed charismatics are basically saying that the only way to change our destructive world is to start with a change in one's own heart. It is not surprising, therefore, to find that charismatics like the Yogi, have often been accused of being aloof and indifferent to the great social problems of war, poverty, pollution, segregation, social injustice, and crime, and of having escaped into a personal garden where they can concentrate on their own souls, experience the stirrings of the Spirit, and make their own conversion the criterion for the solutions of the problems of this world.

But neither the Commissar nor the Yogi, neither the radical Christian reformer nor the charismatic is able to solve the problems of our society. The great task of ministers, rather, is to live and to help live in the tension between both and search for a synthesis. Christian agents of social change are called upon to be social reformers and people who do not lose their own souls, people of action and of prayer at the same time. They are called upon to be concerned with the large issues of our time without losing sight of the children, the poor, the sick, and the old, who ask for our personal care and attention. In a Christian perspective, this careful balance becomes a possibility. Living in this perspective and opening it for the members of their communities, ministers become true agents of social change. And we can even say that insofar as Christians make this perspective visible, they in fact become ministers. I would therefore like now to describe this perspective as one of hope, of creative receptivity, and of shared responsibility.

1. *The perspective of hope*

Gabriel Marcel has made it clear that what many people call hope is in fact a form of wish-fulfillment thinking. The life of any human being is filled with wishes. A child wishes for a bicycle, a boy wishes for a football, a student wishes for a good grade, a woman wishes for a car, a house, a job. A sick man wishes to be cured; a poor woman, to become rich; a prisoner, to become free. This wish-fulfillment thinking is like waiting for a Santa Claus whose task it is to satisfy very specific needs and desires, if possible, immediately. When our lives are filled with this type of specific concrete wish, however, we are in constant danger of becoming disappointed, bitter, angry, or indifferent since more often than not our wishes don't come true, and we come to feel that somewhere and somehow we have been betrayed.

I have the feeling that ministers and priests working for social change are often the victims of this wish-fulfillment thinking. They work for better housing, better schools, or better neighborhoods. They have very concrete goals in mind and very specific ways to realize them. But although the goals are important and the means reasonable, they tend to make the fulfillment of their wishes the criterion for their own self-esteem. Basically, they are still people of little faith, who are more concerned with the gift they want than with the giver from whom they want it.

Only through hope can we overcome this concretionary attitude, for hope is directed not to the gift but to the One who is the giver of all good. We wish *that,* but we hope *in.*[3] Essential to hope, therefore, is that we do not ask for guarantees, do not put conditions on our actions, do not request insurance, but expect everything from the other without putting any limit on our trust. Perhaps the best example of a hopeful attitude is still that of children towards their parents. Children are constantly asking for very concrete things, but their love for their parents does not depend upon the fulfillment of these wishes. Children know that their parents want only the good for them—although they might cry or even be very angry at times, they keep living in the conviction that their parents want only what is good for them.

Those who work for social change usually have very specific things in mind, as they must, but they can only remain a people of faith when they view every result they have achieved as a gift which they are asked to accept in freedom. Nobody can force the soul of a community. The only possibility open is to create conditions in which the community can freely develop and discover the ways that lead to redemption.

People of hope can give all their energy, time, and abilities to those they work for, but when they attach themselves to any specific result they might lose sight of their ultimate objective. Through the attitude of hope, agents of social change do not fall into the temptation of concretism. They do not worry about the results of their work because they believe that God's promises will be fulfilled and that it is only a temptation to desire to know exactly how this will happen. In the same way, a couple who promise faithfulness to each other do not want to know how things will look twenty years later. Only when they leave their future open can they prevent disappointments and receive the results of their mutual relationship as a gift.

When Christians can offer this perspective of hope they make people free to look beyond the immediate needs of the community and understand their activities in a larger perspective. Perhaps there is no better example of this type of leadership than that given by Martin Luther King. He stimulated his people to work for very concrete rights, an equal place on the bus and in the restaurant and an equal right to vote, but at the same time he never made these ultimate values but always looked beyond the results of his actions to the larger issue involved: the total freedom of the human person. Therefore, he could say that not only blacks but whites, who suppressed blacks, were unfree. Therefore, he could prevent people from using violence when a desired goal was not accomplished. Therefore, he could give himself totally for the cause of civil rights even while knowing that he would not see the results. Therefore, he was not afraid of death. In the midst of all activities, he kept reminding his people that although few wishes were fulfilled and few changes brought about, there was no reason for despair. He kept telling his followers that they were on the road to the promised land and that they had to cross the desert first to reach the place where God would make them free. Martin Luther King was able to exercise such a powerful spiritual leadership because, although he asked for freedom NOW, he had learned to be patient and wait until God's will fulfilled the promises.

2. The perspective of creative receptivity

By developing in themselves and others the willingness to receive, ministers can prevent people from falling into the temptation of power. Those who want to bring about change have first of all to learn to be changed by those whom they want to help. This, of course, is exceptionally difficult for those who are undergoing their first exposure to an area of distress. They see poor houses, hungry people, dirty streets, they hear people cry in pain without medical care, they smell unwashed bodies, and in general they are overwhelmed by the misery all around them. But we will never be able to really give if we have not discovered that what we give is only a small thing compared with what we have received. When Jesus says: "Blessed are you who are poor, . . . hungry, . . . weeping" (Lk 6:20–21), we have to be able to *see* that happiness. When Jesus says: "In so far as you did this to one of the least of these brothers of mine, you did to me" (Mt 25:40), he is addressing to us a direct invitation not only to help but also to discover the beauty of God in those who are to be helped.

As long as we see only distasteful poverty, we are not really entitled to give. When, however, we find people who have truly devoted themselves to work in the slums and the ghettos and who feel that their vocation is to be of service there, we see that they have discovered hidden in the smiles of the children, the hospitality of the people, the expressions they use, the stories they tell, the wisdom they show, the goods they share, is so much richness and beauty, so much affection and human warmth, that the work they are doing is only a small return for what they have already received.

In this respect we can better understand those many missionaries who, after living for years in the poorest circumstances, nonetheless became homesick for their missions as soon as they returned to their affluent country. It was not because they wanted to suffer more but because they had found a beauty in their people which they missed in their home community.

There are many countries, cities, and neighborhoods that need help, and it is sad to see that we still believe the best way to motivate others to offer their assistance is to show through books and photographs how inhumanely these people have to live. This certainly creates enough guilt feelings to make people open their wallets and give some money, thereby soothing their consciences for a while. But this is not a Christian response. That the exposure of misery can evoke not only pity but also aggression has become quite clear in concentration camps, in films about dying children in Biafra, and in the endless exposure of emaciated bodies by TV, radio, and newspaper.

As long as we want to change the condition of other people because we feel guilty about our wealth, we are still playing the power game and waiting for thanks. But when we start discovering that in many ways we are the poor and those who need our help are the wealthy, who have a lot to give, then we do not give in to the temptation of power since we have discovered that our task is not a heavy burden or a brave sacrifice but an opportunity to see more and more of the face of the One we want to meet. I wish that more books were written about the so-called poor countries and poor cities, not only to show how poor they are and how much help they need, but also to show the beauty of their lives, their sayings, their customs, their ways of life. Perhaps a new form of Christian "tourism" could then develop in which those who travel can enrich their lives with the wisdom, knowledge, and experience of their hosts.

3. The perspective of shared responsibility

When we think about leaders we still tend to think about individuals with special talents. And indeed, when we think of Pope John XXIII, John F. Kennedy, Martin Luther King, and Dag Hammarskjöld, we easily realize that they were agents of social change with exceptional influence on the lives of many people—even on the course of history. But it would be a mistake to keep waiting for people like them to do the great things. Not too long ago I talked with a black sociologist and asked him about the leadership in the black community. He said: "Perhaps we needed men like King, but now more than ever it is important to look not so much for individuals as for communities which are able to bring about change."

If Christian laypeople, ministers, and priests really want to be agents of social change, the first thing they have to learn is how to share leadership. We are used to saying to people that they have responsibilities. To say that they also have the authority which goes with those responsibilities, however, is something else. It is amazing to find that most priests are still working very much on their own and have not yet found the creative ways to mobilize the potential leadership in their parishes and share their responsibilities with others.

First of all, there are still only a few parishes where the priests really know what the others are doing. While no hospital or school can function without regular staff conferences, it is still a great exception to see parishes where the common concerns are regularly discussed, analyzed, and evaluated and where there is any kind of strategy or long-range planning.

Second, laypeople are rarely, if at all, invited to participate in the pastoral work. While priests are busy complaining that they are overworked with visiting the sick and the old, directing meetings, taking care of the finances and other odds and ends, they are also failing to realize that real leadership means delegation of tasks.

Third, no parish in any city can be considered as its own little kingdom. When pastors and laypeople from different parishes can come together regularly, discuss their common problems, utilize each other's talents, exchange ideas, unite projects, work out common plans in terms of teaching, preaching, pastoral care, and financing; when they can critically evaluate the main problems of their city, raise their voices together when needed, and let the people know that the Christian community is deeply concerned about the crucial issues of the day, then the church cannot be ignored, and although a great deal of irritation and even open hostility might be the result, we could at least be certain that God's Word is again a word that must be taken seriously.

The problem of pride, of course, still remains. The remark "Mind your own business" can also be heard in the mouths of many Christians. It is not easy to say that you cannot do something yourself, that you are in need of constant criticism, that you are willing to be reminded that the problems of the society are also part of your problems. But whenever pastoral workers, ministers, priests, and laypeople come together in a spirit of charity and humility, new things will start happening.

These pastoral staff meetings can, of course, easily be misunderstood as meetings in the spirit of the Commissar, with the primary purpose of working out strategies and planning careful attacks on social problems. But it does not have to be that way. In the middle of a *población* in Santiago, where poverty, hunger, and misery are all around, priests and sisters nonetheless come together for many hours a week, not primarily to formulate a plan of action but to share each other's experiences, to carefully contemplate the reality in which they live, to make each other see why people do what they do and say what they say, and to celebrate the Eucharist together as a thanksgiving for being allowed to be of service to the people. Outsiders might of course say: "Why don't you go to work, why do you spend so much time together when there are still so many people who do not have enough to eat and to drink?" But these men and women know that to be real agents of change they have to be contemplatives at heart, able to hear God's voice in the midst of the crying children and see God's face behind the dirty curtain of misery.

We have now seen how the perspective of hope prevents us from being tempted to look for immediate results, how it can help us avoid the pitfalls of power through the perspective of receptivity, and how it can temper individual pride by a shared responsibility which allows mutual criticism as well as mutual support.

Through living in these perspectives, ministers can become catalysts; that is, people who can uncover the hidden potentials of their communities and channel them into creative social action.

Conclusion

The general question of this chapter was: What is the relationship between spirituality and organization? This question led us to the more specific problem: How can ministers be real agents of change? We discussed the attitude of the Commissar, who wants to change the structures first—even if he has to use power and sacrifice people to come to the concrete results he thinks are indispensable for the new world. We also discussed the attitude of the inward person, who feels that only by changing the hearts of individuals can we change the structures of our society. But just as the social activist is in danger of forgetting that the pains of our society are also to be found in the heart of the reformer, the inward person easily overlooks the colossal problems of our society, which go far beyond the personal insights of any individual.

Christians, laypeople, priests, or ministers who want to be agents of social change, are constantly challenged to look for the creative synthesis between the social activist and the inward person. To avoid concretism, power, and pride, agents of change have to live in the perspectives of hope, receptivity, and shared responsibility—all of which means that they must be contemplatives. The Christian life is not a life divided between times for action and times for contemplation. No. Real social action is a way of contemplation, and real contemplation is the core of social action.

In the final analysis, action and contemplation are two sides of the same reality, which makes one an agent of change. Only the synthesis between the Commissar and the Yogi makes it possible, therefore, to be real agents of social change and to avoid the traps of manipulation. Only this synthesis allows us to look beyond all political, social, and economic developments in order to keep us forever awake and always waiting for a new world to come.

For Christians are only Christians when they unceasingly ask critical questions of the society in which they live and continuously stress the necessity for conversion, not only of the individual but also of the world. Christians are only Christians when they refuse to allow themselves or anyone else to settle into a comfortable rest. They remain dissatisfied with the *status quo*. And they believe that they have an essential role to play in the realization of the new world to come—even if they cannot say how that world will come about. Christians are only Christians when they keep saying to everyone they meet that the Good News of the Kingdom has to be proclaimed to the whole world and witnessed to all nations (Mt 24:14).

As long as Christians live they keep searching for a new order without divisions between people, for a new structure that allows every person to shake hands with every other person, and a new life in which there will be lasting unity and peace. Such Christians will not allow their neighbors to stop moving, to lose courage, or to escape into small, everyday pleasures to which they can cling. They are irritated by satisfaction and content in themselves as well as in others since they know, with an unshakable certainty, that something great is coming of which they have already seen the first rays of light. They believe that this world not only passes but has to pass in order to let the new world be born. They believe that there will never be a moment in this life in which one can rest in the supposition that there is nothing left to do. But they will not despair when they do not see the result they wanted to see. For in the midst of all their work they keep hearing the words of the One sitting on the throne: "I am making the whole of creation new" (Rev 21:5).

5

BEYOND THE
PROTECTIVE RITUAL

■

Celebrating

Obedient Acceptance of Life

Introduction

IN JANUARY OF 1970 students of the Perkins School of Theology in Dallas, Texas, met for an interterm seminar on the Cultural Revolution and the Church. At the end of the course, prepared by the Ecumenical Institute in Chicago, they composed what can be considered a common creed. They wrote the following remarkable words:

> Standing before the mystery—man discovers that he has but one life to live—his own. To accept that fact, and to live it, is to receive grace and to discover that all of life is good. And when we die to our illusions that life is any other way than that, we discover the secret of all life: to die is to live. We are those who name this happening the Jesus Christ Event and reclaim for our time the message of the Biblical people—[1]

This powerful expression of faith makes it clear that ministers are the ones who challenge us to *celebrate* life; that is, to turn away from fatalism and despair and to make our discovery that we have but one life to live into an ongoing recognition of God's work with humanity. But how can this celebration really be a human possibility? Our lives vibrate between two darknesses. We hesitantly come forth out of the darkness of birth and slowly vanish into the darkness of death. We move from dust to dust, from unknown to unknown, from mystery to mystery. We try to keep a vital balance on the thin rope that is stretched between two definitive endings we have never seen or understood. We are surrounded by the reality of the unseen, which fills every part of our lives with a moment of terror but at the same time holds the secret mystery of our being alive.

Christian ministers are the ones whose vocation is to make it possible for us not only to fully face our human situation but also to celebrate it in all its awesome reality.

But how do we celebrate life when we understand neither its ultimate terms nor the full meaning of what happens between them? Celebration seems the least appropriate response to our ambiguous condition. And if we want to celebrate, what kind of person can show us the way to realize our desires? These questions are essential to any attempt to discover the relationship between celebrating and spirituality. Therefore in this chapter I want to raise two questions: (1) how do we celebrate life? and (2) what kind of person makes celebration possible?

I. How Do We Celebrate Life?

When we speak about celebration we tend rather easily to bring to mind happy, pleasant, gay festivities in which we can forget for a while the hardships of life and immerse ourselves in an atmosphere of music, dance, drinks, laughter, and a lot of cozy small talk. But celebration in the Christian sense has very little to do with this. Celebration is only possible through the deep realization that life and death are never completely separate. Celebration can only really come about where fear and love, joy and sorrow, tears and smiles can exist together. Celebration is the acceptance of life in a constantly increasing awareness of its preciousness. And life is precious not only because it can be seen, touched, and tasted but also because it will be gone one day. When we celebrate a wedding, we celebrate a union as well as a departure; when we celebrate death we celebrate lost friendship as well as gained liberty. There can be tears after weddings and smiles after funerals.

We can indeed make our sorrows, just as much as our joys, part of our celebration of life in the deep realization that life and death are not opponents but do, in fact, kiss each other at every moment of our existence. When we are born we become free to breathe on our own but lose the safety of our mothers' bodies; when we go to school we are free to join a greater society but lose a particular place in our families; when we marry we find a new partner but lose the special tie we had with our parents; when we find work we win our independence by making our own money but lose the stimulation of teachers and fellow students; when we receive children we discover a new world but lose much of our freedom to move; when we are promoted we become more important in the eyes of others but lose the chance to take many risks; when we retire we finally have the chance to do what we wanted but lose the support of being wanted. When we have been able to celebrate life in all these decisive moments where gaining and los- ing—that is, life and death—touched each other all the time, we will be able to celebrate even our own dying because we have learned from life that the one who loses it can find it (cf. Mt 16:25).

Those who are able to celebrate life can prevent the temptation to search for clean joy or clean sorrow. Life is not wrapped in cellophane and pro- tected against all infections. Celebration is the opposite of an escape from the realities of the full acceptance of life in its complexity. If we now ask ourselves what the meaning of this acceptance is, we have to look at three main components: affirming, remembering, and expecting.

1. Affirming
Celebrating is first of all the full affirmation of our present condition. We say with full consciousness: We are, we are here, we are now, and let it be that way. We can only really celebrate when we are present in the present. If anything has become clear, it is that we have to a large extent lost the capability to live in the present. Many so-called celebrations are not much more than painful moments between bothersome preparations and boring after-talks. We can only celebrate if there *is* something present that can be celebrated. We cannot celebrate Christmas when there is nothing new born here and now, we cannot celebrate Easter when no new life becomes visible, we cannot celebrate Pentecost when there is no Spirit whatsoever to cele- brate. Celebration is the recognition that something is here and needs to be made visible so that we can all say yes to it.

I found a beautiful illustration of this in the meditation sessions of the members of the so-called *now generation*. Young people gather and for hours try to become present to each other and to recognize their togetherness as a precious reality. But how difficult this is! You can hardly take one step, one breath, without being flooded by thoughts and ideas that pull you away from yourself here and now and make you worry about thousands of little things. You find yourself thinking about your unfinished paper, your plans for tomorrow, or your last conversation. You find yourself asking thousands of unanswerable questions and looking at thousands of invisible pictures. You are not where you are but somewhere where you do not want to be. But when you become able, slowly and carefully, to push all these unwelcome intruders away from your mind you realize that there has been something waiting for you of which you had not been aware, that you really can become present to your own self. At the same time you also become aware of the real presence of the others who are with you because, since they know that their experience will find resonance in yours, they are willing to show you what they have discovered in their own presence.

In this context it becomes clear what praying together really means. It means not worrying together but being present for each other in a very real way. Then it becomes possible to share ideas because they are really ours, to communicate feelings because they are actually there, to talk about concerns because they hurt us and we feel their pains in our own souls. Then the formulation of intentions is much more than a random choice from the many possible problems we can think of. It becomes, rather, an attempt to be visible and available to each other just as we are at this very moment. What we then ask is not, first of all, to solve a problem or to give a hand but to affirm each other in the many different ways we experience life. When this takes place, community starts to form and becomes a reality that can be celebrated as an affirmation of the multiformity of being in which we all take part.

2. Remembering

But nobody can really celebrate life in the present when it is not meaningfully related to the past. The present cannot be experienced as present if the past cannot be remembered as past. A person without a past cannot celebrate the present and own his or her life.

Not too long ago I picked up a hitchhiker who told me that after a serious accident he had lost his memory of all the things that had happened to him during the last ten years. When he came back to the town where he lived, everything was new for him; no feelings, ideas, or associations were connected with the houses he saw and the streets he walked on. His friends had become strangers to him, and the things he did had lost all their connections with his past. He had become a man without a history and, therefore, a man who could no longer give meaning to his present experience.

The way people relate to their own past is of crucial importance for their life experience. The past can become a prison in which you feel you are caught forever or a constant reason to compliment yourself. Your past can make you deeply ashamed or guilt-ridden, but it can also be the cause of pride and contentment. Some people will say with remorse: "If I could live my life again, I certainly would do it differently"; others will say with self-assertion: "You might think I am an old, weak man, but look at those trophies there; I won those when I was young." Memory is one of the greatest sources of human happiness and human suffering. If we want to celebrate our lives in the present, we cannot cut ourselves off from our past. We are instead invited to look at our histories as the sequences of events that brought us where we are now and that help us to understand what it means to be here at this moment in this world.

Those who celebrate life will not make their past a prison or a source of pride but will face the facts of history and fully accept them as the elements that allow them to claim their experience as their own.

When we commemorate during a liturgical celebration those who have gone before us, we do much more than direct a pious thought to our deceased family and friends; we recognize that we stand in the midst of history and that the affirmation of our present condition is grounded in the recognition that we were brought to where we are now by the innumerable people who lived *their* lives before we were given the chance to live *ours*.

3. Expecting

But besides affirming life and remembering it, celebration is filled with expecting the future. If the past had the last word, we would imprison ourselves more and more the older we became. If the present were the ultimate moment of satisfaction, we would cling to it with a hedonistic eagerness, trying to squeeze the last drop of life out of it. But the present holds promises and reaches out to the horizons of life, and this makes it possible for us to embrace our future as well as our past in the moment of celebration.

The truth of this was brought home forcefully to me by a recent painful experience. In January of last year a friend of mine died in Tunisia, where he had gone for a few months to help people who suffered from a terrible flood. His parents, simple farmers living in a small village, expected much from their son, who had been the first university student in the family. His death in a distant country unknown to most of the people of the village paralyzed his family and friends and came as a shock to all.

The most horrible week was when there was nothing but the telegram, that ridiculous piece of paper saying what could not be believed. But when the body was flown back and brought into the village, the death of this student could be celebrated. The fact that he had died while really doing good could be affirmed, and his past could be remembered as a chain of events that had led to the tragic accident. But I am deeply convinced that it became a real celebration only because of the fact that new life became visible around the body of this young man. Suddenly people realized what it means to give one's life for others; men and women who had never heard about Tunisia started to talk about it and to ask what kind of people those strange-looking Muslims really were. People from the city met people from the village and became friends. And after the body was covered with sand people began to be aware that their world had become wider, their ideas larger, and their perspectives deeper. The present indeed held promises for the future. This became clear when a few months later many more students made plans to continue what their friend had begun.

So celebrating means the affirmation of the present, which becomes fully possible only by remembering the past and expecting more to come in the future. But celebrating in this sense very seldom takes place. Nothing is as difficult as really accepting one's own life. More often than not the present is denied, the past becomes a source of complaints, and the future is looked upon as a reason for despair or apathy.

When Jesus came to redeem humankind, he came to free us from the boundaries of time. Through him it became clear not only that God is with us wherever our presence is in time or space but also that our past does not have to be forgotten or denied but can be remembered and forgiven, and that we are still waiting for him to come back and reveal to us what remains unseen. When Jesus left his Apostles he gave them bread and wine in memory of what he did so that he could stay in their presence until the moment of his return.

The word "Eucharist," which means thanksgiving, expresses a way of accepting life in which the past and the future are brought together in the present moment. This thanksgiving is meant to be a way of living that makes it possible to really celebrate life. Frequently, this Eucharistic celebration of life takes place elsewhere than where it is formally planned. Life is not always really celebrated where liturgies are held. Sometimes it is, but quite often it is not. Perhaps we have to become more sensitive to people and places where no one ever talks about liturgical reform or changes but where life is fully affirmed in the deepest Eucharistic sense.

II. What Kind of Person Makes Celebration Possible?

When we now wish to speak about ministers who enable us to celebrate, we are faced with the fact that for people in our culture celebrating has become extremely difficult to do. It seems that the Christian invitation to celebrate, to accept your life as the only life you have, to live it and accept it as good, has become the most difficult challenge we are facing.

We live in a culture in which the words of Jesus "Do not worry about tomorrow: tomorrow will take care of itself" (Mt 6:34) sound beautiful and romantic but completely unrealistic. We live in such a utilitarian society that even our most intimate moments have become subject to the question "What is the purpose of it?"

We do not just eat and drink but have business lunches and fund-raising dinners. We do not just go horseback riding or swimming but also invite our companions to do a little business on horseback or even in the pool. We do not just exercise our bodies or listen to beautiful songs but also become involved in a tremendous industry of sports and music. And we always keep on believing that the real thing is going to happen tomorrow. In this kind of life the past has degenerated into a series of used or misused opportunities, the present into a constant concern about accomplishments, and the future into a make-believe paradise where we hope finally to receive what we always wanted but basically doubt.

A life like this cannot be celebrated because we are constantly concerned with changing it into something else, always trying to do something to it, get something out of it, and make it fit our many plans and projects. We go to meetings, conferences, and congresses. We critically evaluate our part, discuss how to do it better in the future, and worry about whether or not our great design will ever work out. Our culture is a working, hurrying, and worrying culture with many opportunities except the opportunity to celebrate life.

Insofar as this is true, we may wonder how Christian our culture really is. It is a remarkable fact that the first and strongest reactions against this style of life have come not from the churches but from the many people living on the fringes of our society, trying to give shape to what Theodore Roszak has called "the counterculture." It is in the youthful opposition to our technocratic society that we find some authentic elements of a celebrating style of life. In the voices of those who announce the new counterculture we might hear sounds familiar to the Christian ear.

Roszak writes:

> The primary project of our counter-culture is: to proclaim a new heaven and a new earth, so vast, so marvelous, that the inordinate claims of technical expertise must of necessity withdraw in the presence of such splendor to a subordinate and marginal status in the lives of man—we must be prepared to consider the scandalous possibility that wherever the

visionary imagination grows bright, magic, that old antagonist of science, renews itself, transmitting our workday reality into something bigger, perhaps more frightening, certainly more adventurous than the lesser rationality of objective conscience can ever countenance.[2]

This is announcing a new life that can be celebrated. But where does this leave ministers and priests who, though still having many faithful people in their churches, do not find members of the counterculture in their congregations? As long as ministers do no more than use Sunday to soften the pains of the week, their teaching, preaching, counseling, and organizing remain services to a life that cannot be celebrated.

But if they want to show the way to celebration, ministers have to be special kinds of people. They have to be and become more and more obedient—that is, allow themselves to be guided by the voices they hear. They have to be obedient to the voices of nature, to the voices of other people, and to the voice of God.

Let us therefore look next at the spirituality of the celebrant in the perspective of these three areas of obedience.

1. Obedience to the voices of nature

Those who want to help others celebrate first of all have to be obedient to the voices of nature and able to translate their message for other people. Perhaps we have a lot to learn from the Indians here. It seems that we have become so concerned with mastering nature that we no longer hear the voices of the rivers, the trees, the birds, and the flowers, which are constantly telling us about our own condition of life, our beauty, and our mortality.

A Wintu Indian says:

> The white people never cared for land or deer or bear. When we Indians kill meat, we eat it all up. When we dig roots, we make little holes. . . . We shake down acorns and pine nuts. We don't chop down trees. We only use dead wood. But the white people plow up the ground, pull up the trees, kill everything. The tree says, "Don't, I am sore. Don't hurt me." But they chop it down and cut it up. The spirit of the land hates them. . . . The Indians never hurt anything, but the white people destroy all.[3]

Indians know they have to become more and more a part of nature, brothers and sisters of all creatures, so that they can find their real place in this world. They make their artwork in obedience to nature. In their masks human and animal faces merge, in their pottery they use vegetables, such as the gourd, for models. It is nature that teaches them the forms they can make with their own hands.

It is not so difficult to understand why, through all the ages, people searching for the meaning of life tried to live as close to nature as possible. Not only St. Benedict, St. Francis, and St. Bruno in the olden days but also Thomas Merton, who lived in the woods of Kentucky, and the Benedictine monks who built their monastery in an isolated canyon in New Mexico. It is not so strange that many young people are leaving the cities and going out into the country to find peace by listening to the voices of nature. And nature indeed speaks: the birds to St. Francis, the trees to the Indians, the river to Siddhartha. And the closer we come to nature, the closer we touch the core of life when we celebrate. Nature makes us aware of the preciousness of life. Nature tells us that life is precious not only because it is but also because it does not have to be.

I remember sitting day after day at the same table in a dull restaurant where I had to eat my lunch. There was a beautiful red rose in a small vase in the middle of the table. I looked at the rose with sympathy and enjoyed its beauty. Every day I talked with my rose. But then I became suspicious. Because while my mood was changing during the week from happy to sad, from disappointed to angry, from energetic to apathetic, my rose was always the same. And moved by my suspicion I lifted my fingers to the rose and touched it. It was a plastic thing. I was deeply offended and never went back there to eat.

We cannot talk with plastic nature because it cannot tell us the real story about life and death. But if we are sensitive to the voices of nature, we might be able to hear sounds from a world where humanity and nature both find their shape. We will never fully understand the meaning of the sacramental signs of bread and wine when they do not make us realize that the whole of nature is a sacrament pointing to a reality far beyond itself. The presence of Christ in the Eucharist becomes a "special problem" only when we have lost our sense of Christ's presence in all that is, grows, lives, and dies. What happens during a Sunday celebration can only be a real celebration when it reminds us in the fullest sense of what continually happens every day in the world which surrounds us. Bread is more than bread; wine is more than wine: It is God with us—not as an isolated event once a week but as the concentration of a mystery about which all of nature speaks day and night.

Therefore, wasting food is not a sin just because there are still so many hungry people in this world. It is a sin because it is an offense against the sacramental reality of all we eat and drink. But if we become more and more aware of the voices of all that surrounds us and grow in respect and reverence for nature, then we also will be able to truly care for humanity, since we are embedded in nature like a sapphire in a golden ring.

2. Obedience to the voices of other people

For those who want to bring others to the celebration of their lives, however, obedience to people is even more important than obedience to nature. Those who are really able to listen to people will be able to recognize their desire as well as their fear of celebrating. Celebration asks for the willingness to be enraptured by the greatness of the mystery which surrounds us, and for many, who would like to be in real touch with the ground of their own existence, there is a deep-seated anxiety about being absorbed by it and losing their identity. We cannot live without the sun, but we know that by coming too close to it we will be burned. Utilitarians have built a thick wall between themselves and the source of their existence out of fear of total absorption. But that same wall dooms them to cold and alienated lives. They know this and desperately ask the minister, who should know how to be close without being absorbed, to offer a way to participate in what is real life.

Roszak expresses this deep human desire when he writes:

> It is, at last, reality itself that must be participated in, must be seen, touched, breathed with the conviction that here is the ultimate ground of our existence, available to all, capable of ennobling by its majesty the life of every man who opens himself. It is participation of this order— experiential and not merely political—that alone can guarantee the dignity and autonomy of the individual citizen. The strange youngsters who don cowbells and primitive talismans and who take to the public parks or wilderness to improvise outlandish communal ceremonies are in reality seeking to ground democracy safely beyond the culture of expertise.[4]

But what many young people do is, in fact, part of the desire of every human being: to live life to the fullest, on the deepest possible level. Ministers or priests are challenged to offer the way. They are looked upon as people who have closer contact with this reality than many others, not as a personal privilege but as a peculiar gift which they are to share. When Roszak describes the shaman, he describes at the same time the service every minister and priest should offer: to be like an "artist, who lays his work before the community in the hope that through it, as through a window, the reality he has fathomed can be witnessed by all who give attention."[5]

By participating in ritual, the community is able to see, feel, touch, and fully experience without fear of absorption the reality that ministers have discovered for them. In Roszak's words: "Ritual is the [minister's] way of broadcasting his vision, it is his instructive offering. If the [minister's] work is successful, the community's sense of reality will become expansive."[6]

The great temptation is to consider the priests' or ministers' closeness to the mystery of God as a privilege instead of a responsibility, and to turn their vocation into a special status and their ministry into an exploitive enterprise. But when ministers really can be obedient to their people they will recognize the deep desire to see what they saw, to hear what they heard, to touch what they touched, and to break down the wall that separates them from the "Unseen" (William James) Reality of the universe. Then ministers will keep searching for ways and channels, forms and rituals, songs, dances, and gestures that enable their brothers and sisters to come into vibrant contact with the Holy without fear. Then they will make it possible for people to take down their scaffolding and to freely celebrate life.

3. Obedience to the voice of God

But do priests and ministers have any peculiar gift which they can share? Do they have a vision they can offer to help others see? Are they any closer than anyone else to the source of their existence, and do they know, feel, and see more deeply the condition in we are imprisoned but from which we want to become free?

If the answer is *no,* we may rightly wonder if ministers will ever be able to help us celebrate life. Those who are set apart to lead people to the heart of God's mystery will never be able to do so when they are blind, do not know the way, or are afraid to approach the throne of God.

Ordination means the recognition and affirmation of the fact that one has gone beyond the walls of fear, lives in intimate contact with the God of the living, and has a burning desire to show others the way to that Mystery. Ordination does not make anybody anything, but it is the solemn recognition of the fact that this individual has been able to be obedient to God, to hear God's voice and understand the call, and that the ordinand can offer others the way to that same experience. Therefore, ministers who want to make celebration possible are people of prayer. Only people of prayer can lead others to celebration because everyone who comes in contact with them realizes that they draw their powers from a source they cannot easily locate but they know is strong and deep.

The freedom that gives ministers a certain independence is not authoritarian or distant. Rather, it makes them rise above the immediate needs and most urgent desires of the people around them. Ministers are deeply moved by things happening around them, but they do not allow themselves to be crushed by them. They listen attentively, speak with a self-evident authority, but do not easily get excited or nervous. In all they say or do, they prove to have a vision that guides their lives. To that vision they are obedient. It makes them distinguish sharply between what is important and what is not. They are not insensitive to what excites people, but they evaluate people's needs differently by seeing them in the perspective of their vision. Ministers are happy and content when people listen to them, but they do not want to form cliques. They do not attach themselves to anybody exclusively. What they say sounds convincing and obvious, but they do not force their opinions on anybody and are not irritated when people do not accept their ideas or fulfill their will. All this shows that their vision is what counts for them and that they strive to make it come true.

But ministers also have an inner freedom in respect to this ideal. They know they will not see their purpose realized, and they consider themselves only guides to it. They are impressively free toward their own lives. From their actions it becomes clear that they consider their own existence of secondary importance. They do not live to keep themselves alive but to build a new world, of which they have already seen the first images and which so appeals to them that the borderline between life and death loses its definitiveness. These are people who not only celebrate life but also can make others desire to do the same.

And so we have seen how obedience to nature, to other people, and to God are three characteristics of those who want to be servants in the celebration of life. No one can claim to be such a celebrant. Only Jesus could because only he was obedient to God and creation unto death, even death on the Cross. It was on the Cross that Jesus became the celebrant of life in the full sense because it was there that death was conquered and life regained in the total act of obedience. In this way, any who call themselves ministers can only consider themselves weak reflections of the One who gave his life on the Cross and made it available to all who are called to celebrate their lives as children of the same Father.

Conclusion

The main idea of this chapter is that obedience to God and creation is the basic condition for being a celebrant of life. If a minister claims to want others to fully accept their lives as their own by affirmation, remembrance, and expectation, he or she is challenged to be a servant of life who can listen to the voices of nature, other people, and God and announce what has been heard to those who want to join in the act of celebration.

Through celebration we enter the Kingdom. But Jesus said: "Unless you change and become like little children you will never enter the kingdom of Heaven" (Mt 18:3). It is through childlike obedience that life becomes a way to the Kingdom. And if you have ever offered bread and wine to God on the rim of the Grand Canyon, you might have experienced that we can really celebrate when humility has made us free. We are only a very small part of history and have only one short life to live, but when we take the fruits of our labor in our hands and stretch our arms to God in the deep belief that God hears us and accepts our gifts, then we know that all our life is given, given to celebrate.

CONCLUSION

•

A Spirituality of Ministry

IF THERE IS ANY SENTENCE in the Gospel that expresses in a very concentrated way everything I have tried to say in the five chapters of this book, it is the sentence spoken by Jesus to his Apostles the day before his death: "No one can have greater love than to lay down his life for his friends" (Jn 15:13).

For me these words summarize the meaning of all Christian ministry. If teaching, preaching, individual pastoral care, organizing, and celebrating are acts of service that go beyond the level of professional expertise, it is precisely because in these acts ministers are asked to lay down their own lives for their friends. There are many people who, through long training, have reached a high level of competence in terms of understanding human behavior but few who are willing to lay down their own lives for others and make their weakness a source of creativity. For many individuals professional training means power. But ministers, who take off their clothes to wash the feet of their friends, are powerless, and their training and formation are meant to enable them to face their own weakness without fear and make it available to others. It is exactly this creative weakness that gives the ministry its momentum.

Teaching becomes ministry when teachers move beyond the transference of knowledge and are willing to offer their own life experience to their students so that paralyzing anxiety can be removed, new, liberating insight can come about, and real learning can take place. Preaching becomes ministry when preachers move beyond the "telling of the story" and make their own deepest selves available so that their hearers will be able to receive the Word of God. Individual care becomes ministry when those who want to be of help move beyond the careful balance of give-and-take with a willingness to risk their own lives and remain faithful to their suffering sisters and brothers even when their own names and fame are in danger. Organizing becomes ministry when organizers move beyond their desire for concrete results and look at their world with the unwavering hope for a total renewal. Celebrating becomes ministry when celebrants move beyond the limits of protective rituals to an obedient acceptance of life as a gift.

Although none of these tasks of service can ever be fulfilled without careful preparation and proved competence, none can ever be called ministry when this competence is not grounded in the radical commitment to lay down one's own life in the service of others. Ministry means the ongoing attempt to put one's own search for God, with all its moments of pain and joy, despair and hope, at the disposal of those who want to join this search but do not know how. Therefore, ministry is in no way a privilege. Instead, it is the core of the Christian life. No Christian is a Christian without being a minister. There are many more forms of ministry than the five I have discussed in this book, which usually fill the daily life of ordained ministers and priests. But whatever form the Christian ministry takes, the basis is always the same: to lay down one's life for one's friends.

But why do people lay down their lives for their friends? There is only one answer to that question: to give new life. All functions of the ministry are life-giving. Whether one teaches, preaches, counsels, plans, or celebrates, the aim is to open new perspectives, to offer new insight, to give new strength, to break through the chains of death and destruction, and to create new life which can be affirmed. In short—to make the minister's weakness creative.

So, if people want to be ministers, let them be happy to make their weaknesses their special boast so that the power of Christ may rest upon them, for when one is weak then one is strong (cf. St. Paul, 2 Cor 12:9–10).

But although no one can live and keep living without need for this ministry, for many people, who are exposed to the growing destructive potentials of our world and have seen the most ruthless and cruel annihilation of life during their own short history, Christianity does not seem able to offer this indispensable ministry. When they hear about the life of Jesus and his Apostles, they wonder what that story has to do with this age. When they are told that their lives play a meaningful role in the great history of humankind, in which redemption through the death of Jesus has to become more and more visible, they, in fact, do not see much more than an increasing escalation of war, poverty, cruelty, and senseless destruction of the environment. When they are confronted with the idea that this life is not final and that they will find its continuation in a world after this, their question is whether there is much here that calls for continuation and whether it makes sense to think about some new life in a vague future when even words like "tomorrow," "next week," "next year," and "later" are losing their meaning in a world that can kill not only the human race but also our history.

Perhaps the apparent crisis in the Christian ministry is directly related to the fact that humanity today, exposed to so many fearful and widely contrasting experiences and ideas, has hardly any meaningful roots in the past nor much expectation for the future. Robert Jay Lifton speaks of a "worldwide sense of . . . historical dislocation," which he describes as "a break in the sense of connection which men have long felt with the vital and nourishing symbols of their cultural tradition—symbols revolving around family, idea systems, religion, and the life cycle in general."[1]

But if our present age—which is able to destroy not just individuals and families but whole cultures and their histories, whole countries and their chances for rebirth—has caused many people to lose confidence in the Christian ministry, the question is whether we have fully understood what it means today to lay down one's life for one's friends.

Maybe we have to look beyond the institutional church to grasp the full implications of this call, because words such as "concentration," "meditation," and "contemplation" are again used today with great reverence by thousands of young people who would never think of going to a church or consulting a Christian minister. In a great variety of ways they try to break through their confusion and restlessness to find in the center of their own experience something that can make them reach beyond their limited consciousness. They are experimenting with new methods of relating to each other, new ways of nonviolent communication, new approaches to the experience of oneness and union, new means of mutual care, and new attempts to celebrate their lives. They borrow symbols not only from Christian tradition but also from Buddhism and Hinduism; they try to broaden their sensitivities by natural and artificial stimuli such as flowers, incense, and hallucinogenic drugs. They form communities, share their possessions, and read, sing, and prophesy to experience a new sense of freedom.

It is no exaggeration to say that, while the churches become emptier year after year, new forms of ministry are being sought on the periphery of Christianity and that teaching, preaching, caring, planning, and celebrating are appearing in new ways in the many catacombs of our modern cities. In the middle of our chaotic world we have become increasingly aware of the permanent threat of total destruction and cry desperately for a new "spirituality" that enables us to come to terms with our search for meaning.

This new spirituality is described by Lifton as "the path of experiential transcendence—of seeking a sense of immortality in the way the mystics always have, through psychic experience of such great intensity that time and death are, in effect, eliminated."[2]

It is painful to realize that very few ministers are able to offer the rich mystical tradition of Christianity as a source of rebirth for the generation searching for new life in the midst of the debris of a faltering civilization. Perhaps our self-consciousness, fear of rejection, and preoccupation with church quarrels prevent us from being free to experience the transcendent Spirit of God, which can renew our hearts and our world as well. Perhaps we are not ready yet to give the much-needed guidance to the thousands who engage in a risky experimentation with the powers of the unseen. Perhaps we ourselves have lost contact with these powers and can only qualify the stories of the catacombs as weird, dangerous, and signs of immaturity. But I am afraid that the many obvious mistakes, failures, and unintelligible experiments blind us to the fact that underneath all of this is a deep desire for new insight, new understanding, and most of all, new life.

If I can trust my own feelings and limited experiences with young students, it seems that we are approaching a period of an increased search for spirituality that is the experience of God in this very moment of our existence. When there is so little in the past to hold on to and so little in the future to look forward to, the reality that can give meaning to one's life must be experienced here and now.

A twenty-year-old Catholic student who considered his church completely irrelevant for his needs, but who was desperately searching for meaning to his life, said to me: "We tried drugs and they did not work; we tried sex and it did not work; the next thing will be suicide—in the coming years you will see the number of suicides skyrocketing." The only possible response to this seems to be to rediscover the transcending power of the spiritual life by which we are able to stand strong even when surrounded by shifting ideologies, crumbling political, social, and religious structures, and a constant threat of war and total destruction. It may be extremely difficult for those of us living today to feel close to Jesus of Nazareth as a man who lived in another world; it may be even more difficult to look forward to the day of his return; but more than ever it may be possible to experience the Spirit of Christ as a living Spirit who makes it possible to break through the boundaries of our imprisoned existence and frees us to work for a new world.

But this way of the transcendental experience requires ministry. It calls for men and women who do not shy away from careful preparation, solid formation, and qualified training but at the same time are free enough to break through the restrictive boundaries of disciplines and specialties in the conviction that the Spirit moves beyond professional expertise. It calls for Christians who are willing to develop their sensitivity to God's presence in their own lives, as well as in the lives of others, and to offer their experiences as a way of recognition and liberation to their brothers and sisters. It calls for ministers in the true sense, who lay down their own lives for their friends, helping them to distinguish between the constructive and the destructive spirits and making them free for the discovery of God's life-giving Spirit in the midst of this maddening world. It calls for creative weakness.

EPILOGUE

∎

WHEN I LOOK BACK at the way I wrote this book, I begin to realize that it is a very personal book. In fact, it is an attempt to articulate ideas and feelings about the ministry based on the ups and downs of my own experiences. I hoped that a careful reflection on these experiences could throw some light on the different questions I had asked myself and give some insight into the direction I want to go from here.

I also hoped that my "confession" could be of some help to others in the ongoing discussion about the value and meaning of the Christian ministry. Therefore, in concluding this book I want to suggest not the end of a discussion but the beginning of one. In fact, this discussion has already become part of this book, because while presenting the chapters to priests and ministers, to sisters and social workers, to parents and students, I became more and more aware that many people had completely different experiences from those I had and could hardly recognize themselves in the ideas I tried to formulate. When I was confronted with so many questions and criticisms my first inclination was to go back to the text and start all over again. But then I realized that this was impossible, because I could not change my own past and had to accept the limitation attached to being personal. My friend Don McNeill even made me see that it would be much more realistic and in line with my own conviction if I presented the questions and criticisms at the end of this book instead of smuggling the untested answers into the text itself.

Well, there are many unanswered questions. And every chapter has its own. I should like to formulate some of them here.

On teaching:

> What you say about the relationship between student and teacher may be interesting for a college situation, but what about grade school and high school? Does your whole idea not become very romantic when you are confronted with the task of teaching mathematics to small children who can hardly sit quietly for a minute?

On preaching:

> Don't you have to be a trained psychologist to be available to others in the way you suggest? What about the ordinary priest who has to get up into that pulpit every week? Aren't you a little too demanding? And, after all, is the direct presentation of the Word of God, welcome or unwelcome, not more important than the subtle clarification of people's feelings?

On individual pastoral care:

> I work as a chaplain in a prison with twenty men in one cell. When I come into the cell the prisoners fight for the chance to talk to me and to ask me for very concrete help—to find out where their children are, to visit their wives, to ask when their trial will be, to find some medicine, et cetera, et cetera. What does it mean to be a pastor for these men? It seems I do not have to go beyond professionalism to fulfill the task of four different professions at once!

On organizing:

> If you had been a priest in the ghettos you never would have said what you did. You missed the point completely. You are simply soft-pedaling the whole issue. You suggest an unrealistic detachment in an emergency situation.

On celebrating:

> What about the children who never have lived in nature and probably never will? What about the millions of people living in the ever-growing cities? How should they celebrate?

I do not know the answers to these questions and criticisms. They are undoubtedly a convincing illustration of the limitations of my own ideas. But I hope that they also show the value and necessity of sharing experiences as a primary condition for an ongoing search for a spirituality of ministry.

NOTES

1. Beyond the Transference of Knowledge

1. Bernard Lonergan, *Insight* (London: Longmans, Green, 1957), p. 191.
2. Ibid., p. 192.

2. Beyond the Retelling of the Story

1. See Daphne D. C. Pochin Mould, "Let's Abolish the Sunday Sermon," *U.S. Catholic,* July 1970.
2. This example is used with the permission of Mr. Leo Lans, a student at the Catholic Theological Institute in Utrecht, Holland.
3. *Yale Daily News,* Apr. 20, 1970.
4. Carl Rogers, *On Becoming a Person* (Boston: Houghton Mifflin, 1961), p. 26.
5. Thomas Oden, *The Structure of Awareness* (Nashville: Abingdon Press, 1969), pp. 23–24.

3. Beyond the Skillful Response

1. This case is used with the permission of Dr. Seward Hiltner of Princeton Theological Seminary.

2. See Gordon W. Allport, *The Individual and His Religion* (New York: Macmillan, 1960), p. 23.
3. Thomas Merton, *Zen and the Birds of Appetite* (New York: New Directions, 1960), p. 76.
4. H. H. M. Fortmann, *Oosterse Renaissance* (Ambo Bilthoven, 1970), p. 6.
5. Russel Dicks, *The Art of Ministering to the Sick* (New York: Macmillan, 1936), p. 256.
6. Anton Boisen, *The Exploration of the Inner World* (New York: Harper & Row, Harper Torchbooks), p. 135.

4. Beyond the Manipulation of Structures

1. Herbert McCabe, "Priesthood and Revolution," *Commonweal,* Sept. 20, 1968, p. 626.
2. Arthur Koestler, *The Yogi and the Commissar* (New York: Collier Books, 1945).
3. See Paul Pruyser, *A Dynamic Psychology of Religion* (New York: Harper & Row, 1968), pp. 166–70.

5. Beyond the Protective Ritual

1. Bimonthly Newsletter of the Ecumenical Institute, vol. 4, no. 3 (Jan.–Feb. 1970), p. 3.
2. Theodore Roszak, *The Making of a Counter-Culture* (New York: Doubleday, Anchor Books, 1969), p. 240.
3. Ibid., p. 245.
4. Ibid., p. 265.
5. Ibid., p. 260.
6. Ibid.

Conclusion

1. Robert Jay Lifton, "Protean Man," *Partisan Review,* 1968, p. 16.
2. Ibid., p. 27.

THE
WOUNDED HEALER
Ministry in

Contemporary Society

∎

To Colin and Phyllis Williams

ACKNOWLEDGMENTS

■

MANY PEOPLE HAVE PLAYED important roles in the development of the different chapters of this book. Those to whom I presented parts of the manuscript in lecture form have been especially helpful in reorganizing and rephrasing major sections.

I am very grateful to Steve Thomas and Rufus Lusk for their substantial help in the final stage of the manuscript, to Inday Day for her excellent secretarial help, and to Elizabeth Bartelme for her encouragement and competent editorial assistance.

I have dedicated this book to Colin and Phyllis Williams, who by their friendship and hospitality made the Yale Divinity School a real free space for me.

CONTENTS

■

INTRODUCTION

■

The Four Open Doors

WHAT DOES IT MEAN to be a minister in our contemporary society? This question has been raised during the last few years by many men and women who want to be of service but who find the familiar ways crumbling and themselves stripped of their traditional protections.

The following chapters are an attempt to respond to this question. But as Antonio Porchia says: "A door opens to me. I go in and am faced with a hundred closed doors."[1] Any new insight which suggested an answer led me to many new questions, which remained unanswered. But I wanted at least to prevent the temptation of not entering any doors at all out of fear of the closed ones. This explains the structure of this book. The four chapters can be seen as four different doors through which I have tried to enter into the problems of ministry in our modern world. The first door represents the condition of a suffering world (Chapter 1); the second door, the condition of a suffering generation (Chapter 2); the third door, the condition of a suffering individual (Chapter 3); and the fourth door, the condition of a suffering minister (Chapter 4).

The unity of this book lies more in a tenacious attempt to respond to the ministers who are questioning their own relevance and effectiveness than in a consistent theme or a fully documented theoretical argument. Maybe our fragmented life experiences combined with our sense of urgency do not allow for a "handbook for ministers." However, in the middle of all this fragmentation one image slowly arose as the focus: the wounded healer. This image was the last in coming. After all my attempts to articulate the predicament of contemporary humanity, the necessity to articulate the predicament of ministers themselves became most important. For ministers are called to recognize the sufferings of their time in their own hearts and to make that recognition the starting point of their service. Whether they try to enter into a dislocated world, relate to a rootless generation, or speak to a dying individual, their service will not be perceived as authentic unless it comes from hearts wounded by the suffering about which they speak.

Thus nothing can be written about ministry without a deeper understanding of the ways in which ministers can make their own wounds available as sources of healing. Therefore this book is called *The Wounded Healer*.

1

MINISTRY IN A
DISLOCATED WORLD

•

The Search of Nuclear Humanity

Introduction

FROM TIME TO TIME a person enters your life who, by appearance, behavior, and words, intimates in a dramatic way the condition of contemporary humanity. Peter was such a person for me. He came to ask for help, but at the same time he offered a new understanding of my own world! Peter is twenty-six years old. His body is fragile; his face, framed in long blond hair, is thin and has a city pallor. His eyes are tender and radiate a longing melancholy. His lips are sensual, and his smile evokes an atmosphere of intimacy. When he shakes hands he breaks through the formal ritual in such a way that you feel his body as really present. When he speaks, his voice assumes tones that ask to be listened to with careful attention.

As we talk, it becomes clear that Peter feels as if the many boundaries that give structure to life are becoming increasingly vague. His life seems a drifting over which he has no control, a life determined by many known and unknown factors in his surroundings. The clear distinction between himself and his milieu is gone, and he feels that his ideas and emotions are not really his; rather, they are brought upon him. Sometimes he wonders: "What is fantasy and what is reality?" Often he has the strange feeling that small devils enter his head and create a painful and anxious confusion. He also does not know whom he can trust and whom not, what he shall do and what not, why to say yes to one and no to another. The many distinctions between good and bad, ugly and beautiful, attractive and repulsive are losing meaning for him. Even to the most bizarre suggestions he says: "Why not? Why not try something I have never tried? Why not have a new experience, good or bad?"

In the absence of clear boundaries between himself and his milieu, between fantasy and reality, between what to do and what to avoid, it seems that Peter has become a prisoner of the now, caught in the present without meaningful connections with his past or future. When he goes home he feels that he enters a realm which has become alien to him. The words his parents use, their questions and concerns, their aspirations and worries seem to belong to another world, with another language and another mood. When he looks into his future everything becomes an impenetrable cloud. He finds no answers to questions about why he lives and where he is heading. Peter is not working hard to reach a goal, he does not look forward to the fulfillment of a deep desire, nor does he expect that something great or important is going to happen. He looks into empty space and is sure of only one thing: If there is anything worthwhile in life it must be here and now.

I did not paint this portrait of Peter to show you a sick man in need of psychiatric help. No, I think Peter's situation is in many ways typical of the condition of modern men and women. Perhaps Peter needs help, but his experiences and feelings cannot be understood merely in terms of individual psychopathology. They are part of the historical context in which we all live, a context which makes it possible to see in Peter's life the signs of the times, which we too recognize in our own life experiences. What we see in Peter is a painful expression of the situation of what has been called "nuclear" humanity.

In this chapter I would like to arrive at a deeper understanding of our human predicament as it becomes visible through the many men and women who experience life as Peter does. And I hope to discover in the midst of our present ferment new ways to freedom.

I will therefore divide this chapter into two parts: the predicament of nuclear humanity, and the way to liberation.

I. The Predicament of Nuclear Humanity

Nuclear humanity has lost naïve faith in the possibilities of technology and is painfully aware that the same powers that enable us to create new lifestyles carry the potential for self-destruction.

Let me tell you a tale from ancient India which might help us to capture the situation.

Four royal sons were questioning what specialty they should master. They said to one another, "Let us search the earth and learn a special science." So they decided, and after they had agreed on a place where they would meet again, the four brothers started off, each in a different direction. Time went by, and the brothers met again at the appointed meeting place, and they asked one another what they had learned. "I have mastered a science," said the first, "which makes it possible for me, if I have nothing but a piece of bone of some creature, to create straightaway the flesh that goes with it." "I," said the second, "know how to grow that creature's skin and hair if there is flesh on its bones." The third said, "I am able to create its limbs if I have the flesh, the skin, and the hair." "And I," concluded the fourth, "know how to give life to that creature if its form is complete with limbs."

Thereupon the four brothers went into the jungle to find a piece of bone so that they could demonstrate their specialties. As fate would have it, the bone they found was a lion's, but they did not know that and picked up the bone. One added flesh to the bone, the second grew hide and hair, the third completed it with matching limbs, and the fourth gave the lion life. Shaking its heavy mane, the ferocious beast arose with its menacing mouth, sharp teeth, and merciless claws and jumped on his creators. He killed them all and vanished contentedly into the jungle.[1]

Nuclear humanity realizes that our creative powers hold the potential for self-destruction. We see that in this nuclear age vast new industrial complexes enable us to produce in one hour what we labored over for years in the past, but we also realize that these same industries have disturbed the ecological balance and, through air and noise pollution, have contaminated our own milieu. We drive in cars, listen to the radio, and watch TV but have lost the ability to understand the workings of the instruments we use. We see such an abundance of material commodities around us that scarcity no longer motivates us, but at the same time we are groping for a direction and asking for meaning and purpose. In all this we suffer from the inevitable knowledge that in our time it has become possible for us to destroy not only life but also the possibility of rebirth, not only living human beings but also humankind, not only periods of existence but also history itself. For nuclear humanity the future has become an option.

Prenuclear humanity might be aware of the real paradox of a world in which life and death touch each other in a morbid way and in which humanity finds itself on the thin rope which can break so easily, but prenuclear humanity has adapted this knowledge to a previous optimistic outlook on life. For nuclear humanity, however, this new knowledge cannot be adapted to old insights nor be channeled by traditional institutions; rather it radically and definitively disrupts all existing frames of human reference. For nuclear humanity, the problem is not that the future holds a new danger, such as a nuclear war, but that there might be no future at all.

Young people are not necessarily nuclear, and old people are not necessarily prenuclear. The difference is not in age but in consciousness and related lifestyle. The psychohistorian Robert Jay Lifton has given us some excellent concepts to determine the nature of the quandaries of nuclear humanity. In Lifton's terms, nuclear humanity can be characterized by (1) a historical dislocation, (2) a fragmented ideology, and (3) a search for immortality. It might be useful to examine Peter's life in the light of these concepts.

1. Historical dislocation

When Peter's father asks him when he will take his final exam and whether he has found a good girl to marry, and when his mother carefully inquires about confession and communion and his membership in a Catholic fraternity, they both suppose that Peter's expectations for the future are essentially the same as theirs. But Peter thinks of himself more as one of the "last ones in the experiment of living" than as a pioneer working for a new future. Therefore, symbols used by his parents cannot possibly have the unifying and integrating power for him which they have for people with a prenuclear mentality. This experience we call "historical dislocation." Lifton describes it as a "break in the sense of connection, which men have long felt with the vital and nourishing symbol of their cultural tradition; symbols revolving around family, idea-systems, religion, and the life-cycle in general."[2] Why should someone marry and have children, study and build a career; why should someone invent new techniques, build new institutions, and develop new ideas when that person doubts if there will be a tomorrow which can guarantee the value of human effort?

Crucial here is the lack of a sense of continuity, which is so vital for a creative life. Nuclear humanity has become part of a nonhistory in which only the sharp moment of the here and now is valuable. For nuclear humanity life easily becomes a bow whose string is broken and from which no arrow can fly. In this dislocated state we become paralyzed. Our reactions are not anxiety and joy, which were so much a part of existential humanity, but apathy and boredom. Only when people feel themselves responsible for the future can they have hope or despair; when they think of themselves as the passive victims of an extremely complex technological bureaucracy, their motivation falters and they start drifting from one moment to the next, making life a long row of randomly chained incidents and accidents.

When we wonder why the language of traditional Christianity has lost its liberating power, we have to realize that most Christian preaching is still based on the presupposition that people see themselves as meaningfully integrated with a history in which God came to us in the past, is living among us in the present, and will come to liberate us in the future. But when our historical consciousness is broken, the whole Christian message seems like a lecture about the great pioneers to a young person using LSD.

2. Fragmented ideology

One of the most surprising aspects of Peter's life is his fast-shifting value system. For many years he was a very strict and obedient seminarian. He went to daily Mass, took part in the many hours of community prayers, was active on a liturgical committee, and studied with great interest and even enthusiasm the many theological materials for his courses. But when he decided to leave the seminary and study at a secular university, it took him only a few months to shake off his old way of life. He quietly stopped going to Mass even on Sundays, spent long nights drinking and playing with other students, lived with a girlfriend, took up a field of study far removed from his theological interests, and seldom spoke about God or religion.

This is the more surprising since Peter shows absolutely no bitterness toward the old seminary. He even visits his friends there regularly and has good memories of his years as a religious man. But the idea that his two lifestyles are not very consistent hardly seems to hit him. Both experiences are valuable and have their good and bad sides, but why should life be lived in just one perspective, under the guidance of just one idea, and within one unchangeable frame of reference?

Peter neither regrets his seminary days nor glorifies his present situation. Tomorrow it might be different again. Who knows? All depends on the people you meet, the experiences you have, and the ideas and desires which make sense to you at the moment.

Nuclear humanity, like Peter, does not live with an ideology. We have shifted from the fixed and total forms of an ideology to more fluid ideological fragments.[3] One of the most visible phenomena of our time is people's tremendous exposure to divergent and often contrasting ideas, traditions, religious convictions, and lifestyles. Through mass media we are confronted with the most paradoxical human experiences. We encounter not only the most elaborate and expensive attempts to save the life of one person by heart transplantation but also the powerlessness of the world to help when thousands of people die from lack of food. We encounter not only the ability to travel rapidly to another planet but also our impotence to end a senseless war on this planet. We encounter not only high-level discussions about human rights and Christian morality but also torture chambers in Brazil, Greece, and Vietnam. We encounter not only incredible ingenuity that can build dams, change riverbeds, and create fertile new lands but also earthquakes, floods, and tornadoes that can ruin in one hour more than we can build in a generation.

An individual confronted with all this and trying to make sense of it cannot possibly deceive herself or himself with a single idea, concept, or thought system which could bring these contrasting images together into one consistent outlook on life.

"The extraordinary flow of post-modern cultural influences" asks a growing flexibility, a willingness to remain open and live with the small fragments which at the moment seem to offer the best response to a given situation.[4] Paradoxically, this can lead to moments of great exhilaration and exaltation, in which we immerse ourselves totally in the flashing impressions of our immediate surroundings.

Nuclear humanity no longer believes in anything that is always and everywhere true and valid. We live by the hour and create our lives on the spot. The art of nuclear humanity is a collage art, which, though a combination of divergent pieces, is a short impression of how humanity feels at the moment. The music of nuclear humanity is an improvisation, which combines themes from various composers into something fresh as well as momentary. Our lives often look like playful expressions of feelings and ideas that need to be communicated and responded to but that do not attempt to oblige anyone else.

This fragmented ideology can prevent nuclear humanity from becoming fanatics who are willing to die or to kill for an idea. We are primarily looking for experiences that give us a sense of value. Therefore we are very tolerant, since we do not regard a person with a different conviction as a threat but rather as an opportunity to discover new ideas and test our own. We might listen with great attention to a rabbi, a minister, a priest without considering the acceptance of any system of thought but being quite willing to deepen our own understanding of what we experience as partial and fragmentary.

When nuclear humanity feels unable to relate to the Christian message, we may wonder whether this is not due to the fact that, for many people, Christianity has become an ideology. Jesus, a Jew executed by the leaders of his time, is quite often transformed into a cultural hero reinforcing the most divergent and often destructive ideological points of view. When Christianity is reduced to an all-encompassing ideology, nuclear humanity is all too prone to be skeptical about its relevance to our life experience.

3. A search for immortality

Why did Peter come for help? He himself did not know exactly what he was looking for, but he had a general, all-pervading feeling of confusion. He had lost unity and direction in his life. He had lost the boundaries which could keep him together, and he felt like a prisoner of the present, drifting from left to right, unable to decide on a definitive course. He kept studying with a sort of obedient routine to give himself the feeling of having something to do, but the long weekends and many holidays were mostly spent in sleeping, lovemaking, and just sitting around with his friends, gently distracted by music and the free-floating images of his fantasy.

Nothing seemed urgent or even important enough to become involved in. No projects or plans, no exciting goals to work for, no pressing tasks to fulfill. Peter was not torn apart by conflict, was not depressed, suicidal, or anxiety-ridden. He did not suffer from despair, but neither did he have anything to hope for. This paralysis made him suspicious about his own condition. He had discovered that even the satisfaction of his desire to embrace, to kiss, and to hold in a surrendering act of love had not created the freedom to take new steps forward. He started to wonder whether love really is enough to keep us alive in this world and whether, to be creative, we do not need to find a way to transcend the limitations of being human.

Perhaps we can find in Peter's life history events or experiences that throw some light on his apathy, but it seems just as valid to view Peter's paralysis as the paralysis of nuclear humanity, who has lost the source of creativity, which is the sense of immortality. When we are no longer able to look beyond our own deaths and relate ourselves to what extends beyond the time and space of our lives, we lose our desire to create and the excitement of being human. Therefore, I want to look at Peter's problem as that of nuclear humanity, searching for new ways of being immortal.

Robert Lifton sees as the core problem of humanity in the nuclear age the threat to our sense of immortality. This sense of immortality "represents a compelling, universal urge to maintain an inner sense of continuity over time and space, with the various elements of life." It is "man's way of experiencing his connection with all human history."[5] But for nuclear humanity the traditional modes of immortality have lost their connective power. Often people say: "I do not want to bring children into this self-destructive world." This means that the desire to live on in our children is extinguished in the face of the possible end of history. And why should people want to live on in the works of their hands when one atomic blitz may reduce them to ashes in a second? Could an animistic immortality make it possible for humankind to live on in nature? And how can a belief in a "hereafter" be an answer to the search for immortality when there is hardly any belief in the "here"? A life after death can only be thought of in terms of life before it, and nobody can dream of a new earth when there is no old earth to hold any promises.

No form of immortality—neither the immortality through children nor the immortality through works, neither the immortality through nature nor the immortality in heaven—is able to help nuclear humanity project ourselves beyond the limitations of our human existence.

It is therefore certainly not surprising that nuclear humanity cannot find an adequate expression of our experience in symbols such as Hell, Purgatory, Heaven, Hereafter, Resurrection, Paradise, and the Kingdom of God.

A preaching and teaching still based on the assumption that humanity is on the way to a new land filled with promises, and that our creative activities in this world are the first signs of what we will see in the hereafter, cannot find sounding boards in people whose minds are brooding on the suicidal potentials of their own world.

This brings us to the end of our description of nuclear humanity. Peter was our model. We saw his historical dislocation, his fragmented ideology, and his search for a new mode of immortality. Obviously, the level of awareness and visibility is different in different people, but I hope you will be able to recognize in your own experiences and the experiences of your friends some of the traits which are so visible in Peter's lifestyle. And this recognition might also help you to realize that Christianity is challenged not just to adapt itself to a modern age but also to ask itself whether its unarticulated suppositions can still form the basis for its redemptive pretensions.

II. The Way to Liberation

When you recognize nuclear humanity among your colleagues, friends, and family, maybe even in your own self-reflections, you cannot avoid asking if there is not a way to liberation and freedom for this new type of human being. More important than constructing untested answers which tend to create more irritation than comfort, we might be able to uncover, in the midst of the present confusion and stagnation, new trails that point in hopeful directions.

When we look around us we see people paralyzed by dislocation and fragmentation, caught in the prison of their own mortality. However, we also see exhilarating experiments in living by which people try to free themselves of the chains of their predicament, transcend their mortal condition, reach beyond themselves, and experience the source of a new creativity.

My own involvement in the spasms and pains of nuclear humanity makes me suspect that there are two main ways by which we try to break out of our cocoon and fly: the mystical way and the revolutionary way. Both ways can be considered modes of "experiential transcendence," and both ways seem to open new perspectives and suggest new lifestyles.[6] Let me therefore try to describe these two ways and then show how they are interrelated.

1. The mystical way

The mystical way is the inner way. People try to find in their inner lives a connection with the "reality of the unseen," "the source of being," "the point of silence." There they discover that what is most personal is most universal.[7] Beyond the superficial layers of idiosyncrasies, psychological differences, and characterological typologies, they find a center from which they can embrace all other beings at once and experience meaningful connections with all that exists. Many people who have made risky trips on LSD and returned safely from them have spoken about sensations during which they temporarily broke through their alienation, felt an intimate closeness to the mysterious power that brings humanity together, and came to a liberating insight into what lies beyond death. The increasing number of houses for meditation, concentration, and contemplation, and the many new Zen and Yoga centers show that nuclear humanity is trying to reach a moment, a point, or a center in which the distinction between life and death can be transcended and a deep connection with all of nature, as well as with all of history, can be experienced.

In whatever way we attempt to define this mode of "experiential transcendence," it seems that in all its forms people try to transcend their own worldly environment and move one, two, three, or more levels away from the unrealities of daily existence to a more encompassing view, which enables them to experience what is real. In this experience they can cut through their apathy and reach the deep currents of life in which they participate.

There they feel that they belong to a story of which they know neither the beginning nor the end but in which each of them has a unique place. By this creative distance from the unrealities of personal ambitions and urges, nuclear humanity breaks through the vicious circle of the self-fulfilling prophecy that makes us suffer from our own morbid predictions. There we come into contact with the center of our own creativity and find the strength to refuse to become passive victims of our own futurology. There we experience ourselves no longer as isolated individuals caught in the diabolic chain of cause and effect, but as people able to transcend the fences of our own predicament and reach out far beyond the concerns of self. There we touch the place where all people are revealed as equal and where compassion becomes a human possibility. There we come to the shocking, but at the same time self-evident, insight that prayer is not a pious decoration of life but the breath of human existence.

2. The revolutionary way

But there is a second way becoming visible in the present-day world of nuclear humanity. It is the revolutionary way of transcending our human predicament. Here people become aware that the choice is no longer between this world and a better world but between no world and a new world. It is the way of the person who says: Revolution is better than suicide. This individual is deeply convinced that our world is heading for the edge of the cliff, that Auschwitz, Hiroshima, Algeria, Biafra, My Lai, Attica, Bangladesh, and Northern Ireland are only a few of the many names that show how we are killing ourselves with our own absurd technological inventions. For these people no adaptation, restoration, or addition can help any longer. The liberals and progressives are fooling themselves by trying to make an intolerable situation a little more tolerable. They are tired of pruning trees and clipping branches; they want to pull out the roots of a sick society. They no longer believe that integration talks, corporate measures against air and noise pollution, peace corps, antipoverty programs, and civil-rights legislation will save a world dominated by extortion, oppression, and exploitation. Only a total upheaval of the existing order, together with a drastic change of direction, can prevent the end of everything.

But while aiming at a revolution, these people are not just motivated by a desire to liberate the oppressed, alleviate poverty, and end war. While in the past scarcity led people to revolt, present-day revolutionaries see the urgent and immediate needs of their suffering brothers and sisters as part of a much greater apocalyptic scene in which the survival of humanity itself is at stake. Their goal is not a better humanity but a new humanity, people who relate to themselves and their world in ways which are still unexplored but which belong to their hidden potentials. Their lives are not ruled by manipulation and supported by weapons but are ruled by love and supported by new ways of interpersonal communication. These new people, however, do not develop from a self-guiding process of evolution. They might or might not come about. Perhaps it is already too late. Perhaps the suicidal tendencies, visible in the growing imbalance in culture as well as nature, have reached the point of no return.

Still, the revolutionaries believe that the situation is not irreversible and that a total reorientation of humankind is just as possible as is a total self-destruction. They do not think their goal will be reached in a few years or even in a few generations, but they base their commitment on the conviction that it is better to give your life than to take life, and that the value of your actions does not depend on their immediate results. They live by the vision of a new world and refuse to be sidetracked by trivial ambitions of the moment. Thus they transcend their present condition and move from a passive fatalism to a radical activism.

3. The Christian way

Is there a third way, a Christian way? It is my growing conviction that in Jesus the mystical and the revolutionary ways are not opposites but two sides of the same human mode of experiential transcendence. I am increasingly convinced that conversion is the individual equivalent of revolution. Therefore every real revolutionary is challenged to be a mystic at heart, and the one who walks the mystical way is called to unmask the illusory quality of human society. Mysticism and revolution are two aspects of the same attempt to bring about radical change. No mystic can avoid becoming a social critic, since in self-reflection one will discover the roots of a sick society. Similarly, no revolutionary can avoid facing the human condition, since in the midst of the struggle for a new world one will find also the fight against one's own reactionary fears and false ambitions.

Mystics as well as revolutionaries have to cut loose from their selfish needs for a safe and protected existence and have to face without fear the miserable condition of themselves and their world. It is certainly not surprising that the great revolutionary leaders and the great contemplatives of our time meet in their common concern to liberate nuclear humanity from paralysis. Their personalities might be quite different, but they show the same vision, which leads to a radical self-criticism as well as to a radical activism. This vision is able to restore the "broken connection" (Lifton) with past and future, bring unity to a fragmented ideology, and reach beyond the limits of the mortal self. This vision can offer a creative distance from ourselves and our world and help us transcend the limiting walls of our human predicament.

For the mystic as well as for the revolutionary, life means breaking through the veil covering our human existence and following the vision that has become manifest to us. Whatever we call this vision—"The Holy," "The Numion," "The Spirit," or "Father"—we still believe that conversion and revolution alike derive their power from a source beyond the limitations of our own createdness.

For a Christian, Jesus is the one in whom it has indeed become manifest that revolution and conversion cannot be separated in our search for experiential transcendence. His appearance in our midst has made it undeniably clear that changing the human heart and changing human society are not separate tasks but are as interconnected as the two beams of the Cross.

Jesus was a revolutionary who did not become an extremist, since he offered not an ideology but himself. He was also a mystic who did not use his intimate relationship with God to avoid the social evils of his time but shocked his milieu to the point of being executed as a rebel. In this sense he also remains for nuclear humanity the way to liberation and freedom.

Conclusion

In this chapter we saw the predicament of nuclear humanity, characterized by historical dislocation, fragmented ideology, and the search for immortality. We discovered the mystical as well as the revolutionary way by which nuclear humanity tries to reach beyond human limitations. And finally we saw that for a Christian, the human Jesus made it manifest that these ways do not constitute a contradiction but are in fact two sides of the same mode of experiential transcendence.

I suppose you will hesitate to consider yourself a mystic or a revolutionary, but when you have eyes to see and ears to hear you will recognize both of these in your midst. They are sometimes evident to the point of irritation, sometimes only partially visible. You will find them in the eyes of the guerrilla, the young radical, or the girl with the picket sign. You will notice them in the quiet dreamer playing his guitar in the corner of a coffeehouse, in the soft voice of a friendly monk, in the melancholic smile of a student concentrating on her reading. You will see them in the mother who allows her son to go his own difficult way, in the father who reads to his child from a strange book, in the loud laughter of a young girl, and in the determination of a Black Panther.

You will find them in your own town, in your own family, and even in the strivings of your own heart, because they are in every person who draws strength from the vision that dawns on the skyline of our lives and leads to a new world.

It is this new world that fills our dreams, guides our actions, and makes us go on, at great risk, with the increasing conviction that one day we will finally be free—free to love!

2

MINISTRY FOR A ROOTLESS GENERATION

•

Looking into the Fugitive's Eyes

Introduction

TO SET THE TONE for a discussion of Christian ministry in tomorrow's world, I would like to start with a short tale.

One day a young fugitive, trying to hide himself from the enemy, entered a small village. The people were kind to him and offered him a place to stay. But when the soldiers who sought the fugitive asked where he was hiding, everyone became very fearful. The soldiers threatened to burn the village and kill every man in it unless the young man were handed over to them before dawn. The people went to the minister and asked him what to do. The minister, torn between handing over the boy to the enemy and having his people killed, withdrew to his room and read his Bible, hoping to find an answer before dawn. In the early morning his eyes fell on these words: "It is better that one man dies than that the whole people be lost."

Then the minister closed the Bible, called the soldiers, and told them where the boy was hidden. And after the soldiers led the fugitive away to be killed, there was a feast in the village because the minister had saved the lives of the people. But the minister did not celebrate. Overcome with a deep sadness, he remained in his room. That night an angel came to him and asked, "What have you done?" He said: "I handed over the fugitive to the enemy." Then the angel said: "But don't you know that you have handed over the Messiah?" "How could I know?" the minister replied anxiously. Then the angel said: "If, instead of reading your Bible, you had visited this young man just once and looked into his eyes, you would have known."

While versions of this story are very old, it seems the most modern of tales. Like that minister, who might have recognized the Messiah if he had raised his eyes from his Bible to look into the youth's eyes, we are challenged to look into the eyes of the young men and women of today, who are running from our cruel ways. Perhaps that will be enough to prevent us from handing them over to the enemy and enable us to lead them out of their hidden places into the middle of their people, where they can redeem us from our fears.

It would seem, then, that we are faced with two questions. First, how do the men and women of tomorrow look today? And second, how can we lead them to where they can redeem their people?

I. The Men and Women of Tomorrow

If the men and women of today are often thought of as anonymous members of David Riesman's lonely crowd, the men and women of tomorrow will be the children of this lonely crowd. When we look into the eyes of young people, we can catch a glimpse of a shadow of their world. Christian leadership will be shaped by at least three of the characteristics which the men and women of tomorrow share: inwardness, fatherlessness, and convulsiveness. The ministers of tomorrow must indeed take a serious look at those characteristics in their reflections and planning.

We might therefore term this generation the inward generation, the generation without fathers, and the convulsive generation. Let us see how these characteristics help us to understand more fully the men and women of tomorrow.

1. The inward generation

In a study of today's college generation published in October 1969, Jeffrey K. Hadden suggests that the best phrase with which to characterize the coming generation is "the inward generation." It is the generation which gives absolute priority to the personal and which tends in a remarkable way to withdraw into the self. This might surprise those who think of our youth as highly activist, sign-carrying protesters who stage teach-ins, sit-ins, walk-ins, and stay-ins all over the country and think of themselves in many terms but never in terms of inwardness.

First impressions, however, are not always the right ones. Let me describe a recent development in a famous youth center in Amsterdam. This center, called Fantasio, has attracted thousands of young people from all over the world.

Fantasio was divided into many small, cozy, psychedelically painted rooms. Young people with long beards and long hair, in colorful clothing pieced together from old liturgical vestments, were sitting there quietly smoking their sticks, smelling their incense, enthralled by the flesh-and-blood-pervading rock rhythms.

But now things are different. The young leaders have thrown out all pharmaceutical stimuli, remodeled their center into a very sober and more or less severe place, and changed the name from Fantasio to Meditation Center the Kosmos. In the first issue of their newspaper they wrote: "Cut off your long hair, throw away your beards, put on simple clothes, because now things are going to be serious." Concentration, contemplation, and meditation have become the key words of the place. Yogis give classes in body control, people sit and talk for many hours about Chuang Tzu and the Eastern mystics, and everyone is basically trying to find the road that leads inward.

We might be inclined to dismiss this group's transformation as the sort of peripheral oddity found in every modern society. But Jeffrey Hadden shows that this behavior is a symptom of something much more general, basic, and influential. It is the behavior of people who are convinced that there is nothing "out there" or "up there" on which they can get a solid grasp, which can pull them out of their uncertainty and confusion. No authority, no institution, no outer concrete reality has the power to relieve them of their anxiety and loneliness and make them free. Therefore the only way is the inward way. If there is nothing "out there" or "up there," perhaps there is something meaningful, something solid "in there." Perhaps something deep in the most personal self holds the key to the mystery of meaning, freedom, and unity.

The German sociologist, Shelsky speaks about our time as a time of continuing reflection. Instead of an obvious authority telling us how to think and what to do, this continuing reflection has entered into the center of our existence. Dogmas are the hidden realities people have to discover in their inner consciousness as sources of self-understanding. The modern mind, Shelsky says, is in a state of constant self-reflection, trying to penetrate deeper and deeper into the core of its own individuality.

But where does this lead us? What kind of men and women will this inward-moving, self-reflecting generation produce? Hadden writes:

> The prospects are both ominous and promising. If turning inward to
> discover the self is but a step toward becoming a sensitive and honest

person, our society's unfettered faith in youth may turn out to be justified. However, inwardness' present mood and form seems unbridled by any social norm or tradition and almost void of notions for exercise of responsibility toward others.[1]

Hadden is the last one to suggest that the inward generation is on the brink of revitalizing the contemplative life, about to initiate new forms of monasticism. His data show, first of all, that inwardness can lead to a form of privatism, which is not only antiauthoritarian and anti-institutional but also very self-centered, highly interested in material comfort and the immediate gratification of existing needs and desires. But inwardness need not lead to such privatism. It is possible that the new reality discovered in the deepest self can be "molded into a commitment to transform society." The inwardness of the coming generation can lead either to a higher level of hypocrisy or to the discovery of the reality of the unseen, which can make for a new world. The path it takes will depend to a great extent on the kind of ministry given to this generation.

2. The generation without fathers

The many who call themselves father or allow themselves to be called father—from the Holy Father through the many father abbots to the thousands of "priest-fathers" trying to hand over some good news—should know that the last one to be listened to is the father. We are facing a generation which has parents but no fathers, in which all who claim authority—because they are older, more mature, more intelligent, or more powerful—are suspect from the very beginning.

There was a time, and in many ways we see the last spastic movements of this time still around us, when human identity and power were given by the father figure from above. I am good when I am patted on the shoulder by the one who stands above me. I am smart when some teacher gives me a good grade. I am important when I study at a well-known university as the intellectual child of a well-known professor. In short, I am whom I am considered to be by one of my many authority figures.

We could have predicted that the coming generation would reject this, since we have already accepted that individual's worth is dependent not on what is given to them by parents and mentors but on what they make of themselves. We could have expected this, since we have said that faith is not the acceptance of centuries-old traditions but an attitude which grows from within. We could have anticipated this ever since we started saying that all people are free to choose their own future, their own work, their own partners.

Today, seeing that the whole adult world stands helpless before the threat of atomic war, eroding poverty, and the starvation of millions, the men and women of tomorrow see that no one has anything to tell them simply because of having lived longer. An English beat group yells it out:

> The wall on which the prophets wrote
> Is cracking at the seams.
> Upon the instrument of death
> The sunlight brightly gleams.
> When ev'ry man is torn apart
> With nightmares and with dreams
> Will no one lay the laurel wreath
> As silence drowns the screams.[2]

This is what the coming generation is watching, and they know they can expect nothing from above. Looking into the adult world they say:

> I'm on the outside looking inside.
> What do I see?
> Much confusion disillusion all around me.
> You don't possess me
> Don't impress me
> Just upset my mind.
> Can't instruct me
> or conduct me
> Just use up my time.[3]

The only thing left to this generation is to try it alone, not proud or contemptuous of their parents, proclaiming that they will do better, but with the deep-seated fear of complete failure. But they prefer failure to believing in those who have already failed before their eyes. They recognize themselves in the words of a modern song:

> Confusion will be my epitaph
> As I crawl a cracked and broken path.
> If we make it we can all sit back and laugh.
> But I fear tomorrow I'll be crying,
> Yes, I fear tomorrow I'll be crying.[4]

But this fearful generation which rejects its fathers and quite often rejects the legitimacy of every person or institution that claims authority, is facing a new danger: becoming captive to itself. David Riesman says: "As adult authority disintegrates, the young are more and more the captives of each other. . . . When adult control disappears, the young's control of each other intensifies."[5] Instead of the adult, the peer becomes the standard. Many young people who are completely unimpressed by the demands, expectations, and complaints of the big bosses of the adult world show a scrupulous sensitivity to what their peers feel, think, and say about them. Being considered an outcast or a dropout by adults does not worry them. But being excommunicated by the small circle of friends to which they want to belong can be an unbearable experience. Many young people may even become enslaved by the tyranny of their peers. While they seem indifferent, casual, and even dirty to their elders, their indifference is often carefully calculated, their casualness studied in the mirror, and their dirty appearance based on a detailed imitation of their friends.

But the tyranny of adults is not the same as the tyranny of one's peers. Not following older authorities is quite different from not living up to the expectations of one's peers. The first means disobedience; the second, nonconformity. The first creates guilt feelings; the second, feelings of shame. In this respect there is an obvious shift from a guilt culture to a shame culture.

This shift has very deep consequences, for if youth no longer aspire to mature and take their adult places in the world, and if the main motivation is conformity to the peer group, we might witness the death of a future-oriented culture or—to use a theological term—the end of an eschatology. Then we no longer witness any desire to leave the safe place and travel to the Father's house, which has so many rooms, any hope to reach the promised land or to see the one who is waiting for his prodigal son, any ambition to sit at the right or the left side of the heavenly throne. Then staying home, keeping in line, and being in with your little group become most important. But that also is an absolute vote for the status quo.

This aspect of the coming generation raises serious questions for the Christian leadership of tomorrow. But we would be getting a very one-sided picture if we did not first take a careful look at the third aspect of the coming generation, convulsiveness.

3. The convulsive generation
The inwardness and fatherlessness of the coming generation might lead us to expect a very quiet and contented future in which people keep to them-

selves and try to conform to their own little in-groups. But then we must take into account the fact that these attributes are closed related to a deep-seated unhappiness with the society in which the young find themselves. Many young people are convinced that there is something terribly wrong with the world in which they live and that cooperation with existing models of living would constitute betrayal of themselves. Everywhere we see restless and nervous people, unable to concentrate and often suffering from a growing sense of depression. They know that what is shouldn't be the way it is, but they see no workable alternative. Thus they are saddled with frustration, which often expresses itself in undirected violence, or in suicidal withdrawal from the world, both of which are signs more of protest than of the results of a new-found ideal.

Immediately after the surrender of the exhausted state of Biafra, two high-school boys in France—Robert, nineteen years old, and Regis, sixteen years old—burned themselves to death and urged many of their peers to do the same. Interviews with their parents, pastors, teachers, and friends revealed the horrifying fact that both of these sensitive students had become so overwhelmed by the hopeless misery of humankind and by the incapacity of adults to offer any real faith in a better world that they chose to set their bodies afire as their ultimate way of protest.

To reach a better understanding of the underlying feelings of such young people, let me quote from the letter of a student who had stopped studying and was still trying to find a new world. He wrote to his mother on January 1, 1970:

> Society forces me to live an unfree life, to accept values which are not values to me. I reject the society as it now exists as a whole, but since I feel compassion for people living together, I try to look for alternatives. I have given myself the obligation to become aware of what it means to be a man and to search for the source of life. Church people call it "God." You see that I am traveling a difficult road to come to self-fulfillment, but I am proud that I seldom did what others expected me to do in line with a so-called "normal development." I really hope not to end up on the level of a square, chained to customs, traditions, and the talk of next-door neighbors . . .

This letter seems to me a very sensitive expression of what many young people feel. They share a fundamental unhappiness with their world and a strong desire to work for change, but they doubt deeply that they will do better than their parents did and almost completely lack any kind of vision or perspective. Within this framework I think that much erratic and undirected behavior is understandable. A person who feels caught like an animal in a trap may be dangerous and destructive, because of undirected movements caused by panic.

This convulsive behavior is often misunderstood by those who have power and feel that society should be protected against protesting youth. They do not recognize the tremendous ambivalence behind much of this convulsive behavior, and, rather than offering creative opportunities, they tend to polarize the situation and alienate even more those who are in fact only trying to find out what is worthwhile and what is not.

Similarly, sympathetic adults may misread the motives of the young. David Riesman, in an article about radical students on campus, writes that many

> *adults* fear to be thought old-fashioned or square and, by taking the part of the radical young without seeing the latter's own ambivalence, they are often no help to them but contribute to the severity of pressures from the peer group. And I expect to see that some faculty who have thought of themselves as very much on the side of students will themselves join the backlash when many students fail to reciprocate and are especially hostile towards the permissive faculty who have in the past been on their side.[6]

The generation to come is seeking desperately for a vision, an ideal to dedicate themselves to—a "faith," if you want. But their drastic language is often misunderstood and considered more a threat or a sturdy conviction than a plea for alternative ways of living.

Inwardness, fatherlessness, and convulsiveness—these three characteristics of today's young people draw the first lines on the face of the coming generations. Now we are ready to ask what is expected of those who aspire to be Christian leaders in the world of tomorrow.

II. Tomorrow's Ministers

When we look for the implications of our prognosis for the Christian ministry of the future, it appears as though three roles ask for special attention: (1) the articulator of inner events; (2) the person of compassion; and (3) the contemplative critic.

1. The articulator of inner events

Inward people are faced with a new and often dramatic task: They must come to terms with the inner tremendum. Since the God "out there" or "up there" is more or less dissolved in the many secular structures, the God within asks attention as never before. And just as the God outside could be experienced not only as a loving father but also as a horrible demon, the God within can be not only the source of a new, creative life but also the cause of a chaotic confusion.

The greatest complaint of the Spanish mystics St. Teresa of Avila and St. John of the Cross was that they lacked spiritual guides to lead them along the right paths and enable them to distinguish between creative and destructive spirits. We hardly need emphasize how dangerous experimentation with the interior life can be. Drugs as well as different concentration practices and withdrawal into the self often do more harm than good. On the other hand it is becoming obvious that those who avoid the painful encounter with the unseen are doomed to live supercilious, boring, and superficial lives.

The first and most basic task required of the ministers of tomorrow therefore is to clarify the immense confusion which can arise when people enter this new internal world. It is painful indeed to realize how poorly prepared most Christian leaders prove when they are invited to be spiritual leaders in the true sense. Most of them are used to thinking in terms of large-scale organization: getting people together in churches, schools, and hospitals, and running the show as a circus director. They have become unfamiliar with, and even somewhat afraid of, the deep and significant movements of the Spirit. I am afraid that in a few decades the Church will be accused of having failed in its most basic task: to offer people creative ways to communicate with the source of human life.

But how can we avoid this danger? I think by no other way than to enter the center of our existence and become familiar with the complexities of our inner lives. As soon as we feel at home in our own houses, discover the dark corners as well as the light spots, the closed doors as well as the drafty rooms, our confusion will evaporate, our anxiety will diminish, and we will become capable of creative work.

The key word here is articulation. People who can articulate the movements of their inner lives, who can give names to their varied experiences, need no longer be victims of themselves but are able slowly and consistently to remove the obstacles that prevent the Spirit from entering. They can create space for the One whose heart is greater than theirs, whose eyes see more than theirs, and whose hands can heal more than theirs.

This articulation, I believe, is the basis for a spiritual leadership of the future, because only those who are able to articulate their own experience can offer themselves to others as sources of clarification. Christian leaders are, therefore, first of all, people who are willing to put their own articulated faith at the disposal of those who ask their help. In this sense they are servants of servants, because they are the first to enter the promised but dangerous land, the first to tell those who are afraid what they have seen, heard, and touched.

This might sound highly theoretical, but the concrete consequences are obvious. In practically all priestly functions, such as pastoral conversation, preaching, teaching, and liturgy, ministers try to help people recognize the work of God in themselves. Christian leaders, ministers or priests, are not ones who reveal God to their people—who give something they have to those who have nothing—but ones who help those who are searching to discover reality as the source of their existence. In this sense we can say that Christian leaders lead people to confession, in the classic sense of the word: to the basic affirmation that humanity is humanity and God is God, and that without God, humanity cannot be called human.

In this context pastoral conversation is not merely a skillful use of conversational techniques to manipulate people into the Kingdom of God but a deep human encounter in which a minister is willing to put his own faith and doubt, her own hope and despair, his own light and darkness at the disposal of others who want to find a way through their confusion and touch the solid core of life. In this context preaching means more than handing over a tradition; it is rather the careful and sensitive articulation of what is happening in the community so that those who listen can say: "You say what I suspected, you express what I vaguely felt, you bring to the fore what I fearfully kept in the back of my mind. Yes, yes—you say who we are, you recognize our condition."

When listeners are able to say this, then the ground is broken for others to receive the Word of God. And no minister need doubt that the Word will be received! The young especially do not have to run away from their fears and hopes but can see themselves in the face of the one who leads them; the minister will make them understand the words of salvation which in the past often sounded to them like words from a strange and unfamiliar world.

Teaching in this context means not telling the old story over and over again but offering channels through which people can discover themselves, clarify their own experiences, and find the niches in which the Word of God can take firm hold. And finally in this context liturgy is much more than ritual. It can become a true celebration when the liturgical leader is able to name the space where joy and sorrow touch each other as the place in which it is possible to celebrate both life and death.

So the first and most basic task of Christian leaders in the future will be to lead people out of the land of confusion into the land of hope. Therefore, ministers must first have the courage to be explorers of the new territory in themselves and to articulate their discoveries as a service to the inward generation.

2. The person of compassion

By speaking about articulation as a form of leadership we have already suggested the place where future leaders will stand. Not "up there," far away or secretly hidden, but in the midst of the people, with the utmost visibility.

If we now realize that the future generation is not only an inward generation asking for articulation but also a fatherless generation looking for a new kind of authority, we must consider what the nature of this authority will be. To name it, I cannot find a better word than compassion. Compassion must become the core and even the nature of authority. Christian leaders can be people of God for the future generation only insofar as they are able to make the compassion of God with humanity—which is visible in Jesus Christ—credible in their own world.

Compassionate ministers stand in the midst of their people but do not get caught in the conformist forces of the peer group, because through their compassion they are able to avoid the distance of pity as well as the exclusiveness of sympathy. Compassion is born when we discover in the center of our own existence not only that God is God and humanity is humanity, but also that our neighbor is really our brother or sister.

Through compassion it is possible to recognize that people's craving for love resides also in our own hearts, that the world's cruelty is also rooted in our own impulses. Through compassion we also sense our hope for forgiveness in our friends' eyes and our hatred in their bitter mouths. When they kill, we know that we could have done it; when they give life, we know that we can do the same. For a compassionate person nothing human is alien: no joy and no sorrow, no way of living and no way of dying.

This compassion is authority because it does not tolerate the pressures of the in-group but breaks through the boundaries between languages and countries, rich and poor, educated and illiterate. This compassion pulls people away from the fearful clique into the large world, where they can see that every human face is the face of a neighbor. Thus the authority of compassion is the possibility to forgive one another, because forgiveness is only real for those who have discovered the weakness of their friends and the sins of their enemies in their own hearts and are willing to call every human being friend. A fatherless generation looks for brothers and sisters who are able to take away their fear and anxiety, who can open the doors of their narrowmindedness and show them that forgiveness is a possibility which dawns on the horizon of humanity.

Compassionate ministers who point to the possibility of forgiveness help others to free themselves from the chains of their restrictive shame, allow them to experience their own guilt, and restore their hope for a future in which the lamb and the lion can sleep together.

But here we must be aware of the great temptation that will face the Christian ministers of the future. Everywhere Christian leaders have become increasingly aware of the need for more specific training and formation. This need is realistic, and the desire for more professionalism in the ministry is understandable. But the danger is that instead of becoming free to let the spirit grow, future ministers may entangle themselves in the complications of their own assumed competence and use their specialization as an excuse to avoid the much more difficult task of being compassionate. The task of Christian leaders is to bring out the best in all people and to lead them forward to a more human community; the danger is that their skillful diagnostic eye will become more an eye for distant and detailed analysis than the eye of a compassionate partner. And if priests and ministers of tomorrow think that more skill training is the solution for the problem of future Christian leadership, they may end up being more frustrated and disappointed than the leaders of today. More training and structure are as necessary as more bread for the hungry. But just as bread given without love can bring war instead of peace, professionalism without compassion will turn forgiveness into a gimmick, and the Kingdom to come into a blindfold.

This brings us to the final characteristic of the Christian leaders of the future generation. If they are to be not just members of the long row of professionals who try to help people with their specific skills, if they are really to be agents leading from confusion to hope and from chaos to harmony, they must be not only articulate and compassionate but contemplatives as well.

3. The contemplative critic
We have said that the inward, fatherless generation desperately want to change the world in which they live but tend to act spastically and convulsively in the face of a lack of a credible alternative. How can Christian leaders direct their explosive energy into creative channels and really be

agents of change? It might sound surprising and even contradictory, but I think that what is asked of the Christian leaders of the future is that they be contemplative critics.

I hope I will be able to prevent the free association of the word "contemplative" with a life lived behind walls, in minimal contact with what is going on in the fast-moving world. What I have in mind is a very active, engaged form of contemplation of an evocative nature. This needs some explanation.

Those who do not know where they are going or what kind of world they are heading toward, who wonder if bringing forth children in this chaotic world is not an act of cruelty rather than love, will often be tempted to become sarcastic or even cynical. They laugh at their busy friends but offer nothing in place of their activity. They protest against many things but do not know what to witness for.

But Christian ministers who have discovered in themselves the voice of the Spirit and have rediscovered their brothers and sisters with compassion might be able to look at the people they meet, the contacts they make, and the events they become a part of in a different way. They might reveal the first lines of the new world behind the veil of everyday life. As contemplative critics they keep a certain distance to prevent their becoming absorbed in what is most urgent and most immediate, but that same distance allows them to bring to the fore the real beauty of humanity and our world, which is always different, always fascinating, always new.

It is not the task of Christian leaders to go around nervously trying to redeem people, to save them at the last minute, to put them on the right track. For we are redeemed once and for all. Christian leaders are called to help others affirm this great news, and to make visible in daily events the fact that behind the dirty curtain of our painful symptoms there is something great to be seen: the face of the One in whose image we are shaped. In this way contemplatives can be leaders for a convulsive generation because they can break through the vicious circle of immediate needs asking for immediate satisfaction. They can direct the eyes of those who want to look beyond their impulses and steer their erratic energy into creative channels.

Here we see that future Christian ministers can in no way be considered concerned only about helping individuals to adapt themselves to a demanding world. In fact, the Christian leaders who are able to be critical contemplatives will be revolutionaries in the most real sense. Because by testing all they see, hear, and touch for its evangelical authenticity, they can change the course of history and lead their people away from their panic-stricken convulsions to the creative action that will make a better world.

These Christian leaders do not shoulder every protest sign in order to be in with those who express their frustration more than their ideas, nor do they easily join those asking for more protection, more police, more discipline, and more order. But they will look critically at what is going on and make their decisions based on insight into their own vocation, not on the desire for popularity or the fear of rejection. They will criticize the protesters as well as the rest seekers when their motives are false and their objectives dubious.

Contemplatives are not needy or greedy for human contacts but are guided by a vision of what they have seen beyond the trivial concerns of a possessive world. They do not bounce up and down with the fashions of the moment, because they are in contact with what is basic, central, and ultimate. They do not allow anybody to worship idols, and they constantly invite their sisters and brothers to ask real, often painful and upsetting questions, to look behind the surface of smooth behavior, and to take away all the obstacles that prevent people from getting to the heart of the matter. Contemplative critics take away the illusory mask of the manipulative world and have the courage to show what the true situation is. They know that they are considered by many as foolish, insane dangers to society and threats to humankind. But they are not afraid to die, since their vision transcends the difference between life and death and makes them free to do what has to be done here and now, notwithstanding the risks involved.

More than anything else, contemplative critics will look for signs of hope and promise in the situations in which they find themselves. They have the sensibility to notice the small mustard seed and the trust to believe that "when it has grown it is the biggest of shrubs and becomes a tree, so that the birds of the air come and shelter in its branches" (Mt 13:32). They know that if there is hope for a better world in the future the signs must be visible in the present, and they will never curse the now in favor of the later. They are not naïve optimists who expect their frustrated desires to be satisfied in the future, or bitter pessimists who keep repeating that the past has taught them that there is nothing new under the sun; they are rather people of hope who live with the unshakable conviction that now they are seeing a dim reflection in a mirror but that one day they will see the future face to face.

Christian leaders who are able not only to articulate the movements of the Spirit but also to contemplate their world with a critical but compassionate eye may expect that the convulsive generation will choose not death as the ultimate form of protest but instead the new life of which they have made visible the first hopeful signs.

Conclusion

We looked into the eyes of the young fugitive and found him inward, fatherless, and convulsive. We wanted to prevent ourselves from handing him over to the enemy to be killed; we wanted instead to lead him to the center of our village and to recognize in this coming man the redeemer of a fearful world. To do this we are challenged to be articulate, compassionate, and contemplative.

Is this too much of a task? Only if we feel we have to accomplish this individually and separately. But if anything has become clear in our day, it is that leadership is a shared vocation, which develops by working closely together in a community where men and women can help one another realize that, as Teilhard de Chardin remarked, "to him who can see, nothing is profane."

Having said all this, I realize that I have done nothing more than rephrase the fact that Christian leaders must be in the future what they have always had to be in the past: people of prayer, people who have to pray, and who have to pray always. That I bring up this simple fact at this point may be surprising, but I hope I have succeeded in taking away all the sweet, pietistic, and churchy aura attached to this often misused word.

For people of prayer are, in the final analysis, those who are able to recognize in others the face of the Messiah and make visible what was hidden, make touchable what was unreachable. People of prayer are leaders precisely because through their articulation of God's work within themselves they can lead others out of confusion to clarification; through their compassion they can guide them out of the closed circuits of their in-groups to the wide world of humanity; and through their critical contemplation they can convert their convulsive destructiveness into creative work for the new world to come.

3

MINISTRY TO
A HOPELESS INDIVIDUAL

■

Waiting for Tomorrow

Introduction

WHEN WE THINK about leadership we usually think about one person offering ideas, suggestions, or directions to many others. We think of Mahatma Gandhi, Martin Luther King, John F. Kennedy, Dag Hammarskjöld, Charles de Gaulle—all men who played an important role in modern history and found themselves at the center of public attention. But when we want to determine what kind of leadership Christians can claim for themselves, it sometimes seems better to start closer to home. There one has no chance to hide behind the excuse that one is not striving for worldwide change.

There is hardly a man or woman who does not exercise some leadership over other men or women. Among parents and children, teachers and students, bosses and employees, many different patterns of leadership can be found. In less formal settings—playgrounds, street gangs, academic and social societies, hobby and sports clubs—we also see how much of our life is dependent on the way leadership is given and accepted.

In this chapter I would like to concentrate on the simplest structure in which leadership plays a role: the encounter between people. In this one-to-one relationship, we realize that we are involved in leading one another from point to point, from view to view, from one conviction to another. We need not name people like Hitler or Gandhi to demonstrate how destructive or creative this leadership can be. Even in the simple form of a conversation between two people, leadership can be a question of life and death. Indeed, in precisely this one-to-one encounter we discover some of the principles of Christian leadership, which also have implications for more complex leadership relationships.

Let a short conversation between a hospital patient and his visitor serve as a starting point for our discussion. The patient, Mr. Harrison, is a forty-eight-year-old farm laborer, stocky, tough looking, and not used to expressing himself verbally. He comes from a very simple Baptist family and feels completely disoriented in the big-city hospital where he was brought for an operation on his legs. He suffers from an insufficient functioning of his arteries. The visitor, John Allen, is a theology student who is taking a year of clinical-pastoral training under the supervision of the hospital chaplain.

This is John's second visit to Mr. Harrison. The patient sits in a wheelchair in the middle of the ward; other patients are present, some of them talking with each other. The following conversation takes place:

JOHN: Mr. Harrison, I'm . . . I came by . . . to see you the other day.

MR. HARRISON: Oh yes, I remember.

JOHN: How are things going?

MR. HARRISON: Well, I'll tell you. They were supposed to operate on me last week. They got me drugged, took me up there, and my heart flew up. They decided they'd better not try it then. They brought me back down here and I'm supposed to have the operation tomorrow.

JOHN: You say your heart flew up?

MR. HARRISON: Yes, they thought it might be too risky to go through with it. [*Pause*] I guess I'm ready for the operation. I think I can make it.

JOHN: You feel you're ready for it.

MR. HARRISON: Well, I'm not ready to die. But I think the operation is necessary or I'll lose my legs.

JOHN: You're not ready for the end, but you want something to be done if possible so you won't lose your legs.

MR. HARRISON: Yeah [nodding]. If this is the end, this is one who's gonna be lost.

JOHN: You feel the cause is lost if you don't make it through the operation.

MR. HARRISON: Yeah! Of course they tell me there's not too much to the operation. They're gonna dope me up right here and keep me here until it's time for the operation. They said they're going to put some plastic tubes inside me and that oughta save my legs. You see my foot here [takes shoe off and shows his foot]. This toe here gets blue when I stand on it. They could amputate here by the ankle, but this way they might save my legs.

JOHN: It's worth the operation if you can use your legs again.

MR. HARRISON: Yeah. Course I don't want to die during the operation. I'd rather die a natural death than die through anesthesia.

JOHN: You know the possibility of death is present during the operation, but the only way you can get well is to have the operation.

MR. HARRISON: Yeah, that's right.

Pause.

JOHN: You got much waiting for you when you leave the hospital?

MR. HARRISON: Nothing and nobody. Just hard work.

JOHN: Just a lot of hard labor.

MR. HARRISON: Yeah, that's right. Course I got to gain my strength back. I figure I'll be ready about the time the tobacco crop is ready.

JOHN: You'll be working with the tobacco crop?

MR. HARRISON: Yeah, picking starts around August.

JOHN: Mmm-hm.

Pause.

JOHN: Well, Mr. Harrison, I hope things go well for you tomorrow.

MR. HARRISON: Thank you. Thanks for coming by.

JOHN: I'll be seeing you. Good-by.

MR. HARRISON: Good-by.

John did not speak to Mr. Harrison again. The next day, during the operation, Mr. Harrison died. Perhaps we might better say: "He never woke up from the anesthesia."

John had been asked to guide Mr. Harrison in this critical moment, to lead him to a new tomorrow. And what did "tomorrow" mean? For Mr. Harrison it meant a beginning of his return to the tobacco crop or . . . an entry into the realm beyond death.

In order to come to a deeper understanding of the meaning of Christian leadership we will study in more detail the encounter between Mr. Harrison and John Allen. First we will consider Mr. Harrison's condition, then we will raise the question how John could have led Mr. Harrison to tomorrow. Finally we will discuss the main principles of Christian leadership which became visible in this encounter.

I. Mr. Harrison's Condition

John was irritated and even a little angry when he came to the chaplain supervisor shortly after his visit to Mr. Harrison. He had the feeling that

Mr. Harrison was a stubborn, indifferent man, with whom a decent conversation was hardly possible. He did not believe that Mr. Harrison had really appreciated his visit and felt that in his bitter and somewhat coarse way of talking this patient had in fact expressed more hostility toward his visitor than gratitude. John was disappointed and did not hesitate to call Mr. Harrison an impossible man, that is, not a likely candidate for pastoral help.

John's reaction is quite understandable. As a young theology student he had hoped for a meaningful conversation with his patient, in which he could offer some hope and consolation. But he had felt frustrated, let down, and unable to "get anywhere." Only when he started to write, read, and reread his conversation, and to discuss with his supervisor what had actually happened, was he able to develop the distance necessary to see the painful condition of Mr. Harrison. Through that distance he could see that Mr. Harrison found himself in an impersonal-mechanical situation, afraid to die but also afraid to live again. It is this paralyzing condition which John had to feel and taste deeply before he could be of help.

1. The impersonal milieu

For a theology student who went through grade school, high school, college, and divinity school, it was hard to imagine what it meant for a forty-eight-year-old man to be placed in the middle of the technocracy of a modern hospital. It must have been like coming to another planet, where the people dress, behave, talk, and act in a frightfully strange way. The white nurses, with their efficient way of washing, feeding, and dressing patients; the doctors with their charts, making notes and giving orders in an utterly strange language; the many unidentifiable machines with bottles and tubes; and all the strange odors, noises, and foods must have made Mr. Harrison feel like a little child who has lost his way in a fearful forest. For him nothing was familiar, nothing understandable, nothing even approachable. Suddenly this tough man who could maintain his own independence through hard manual labor found himself the passive victim of many people and operations which were totally alien to him. He had lost control over himself. An anonymous group of "they people" had taken over: "*They* got me drugged, took me up there . . . *they* decided they'd better not try it then. *They* brought me back down here . . ."

This language shows that Mr. Harrison felt that strange powers had taken away his identity. The operation on his legs became a mysterious, otherworldly manipulation. His own presence seemed unwanted in the process: "They're gonna dope me up right here and keep me here until it's time for the operation. They said they're going to put some plastic tubes inside me and that oughta save my legs."

For Mr. Harrison, "they" were working as if his very presence were only an incidental fact. No self-initiative was required or appreciated, no question expected or answered, no interest respected or stimulated. In Mr. Harrison's own experience: "They do things to it."

It was in this impersonal milieu that John Allen desired to offer his pastoral help.

2. *The fear of death*

While studying the verbatim report of his conversation with Mr. Harrison, John discovered that death had been at the center of his patient's concern. In some way Mr. Harrison had realized that his condition was a matter of life and death. Three times during their short interchange Mr. Harrison spoke about his fear of death, while John seemed constantly to avoid the subject or at least to cover up its painful reality.

Mr. Harrison feared an impersonal death, a death in which he did not have a part, of which he was not aware, and which was more real in the minds of the many powers around him than in his own mind.

Mr. Harrison must have sensed that the opportunity to die as a man was to be denied him: "Course I don't want to die during the operation. I'd rather die a natural death than die through anesthesia." Mr. Harrison realized that in the mechanical, incomprehensible milieu to which "they" had brought him, his death was but a part of the process of human manipulation to which he remained an outsider. There was a moment of protest in his hopeless remark. He, a man from the fields who had worked hard to make a living, who had had to rely wholly on his own body, knew that he had a right to die his own death, a natural death. He wanted to die the way he had lived.

But his protest was weak, and he must have realized that there was no choice. He would just vanish, slip away, stop living in a dreamlike state brought on by those who were going "to dope him up." He knew that if he died, he would be absent in that most crucial moment of human existence. It was not just the possibility of death during the operation which frightened Mr. Harrison but also the fact that a chance to make death his own would be taken away from him, that in fact he would not die but simply fail to regain consciousness.

But there is more, much more. Mr. Harrison was not ready to die. Twice he tried to make his utter despair known to John, but John did not hear him. When John said, "You feel like you're ready for it," meaning the operation, Mr. Harrison revealed what was really on his mind: "Well, I'm not ready to die. . . . If this is the end, this is one who's gonna be lost." We can only guess what lay behind these desperate words, full of agony. Perhaps something too difficult for John to address. He tried to soften the hard realities. He called death "the end" and transformed "this is one who's gonna be lost" into "the cause." By softening the words of Mr. Harrison, John evaded confrontation with the personal agony of his patient.

Nobody can understand all the implications of Mr. Harrison's cry: "If this is the end, this is one who's gonna be lost." For what does "being lost" really mean? We do not know, but his Baptist background and his rough, lonely life imply that he might well have been speaking about being condemned, facing an eternal life in hell. This forty-eight-year-old man, without family or friends, without anybody around to talk with him, to understand or forgive him, faced death with the burden of a painful past on his shoulders. We have no idea of the many images which came to his mind at this hour, but a man as lonely and desperate as Mr. Harrison probably could not draw on past experiences that had established in him an awareness of God's love and forgiveness.

Further, if the hour of death often brings back early memories, it might well be that the Baptist sermons of his childhood, threatening with eternal punishment the person who yields to the "pleasures of this world," returned with horrifying vividness, forcing Mr. Harrison to identify himself in retrospect as "one who's gonna be lost." Maybe Mr. Harrison had not visited a church for years and had not met a minister since he was a boy. When the young chaplain, John, appeared at his wheelchair, it is likely that all the warnings, prohibitions, and admonitions of his childhood returned to him and made the transgressions of his adulthood seem a heavy burden that could lead only to hell.

We do not know what really took place in Mr. Harrison's mind; however, there is no reason to underestimate the agonizing quality of his own words. Our "maybes" and "perhapses" can at least make us aware of what it means for a man to bring his forty-eight years of life to the day of judgment.

"I'm not ready to die." This means that Mr. Harrison was not prepared for a faithful act of surrender. He was not prepared to give his life away in faith and hope. His present suffering was small compared with what he expected beyond the boundary of life. Mr. Harrison feared death in the most existential way. But did he desire to live?

3. The fear of life

There are few patients who do not hope for a recovery when they face an operation. The complex hospital industry exists to heal, to restore, to bring people back to "normal life." Everyone who has paid a visit to a hospital and talked with patients knows that "tomorrow" means the day closer to home, to old friends, to the job, to everyday life. General hospitals are places that people want and expect to leave as soon as possible. It is in this context—the context of the healing power of human hope—that doctors, nurses, and aides do their work.

A person who does not want to leave the hospital does not cooperate with the overall purpose of the institution and limits the power of all those who want to help. Did Mr. Harrison strive to recuperate? We know he was afraid to die; however, that does not mean he wanted to live. Returning to normal life means in part returning to those who are waiting for you. But who was waiting for Mr. Harrison? John sensed Mr. Harrison's loneliness when he asked, "You got much waiting for you when you leave the hospital?" This question opened a deep wound, and Mr. Harrison replied, "Nothing and nobody. Just hard work."

It is very difficult if not impossible for a healthy young man to realize what it means when nobody cares whether you live or die. Isolation is among the worst of human sufferings, and for a man like John the experience of isolation is endless miles away. He has his supervisor to talk to, his friends to share his ideas with, his family and all the people who in one way or another are interested in his well-being. In contrast, what is life to one for whom no one waits, who expects only hard work in the tobacco crop, whose only motive for cure is to recover enough strength for the picking season? Certainly life does not call, does not pull the isolation away from the destructive processes in his body. Why should Mr. Harrison return to life? Only to spend a few more years struggling in the hot sun to make just enough money to feed and dress himself until he is considered unfit for hard labor and can die a "natural death"? Death may be hell, but life is no less.

Mr. Harrison did not really want to live any longer. He feared that life which gave him so little happiness and so much pain. His legs hurt, and he knew that without legs there was no life for him. But his legs couldn't bring him love; they promised only hard work, and that was a frightening thought.

Thus John found Mr. Harrison in an impersonal milieu, afraid to die and afraid to live. We do not know how serious Mr. Harrison's illness was, and we do not know how much chance he had to survive the operation. But Mr. Harrison was not ready for it. He did not understand what was going on around him; he wanted neither to die nor to live. He was caught in a terrible trap. Any option would have been fatal, condemnation either to hell or to hard work.

This was Mr. Harrison's condition. Like many, he suffered from a psychic paralysis in which his deepest aspirations were cut, his desires blocked, his strivings frustrated, his will chained. Instead of a man filled with love and hate, desire and anger, hope and doubt, he had become a passive victim unable to give any direction to his own history. When the hands of doctors touch a person in this condition they touch a body which no longer speaks a language and has given up every form of cooperation. Such a patient cannot struggle to win the battle of life or surrender peacefully if the chances to win diminish. Under the surgeon's hands Mr. Harrison indeed did not have a name, nor did he claim one for himself. He had become an anonymous body which had lost even the ability to live. It simply stopped functioning.

As we all know, Mr. Harrison's is not an isolated case. Many people are the prisoners of their own existence. Mr. Harrison's condition is the condition of all men and women who do not understand the world in which they find themselves, and for whom death as well as life is loaded with fear.

And there are many like John as well. There are many idealistic, intelligent men and women who want to make others free and lead them to tomorrow. How then to free people like Mr. Harrison from their paralysis and lead them to tomorrow, when a new life can start? This is the question we now have to consider.

II. How to Lead Mr. Harrison to Tomorrow

John visited Mr. Harrison. The obvious question is: What could or should John have done for Mr. Harrison? But this question is really not fair. For the condition of Mr. Harrison was not immediately clear and comprehensible. Perhaps even now, after many hours of careful analysis of this short interchange, we still have nothing but a very partial understanding of what was happening to the patient.

It is too easy to criticize John's responses and to show how often he failed to come close to Mr. Harrison. What we in fact see is John's serious attempt to listen to Mr. Harrison and to apply the rules of nondirective counseling which he learned in class. It is academic, awkward, and obviously filled with feelings of fear, hesitation, confusion, self-preoccupation, and distance. John and Mr. Harrison represent two worlds so different in history, thought, and feeling that it is totally unrealistic, if not inhuman, to expect that they would be able to understand each other in two rather casual conversations. It is even pretentious to think that we, with our academic distinctions, will ever know who this farmworker was and how he faced his death.

The mystery of one man is too immense and too profound to be explained by another man. And still the question: "How could Mr. Harrison be led to tomorrow?" is a valid question. For one person needs another to live and the more deeply we are willing to enter into the painful condition which we and others know, the more likely it is that we can be leaders, leading our people out of the desert into the promised land.

Therefore, what follows is not a lesson, to show John how miserably he failed to help Mr. Harrison and to tell him what he should have done, but an attempt to recognize in Mr. Harrison's condition the agony of all human beings: the desperate cry for a human response.

Probably John couldn't have done much more than he did during his talk with Mr. Harrison, but the study of his tragic human situation may reveal that indeed a human response is a matter of life and death.

The response which might have been within the reach of human possibility is a personal response in an impersonal milieu, by which one individual can wait for an another in life as well as in death.

1. A personal response

When theology students read the conversation between John and Mr. Harrison, they usually have strong criticism of John's responses and offer ideas about what they themselves might have said. They explain: "I would have told him to think about the good experiences he had in life and would have attempted to offer him hope for a better life" or: "I would have explained to him that God is merciful and will forgive him his sins" or: "I would have tried to find out more about the nature of his illness and showed him that he really had a good chance to recover" or: "I would have talked more with him about his fear of dying and would have talked about his past so that he could unburden his guilty conscience" or: "I would have talked about death as a way to new life for a person who can put his faith in Christ."

All these and other proposed responses are grounded in a deep desire to help and to offer a message of hope which can alleviate the pains of this suffering man. But still the question remains: What use can an illiterate man in the hour of agony make of the words, explanations, exhortations, and arguments of a theology student? Can anyone change a person's ideas, feelings, or perspectives a few hours before death? To be sure, forty-eight years of living are not ruffled by a few intelligent remarks by a well-meaning seminarian. John may have been too nondirective, he may have lacked the courage for clear witness or for deeper concern. But what difference would it really have made?

The possibilities of John's visit to Mr. Harrison will never be made manifest if we expect any salvation from a change in terminology, or a new twist in the order or the nature of the words we use. We might even ask ourselves: "Wouldn't it have been better for John to stay away from Mr. Harrison, to leave him alone, to prevent him from making morbid associations with the appearance of a preacher?"

Yes . . . unless in the middle of the anonymity caused by his surroundings Mr. Harrison were to meet someone with a clear face who called him by his name and became his brother . . . unless John were to become a person Mr. Harrison could see, touch, smell, and hear, and whose real presence would in no way be denied. If a minister were to appear from out of the cloudiness of Mr. Harrison's existence who looked at him, spoke to him, and pressed his hands in a gesture of real concern, that would have mattered. The emptiness of the past and the future can never be filled by words but only by a human presence. Because only then can the hope be born that there might be at least one exception to the "nobody and nothing" of his complaint—a hope that will make him whisper, "Maybe, after all, someone is waiting for me."

2. Waiting in life

We cannot offer leadership to anyone unless we make our presence known—that is, unless we step forward out of the anonymity and apathy of our milieu and make the possibility of fellowship visible.

But how could John, even when really present to Mr. Harrison, even when able to express his real concern to him, lead him out of his fear into the hope for tomorrow? We might as well start by realizing that neither John nor any other concerned person would want Mr. Harrison to die. The operation was meant to save his legs, and when Mr. Harrison said, "I think I can make it," only a heartless person would have criticized his careful guess. For a patient facing surgery, tomorrow must be the day of recovery, not the day of death.

John's task was therefore to reinforce his patient's desire to recover and to reinforce what little strength he had in the struggle for life.

But how? By making Mr. Harrison's dangerous generalization, "Nothing and nobody is waiting for me," untrue, by reducing it to a paralyzing self-complaint; and by a frontal attack against his false self-concept: "Look at me, and try to say that again—you will see in my eyes that you are wrong—I am here, and I am waiting for you—I will be here tomorrow and the day after tomorrow—and you are not going to let me down."

We cannot stay alive when nobody is waiting for us. Everyone who returns from a long and difficult trip is looking for someone waiting at the station or the airport. We all want to tell our stories and share our moments of pain and exhilaration with someone who stayed home, waiting for us to come back.

Alexander Berkman, the anarchist who attempted to kill the industrial captain Henry Clay Frick in 1892, would have gone insane during his four-teen years of brutal prison life had there not been a few friends waiting for him outside.[1] George Jackson, Soledad brother who was imprisoned in 1960 when he was eighteen years old for robbing a gas station of seventy dollars, and who was killed in 1971 while trying to escape, would never have been able to write the impressive human document he did if his mother, his father, his brothers Robert and Jonathan, and his friend Fay Stender had not been waiting outside, receiving his letters and constantly reacting to his thoughts.[2]

We can keep our sanity and stay alive as long as there is at least one person who is waiting for us. The mind can indeed rule the body, even when there is little health left. A dying mother can stay alive to see her son before she gives up the struggle, a soldier can prevent his mental and physical disintegration when he knows that his wife and children are waiting for him. But when "nothing and nobody" is waiting, there is no chance to survive in the struggle for life. Mr. Harrison had no reason to come out of the anesthesia if returning to consciousness meant arriving at a station where thousands of people ran left and right but where no one raised a hand, approached him with a smile of recognition, or welcomed him back into the land of the living. John might have been that one man. He might have saved Mr. Harrison's life by making him realize that returning to life is a gift to the one who is waiting. Thousands of people commit suicide because there is nobody waiting for them tomorrow. There is no reason to live if there is nobody to live for.

But when one human being says to another, "I will not let you go. I am going to be here tomorrow waiting for you and I expect you not to disap-point me," then tomorrow is no longer an endless dark tunnel. It becomes flesh and blood in the one who is waiting and for whom that one wants to give life one more chance. When tomorrow only meant the tobacco crop and hard labor and a lonely life, Mr. Harrison could hardly have been ex-pected to cooperate with the surgeon's work. But if John had stood on the threshold of tomorrow, Mr. Harrison might have wanted to know what he would have to say about the day after, and might have given the doctor a helping hand.

Let us not diminish the power of waiting by saying that a lifesaving relationship cannot develop in an hour. One eye movement or one hand-shake can replace years of friendship when a person is in agony. Not only does love last forever but it needs only a second to come about.

John might indeed have saved Mr. Harrison's life by becoming his tomorrow.

3. Waiting in death

But Mr. Harrison's recovery was far from sure. Mr. Harrison himself was the first to realize this. Three times he explicitly spoke about his death, and he knew that his illness was serious enough to question a positive outcome from the operation. In the short interchange with John Allen, Mr. Harrison seemed to fear death even more than a return to life. Do not John's presence and faithful waiting become ridiculous in the face of a man who quite possibly will not live the next day? Many patients have been fooled with stories about recovery and the better life after that, while few consoling people believed in their own words. What sense does it make to speak about waiting for tomorrow when those words will quite likely be the last words spoken to the patient?

Here we touch upon the most sensitive spot of John's encounter with Mr. Harrison. Why should a healthy-looking, intelligent man show himself and make himself really present to a man in whom the forces of death are at work? What does it mean for a dying man to be confronted with another man for whom life has hardly begun? This looks like psychological torture, in which a dying man is reminded by a young fellow that his life could have been so different but that it is too late to change.

Most people in our society do not want to disturb each other with the idea of death. They want people to die without ever having realized that death was approaching. Surely John could not lead Mr. Harrison to tomorrow by playing this false game. Instead of leading him he would have been misleading him. He would have stolen his human right to die.

Can John really say, "I will be waiting for you," if this would only be true in the case of Mr. Harrison's recovery? Or can one human being wait for another, whatever happens, death included? In the face of death there is hardly any difference between John and Mr. Harrison. They will both die. The difference is time, but what does time mean when two people have discovered each other as fellows? If John's waiting could have saved Mr. Harrison's life, the power of his waiting would not be conditioned by Mr. Harrison's recovery, because when two people have become present to each other, the waiting of one must be able to cross the narrow line between the living and dying of the other.

Mr. Harrison was afraid to die because he was afraid of condemnation, of an eternal prolongation of his isolation. Whatever else hell may have meant to Mr. Harrison, it certainly entailed his total rejection. But were he able to accept John's presence, he might have felt that someone at least protested against his fear and that in the hour of death he was not alone.

It is indeed possible to be faithful in death, to express a solidarity based not just on a return to everyday life but also on a participation in the death experience which belongs in the center of the human heart. "I will be waiting for you" means much more than "If you make it through the operation I will be there to be with you again." There will be no "ifs." "I will wait for you" goes beyond death and is the deepest expression of the fact that faith and hope may pass but that love will remain forever. "I will wait for you" is an expression of solidarity which breaks through the chains of death. At that moment John is no longer a chaplain trying to do a good piece of counseling, and Mr. Harrison is no longer a farmworker doubting if he will make it through the operation; rather they are two human beings who reawaken in each other the deepest human intuition, that life is eternal and cannot be made futile by a biological process.

One can lead another to tomorrow even when tomorrow is the day of the other's death, because we can wait for each other on both sides. But would it have been so meaningful for John to have led Mr. Harrison back to the tobacco crop if this was just another delay for a man on death row?

We protest against death, for we are not content with a postponement of the execution. And it is this protest that might have mobilized in Mr. Harrison both the powers of recovery and the ability to break through the wall of his fears, making his death an entry into a life where he is awaited.

So John might indeed have led Mr. Harrison to tomorrow by making himself present to him and waiting for him in life and death. It is exactly John's willingness to enter with Mr. Harrison into his paralyzing condition which would have enabled him to be a guide or leader in the best sense. Only by this personal participation could he have freed Mr. Harrison of his paralysis and made him responsible again for his own history. In this sense he indeed could have saved Mr. Harrison's life, whether or not that entailed recovery. With John waiting, the surgeon would have worked not on a passive victim but on a man able to make decisions that count.

Mr. Harrison's condition is more than the condition of one person in a particular hospital. It is an image of the condition of all. The leadership potential is not just a possibility to be actualized by a well-trained theologian but the responsibility of every Christian. Therefore let us now finally discuss the main principles of Christian leadership which become visible in this encounter.

III. Principles of Christian Leadership

How could we speak about Christian leadership without mentioning Jesus Christ, his life, his crucifixion, and his resurrection? The only answer is: He has been here from the first page of this chapter. The understanding of Mr. Harrison's condition and the search for a creative response were based on God's revelation in Jesus Christ. This revelation shows in the paralyzing condition of Mr. Harrison, the condition of all humanity. It also reveals to us the possibility of following Christ in a faithful waiting for another beyond the boundaries which separate life from death.

Therefore we can discover and rediscover in the encounter between Mr. Harrison and John the basic principles of Christian leadership: first, personal concern, which asks one person to give his or her life for others; second, a deep-rooted faith in the value and meaning of life, even when the days look dark; and third, an outgoing hope which always looks for tomorrow, even beyond the moment of death. And all these principles are based on the one and only conviction that, since God has become human, we have the power to lead our fellow human beings to freedom. Let us now pay special attention to these three principles which we derived from John's visit to Mr. Harrison.

1. Personal concern

If there is any posture that disturbs a suffering man or woman, it is aloofness. The tragedy of Christian ministry is that many who are in great need, many who seek an attentive ear, a word of support, a forgiving embrace, a firm hand, a tender smile, or even a stuttering confession of inability to do more often find their ministers distant people who do not want to burn their fingers. They are unable or unwilling to express their feelings of affection, anger, hostility, or sympathy. The paradox indeed is that those who want to be for "everyone" find themselves often unable to be close to anyone. When everybody becomes my "neighbor," it is worth wondering whether anybody can really become my "proximus," that is, the one who is most close to me.

After so much stress on the necessity of leaders to prevent their own personal feelings and attitudes from interfering in a helping relationship (see the excellent study by Seward Hiltner: *Counselor on Counseling*)[3] it seems necessary to reestablish the basic principle that no one can help anyone without becoming involved, without entering wholly into the painful situation, without taking the risk of becoming hurt, wounded, or even destroyed in the process. The beginning and the end of all Christian leadership is to give your life for others. Thinking about martyrdom can be an escape unless we realize that real martyrdom means a witness that starts with the willingness to cry with those who cry, laugh with those who laugh, and make one's own painful and joyful experiences available as sources of clarification and understanding.

Who can save a child from a burning house without taking the risk of being hurt by the flames? Who can listen to a story of loneliness and despair without taking the risk of experiencing similar pains in her own heart and even losing her precious peace of mind? In short: Who can take away suffering without entering it?

The great illusion of leadership is to think that people can be led out of the desert by someone who has never been there. Our lives are filled with examples which tell us that leadership asks for understanding and that understanding requires sharing. So long as we define leadership in terms of preventing or establishing precedents, or in terms of being responsible for some kind of abstract "general good," we have forgotten that only a suffering God can save us, and that only a leader crushed by their sins can lead the people. Personal concern means making Mr. Harrison the only one who counts, the one for whom I am willing to forget my many other obligations, my scheduled appointments and long-prepared meetings, not because they are not important but because they lose their urgency in the face of Mr. Harrison's agony. Personal concern makes it possible to experience that going after the "lost sheep" is really a service to those who were left alone.

Many will put their trust in the one who went all the way out of concern for just one of them. The remark "He really cares for us" is often illustrated by stories which show that forgetting the many for the one is a sign of true leadership.

It is not just curiosity which makes people listen to preachers when they speak directly to a man and a woman whose marriage they bless or to the children of the parent they bury. They listen in the deep-seated hope that a personal concern might give preachers words that carry beyond the ears of those whose joy or suffering they share. Few listen to a sermon which is intended to be applicable to everyone, but most pay careful attention to words born out of concern for only a few.

All this suggests that when one has the courage to enter where life is experienced as most unique and most private, one touches the soul of the community. The one who has spent many hours trying to understand, feel, and clarify the alienation and confusion of another human being might well be the best equipped to speak to the needs of the many, because all people are one at the wellspring of pain and joy.

This is what Carl Rogers pointed out when he wrote: "I have . . . found that the very feeling which has seemed to me most private, most personal and hence most incomprehensible by others, has turned out to be an expression for which there is a resonance in many other people. It has led me to believe that what is most personal and unique in each one of us is probably the very element which would, if it were shared or expressed, speak most deeply to others. This has helped me to understand artists and poets who have dared to express the unique in themselves."[4] It indeed seems that Christian leaders are first of all the artists who can bind together many people by their courage in giving expression to their most personal concern.

2. Faith in the value and meaning of life

Faith in the value and meaning of life, even in the face of despair and death, is the second principle of Christian leadership. This seems so obvious that it is often taken for granted and overlooked.

John's visit to Mr. Harrison asks for a personal concern, but this concern can only be sustained by a growing faith in the value and meaning of the life which takes shape in the encounter itself. Christian leadership is a dead-end street when nothing new is expected, when everything sounds familiar, and when ministry has regressed to the level of routine. Many have walked into that dead-end street and found themselves imprisoned in a life where all the words were already spoken, all the events had already taken place, and all the people had already been met.

But for people with deep-rooted faith in the value and meaning of life, every experience holds a new promise, every encounter carries a new insight, and every event brings a new message. These promises, insights, and messages, however, have to be discovered and made visible. Christian leaders are not leaders because they announce a new idea and try to convince others of its worth; they are leaders because they face the world with eyes full of expectation, with the expertise to take away the veil that covers its hidden potential.

Christian leadership is called ministry precisely to express that in the service of others new life can be brought about. It is this service which gives eyes to see the flower breaking through the cracks in the street, ears to hear a word of forgiveness muted by hatred and hostility, and hands to feel new life under the cover of death and destruction. Mr. Harrison was not just a bitter and hostile man, resistant to pastoral help. For a real minister he incarnates the truth that it belongs to dignity to die a human death, to surrender life instead of allowing it to be taken away in a state of unconsciousness. Underneath Mr. Harrison's coarse and bitter remarks, a Christian hears a cry for help in facing what is hidden behind his imminent death, and above all the cry for someone who will be with him in life and in death.

The encounter between these two men in a crisis situation therefore is not an accidental event but a direct appeal to both of them to discover or rediscover the basic search of the human heart. But this appeal can only be heard by one who has a deep-rooted faith in the value and meaning of life, by one who knows that life is not a static given but a mystery which reveals itself in the ongoing encounter between humanity and the world.

3. Hope

While personal concern is sustained by a continuously growing faith in the value and meaning of life, the deepest motivation for leading our brothers and sisters to the future is hope. For hope makes it possible to look beyond the fulfillment of urgent wishes and pressing desires and offers a vision beyond human suffering and even death. Christian leaders are people of hope whose strength in the final analysis is based neither on self-confidence derived from personality nor on specific expectations for the future, but on a promise given.

This promise not only made Abraham travel to unknown territory; it not only inspired Moses to lead his people out of slavery; it is also the guiding motive for any Christian who keeps pointing to a new life even in the face of corruption and death.

Without this hope, we will never be able to see value and meaning in the encounter with a decaying human being and become personally concerned. This hope stretches far beyond the limitations of one's own psychological strength, for it is anchored not just in the soul of the individual but in God's self-disclosure in history. Leadership therefore is not called Christian because it is permeated with optimism against all the odds of life but because it is grounded in the historic Christ-event, which is understood as a definitive breach in the deterministic chain of human trial and error and as a dramatic affirmation that there is light on the other side of darkness.

Every attempt to attach this hope to visible symptoms in our surroundings becomes a temptation when it prevents us from the realization that promises, not concrete successes, are the basis of Christian leadership. Many ministers, priests, and Christian laypeople have become disillusioned, bitter, and even hostile when years of hard work bear no fruit, when little change is accomplished. Building a vocation on the expectations of concrete results, however conceived, is like building a house on sand instead of on solid rock, and it takes away even the ability to accept successes as free gifts.

Hope prevents us from clinging to what we have and frees us to move away from the safe place and enter unknown and fearful territory. This might sound romantic, but when someone enters with another into the fear of death and is able to wait for him or her right there, leaving the safe place might turn out to be a very difficult act of leadership. It is an act of discipleship in which we follow the hard road of Jesus, who entered death with nothing but bare hope.

Conclusion

Thus, waiting for tomorrow, as an act of Christian leadership, asks for personal concern, a deep faith in the value and meaning of life, and a strong hope, which breaks through the boundaries of death. In this analysis it has become clear that Christian leadership is accomplished only through service. This service requires the willingness to enter into a situation, with all the human vulnerabilities we have to share with one another. This is a painful and self-denying experience but an experience which can indeed lead us out of our prison of confusion and fear. Indeed, the paradox of Christian leadership is that the way out is the way in, that only by entering into communion with human suffering can relief be found. As John Allen was invited to enter into Mr. Harrison's agony and wait for him there, all Christians are constantly invited to overcome their neighbors' fear by entering into it with them, and to find in the fellowship of suffering the way to freedom.

4

MINISTRY BY
LONELY MINISTERS

■

The Wounded Healer

Introduction

IN THE MIDDLE of our convulsive world men and women raise their voices time and again to announce with incredible boldness that we are waiting for a Liberator. We are waiting, they announce, for a Messiah who will free us from hatred and oppression, from racism and war—a Messiah who will let peace and justice take their rightful place.

If the ministry is meant to hold the promise of this Messiah, then whatever we can learn of his coming will give us a deeper understanding of what is called for in ministry today.

How does our Liberator come? I found an old legend in the Talmud which may suggest to us the beginning of an answer:

> Rabbi Yoshua ben Levi came upon Elijah the prophet while he was standing at the entrance of Rabbi Simeron ben Yohai's cave. . . . He asked Elijah, "When will the Messiah come?"
> Elijah replied, "Go and ask him yourself."
> "Where is he?"
> "Sitting at the gates of the city."
> "How shall I know him?"
> "He is sitting among the poor covered with wounds. The others unbind all their wounds at the same time and then bind them up again. But he unbinds one at a time and binds it up again, saying to himself, 'Perhaps I shall be needed: if so I must always be ready so as not to delay for a moment.'"[1]

The Messiah, the story tells us, is sitting among the poor, binding his wounds one at a time, waiting for the moment when he will be needed. So it is too with ministers. Since it is our task to make visible the first vestiges of liberation for others, we must bind our own wounds carefully in anticipation of the moment when we will be needed. We are called to be the wounded healers, the ones who must look after our own wounds but at the same time be prepared to heal the wounds of others.

We are both wounded ministers and healing ministers, two concepts I would like to explore in this last chapter.

I. The Wounded Minister

The Talmud story suggests that, because he binds his own wounds one at a time, the Messiah would not have to take time to prepare himself if asked to help someone else. He would be ready to help. Jesus has given this story a new fullness by making his own broken body the way to health, to liberation and new life. Thus like Jesus, those who proclaim liberation are called not only to care for their own wounds and the wounds of others but also to make their wounds into a major source of their healing power.

But what are our wounds? They have been spoken about in many ways by many voices. Words such as "alienation," "separation," "isolation," and "loneliness" have been used as the names of our wounded condition. Maybe the word "loneliness" best expresses our immediate experience and therefore most fittingly enables us to understand our brokenness. The loneliness of ministers is especially painful; for over and above their experience as individuals in modern society, they feel an added loneliness resulting from the changing meaning of the ministerial profession itself.

1. Personal loneliness

We live in a society in which loneliness has become one of the most painful human wounds. The growing competition and rivalry which pervade our lives from birth have created in us an acute awareness of our isolation. This awareness has in turn left many with a heightened anxiety and an intense search for the experience of unity and community. It has also led people to ask anew how love, friendship, brotherhood, and sisterhood can free them from isolation and offer them a sense of intimacy and belonging. All around us we see the many ways by which the people of the Western world are trying to escape this loneliness. Psychotherapy, the many institutes which offer group experiences with verbal and nonverbal communication techniques, summer courses and conferences supported by scholars, trainers, and "huggers" where people can share common problems, and the many experiments which seek to create intimate liturgies where peace is not only announced but also felt—these increasingly popular phenomena are all signs of a painful attempt to break through the immobilizing wall of loneliness.

But the more I think about loneliness, the more I think that the wound of loneliness is like the Grand Canyon—a deep incision in the surface of our existence which has become an inexhaustible source of beauty and self-understanding.

Therefore I would like to voice loudly and clearly what might seem unpopular and maybe even disturbing: The Christian way of life does not take away our loneliness; it protects and cherishes it as a precious gift. Sometimes it seems as if we do everything possible to avoid the painful confrontation with our basic human loneliness, and allow ourselves to be trapped by false gods promising immediate satisfaction and quick relief. But perhaps the painful awareness of loneliness is an invitation to transcend our limitations and look beyond the boundaries of our existence. The awareness of loneliness might be a gift we must protect and guard, because our loneliness reveals to us an inner emptiness that can be destructive when misunderstood but filled with promise for the one who can tolerate its sweet pain.

When we are impatient, when we want to give up our loneliness and try to overcome the separation and incompleteness we feel too soon, we easily relate to our human world with devastating expectations. We ignore what we already know with a deep-seated, intuitive knowledge—that no love or friendship, no intimate embrace or tender kiss, no community, commune, or collective, no man or woman, will ever be able to satisfy our desire to be released from our lonely condition. This truth is so disconcerting and painful that we are more prone to play games with our fantasies than to face the truth of our existence. Thus we keep hoping that one day we will find the man who really understands our experiences, the woman who will bring peace to our restless life, the job where we can fulfill our potentials, the book which will explain everything, and the place where we can feel at home. Such false hope leads us to make exhausting demands and prepares us for bitterness and dangerous hostility when we start discovering that nobody, and nothing, can live up to our absolutist expectations.

Many marriages are ruined because neither partner was able to fulfill the often hidden hope that the other would take his or her loneliness away. And many celibates live with the naïve dream that in the intimacy of marriage their loneliness will be taken away.

When ministers live with these false expectations and illusions they prevent themselves from claiming their own loneliness as a source of human understanding and are unable to offer any real service to the many who do not understand their own suffering.

2. Professional loneliness

The wound of loneliness in the lives of ministers hurts all the more since they not only share in the human condition of isolation but also find that their professional impact on others is diminishing. Ministers are called to speak to the ultimate concerns of life: birth and death, union and separation, love and hate. They have an urgent desire to give meaning to people's lives. But they find themselves standing on the edges of events and only reluctantly admitted to the spot where the decisions are made.

In hospitals, where many utter their first cry as well as their last words, ministers are often more tolerated than required. In prisons, where people's desire for liberation and freedom is most painfully felt, chaplains feel like guilty bystanders whose words hardly move the wardens. In the cities, where children play between buildings and old people die isolated and forgotten, the protests of priests are hardly taken seriously and their demands hang in the air like rhetorical questions. Many churches decorated with words announcing salvation and new life are often little more than parlors for those who feel quite comfortable in the old life and who are not likely to let the minister's words change their stone hearts into furnaces where swords can be cast into plowshares and spears into pruning hooks.

The painful irony is that ministers, who want to touch the center of people's lives, find themselves on the periphery, often pleading in vain for admission. They never seem to be where the action is, where the plans are made and the strategies discussed. They always seem to arrive at the wrong places at the wrong times with the wrong people, outside the walls of the city when the feast is over.

A few years ago, when I was chaplain of the Holland–America line, I was standing on the bridge of a huge Dutch ocean liner which was trying to find its way through a thick fog into the port of Rotterdam. The fog was so thick, in fact, that the steersman could not even see the bow of the ship. The captain, carefully listening to a radar station operator who was explaining his position between other ships, walked nervously up and down the bridge and shouted his orders to the steersman. When he suddenly stumbled over me, he blurted out: "God damn it, Father, get out of my way." But when I was ready to run away, filled with feelings of incompetence and guilt, he came back and said: "Why don't you just stay around? This might be the only time I really need you."

There was a time, not too long ago, when we felt like captains running our own ships with a great sense of power and self-confidence. Now we are standing in the way. That is our lonely position: We are powerless, on the side, liked maybe by a few crew members who swab the decks and drink a beer with us, but not taken very seriously when the weather is fine.

The wound of our loneliness is indeed deep. Maybe we had forgotten it, since there were so many distractions. But our failure to change the world with our good intentions and sincere actions and our undesired displacement to the edges of life have made us aware that the wound is still there.

So we see how loneliness is the ministers' wound not only because we share in the human condition but also because of the unique predicament of the profession. It is this wound which we are called to bind with more care and attention than others usually do. For a deep understanding of our own pain makes it possible for us to convert our weakness into strength and to offer our own experience as a source of healing to those who are often lost in the darkness of their own misunderstood sufferings. This is a very hard call, because for ministers who are committed to forming a community of faith, loneliness is a painful wound, which is easily subject to denial and neglect. But once the pain is accepted and understood, a denial is no longer necessary, and ministry can become a healing service.

II. The Healing Minister

How can wounds become a source of healing? This is a question which requires careful consideration. For when we want to put our wounded selves in the service of others, we must consider the relationship between our professional and personal lives.

On the one hand, no ministers can keep their own experiences of life hidden from those they want to help. Nor should they want to keep them hidden. While doctors can still be good doctors when their private lives are severely disrupted, ministers cannot offer service without a constant and vital acknowledgment of their own experiences. On the other hand, it would be very easy to misuse the concept of the wounded healer. Ministers who talk in the pulpit about their own personal problems are of no help to their congregations, for no suffering human being is helped by someone who says that he or she has the same problems. Remarks such as "Don't worry because I suffer from the same depression, confusion, and anxiety as you do" help no one. This spiritual exhibitionism adds little faith to little faith and creates narrow-mindedness instead of new perspectives. Open wounds stink and do not heal.

Making one's own wounds a source of healing, therefore, calls not for a sharing of superficial personal pains but for a constant willingness to see one's own pain and suffering as rising from the depth of the universal human condition.

To some, the concept of the wounded healer might sound morbid and unhealthy. They might feel that the ideal of self-fulfillment is replaced by an ideal of self-castigation, and that pain is romanticized instead of criticized. I would like to show how the idea of the wounded healer does not contradict the concept of self-realization, or self-fulfillment, but deepens and broadens it.

How does healing take place? Many words, such as care and compassion, understanding and forgiveness, fellowship and community, have been used for the healing task of the Christian minister. I like to use the word hospitality, not only because it has such deep roots in the Judeo-Christian tradition but also, and primarily, because it gives us more insight into the nature of response to the human condition of loneliness. Hospitality is the virtue which allows us to break through the narrowness of our own fears and to open our houses to the stranger, with the intuition that salvation comes to us in the form of a tired traveler. Hospitality makes anxious disciples into powerful witnesses, makes suspicious owners into generous givers, and makes closed-minded sectarians into interested recipients of new ideas and insights.

But it has become very difficult for us today to fully understand the implications of hospitality. Like the Semitic nomads, we live in a desert with many lonely travelers who are looking for a moment of peace, for a fresh drink, and for a sign of encouragement so that they can continue their mysterious search for freedom.

What does hospitality as a healing power require? It requires first of all that hosts feel at home in their own houses, and second, that they create a free and fearless place for the unexpected visitor. Therefore, hospitality embraces two concepts: concentration and community.

1. Hospitality and concentration
Hospitality is the ability to pay attention to the guest. This is very difficult, since we are preoccupied with our own needs, worries, and tensions, which prevent us from getting distance from ourselves in order to pay attention to others.

Not long ago I met a parish priest. After describing his hectic daily schedule—religious services, classroom teaching, luncheon and dinner engage-
ments, and organizational meetings—he said apologetically: "Yes . . . but
there are so many problems." When I asked, "Whose problems?" he was
silent for a few minutes, and then more or less reluctantly said, "I guess—
my own." Indeed, his incredible activities seemed in large part motivated
by fear of what he would discover when he came to a standstill. He actually
said: "I guess I am busy in order to avoid a painful self-concentration."

So we find it extremely hard to pay attention because of our intentions.
As soon as our intentions take over, the question no longer is "Who is she?"
but "What can I get from her?"—and then we no longer listen to what she
is saying but to what we can do with what she is saying. Then the fulfillment
of our unrecognized need for sympathy, friendship, popularity, success,
understanding, money, or a career becomes our concern, and instead of
paying attention to the other person we impose ourselves upon him or her
with intrusive curiosity.[2]

If we want to pay attention without intention we have to be at home in
our own houses—that is, we have to discover the center of our lives in our
own hearts. Concentration, which leads to meditation and contemplation,
is therefore the necessary precondition for true hospitality. When our souls
are restless, when we are driven by thousands of different and often conflict-
ing stimuli, when we are always "over there" between people, ideas, and
the worries of this world, how can we possibly create the space where
someone else can enter freely without feeling like an unlawful intruder?

Paradoxically, by withdrawing into ourselves, not out of self-pity but out
of humility, we create the space for another to be and to come to us on his
or her own terms. James Hillman, director of studies at the C. G. Jung
Institute in Zurich, speaking about counseling, has written:

> For the other person to open and talk requires a withdrawal of the coun-
> selor. I must withdraw to make room for the other. . . . This withdrawal,
> rather than going-out-to-meet the other, is an intense act of concentra-
> tion, a model for which can be found in the Jewish mystical doctrine of
> Tsimtsum. God as omnipresent and omnipotent was everywhere. He
> filled the universe with his Being. How then could the creation come
> about? . . . God had to create by withdrawal; He created the not-Him,
> the other, by self-concentration. . . . On the human level, withdrawal of
> myself aids the other to come into being.[3]

But human withdrawal is a very painful and lonely process, because it
forces us to face directly our own condition in all its beauty as well as misery.

When we are not afraid to enter into our own center and to concentrate on the stirrings of our own souls, we come to know that being alive means being loved. This experience tells us that we can only love because we are born out of love, that we can only give because our lives are gifts, and that we can only make others free because we are set free by the One whose heart is greater than ours. When we have found the anchor places for our lives in our own center, we can be free to let others enter into the space created for them and allow them to dance their own dance, sing their own song, and speak their own language without fear. Then our presence is no longer threatening and demanding but inviting and liberating.

2. Hospitality and community

Minister who have come to terms with their own loneliness and are at home in their own houses are hosts who offer hospitality to their guests. They give them a friendly space, where they may feel free to come and go, to be close and distant, to rest and to play, to talk and to be silent, to eat and to fast. The paradox indeed is that hospitality asks for the creation of an empty space where guests can find their own souls.

Why is this a healing ministry? It is healing because it takes away the illusion that wholeness can be given by one to another. It is healing because it does not take away the loneliness and the pain of others but invites them to recognize their loneliness on a level where it can be shared. Many people in this life suffer because they are anxiously searching for the man or woman, the event or encounter, which will take their loneliness away. But when they enter a house with real hospitality they soon see that their own wounds must be understood not as sources of despair and bitterness but as signs that they have to travel on in obedience to the calling of those wounds.

From this we get an idea of the kind of help ministers may offer. Ministers are not doctors whose primary task is to take away pain. Rather, ministers deepen the pain to a level where it can be shared. When someone comes with his loneliness to the minister, he can only expect that his loneliness will be understood and felt, so that he no longer has to run away from it but can accept it as an expression of his basic human condition. When a woman suffers the loss of her child, the minister is not called upon to comfort her by telling her that she still has two beautiful healthy children at home; the minister is challenged to help her realize that the death of her child reveals her own mortal condition, the same human condition which the minister and others share with her.

Perhaps the main task of ministers is to prevent people from suffering for the wrong reasons. Many people suffer because of the false supposition on which they have based their lives. That supposition is that there should be no fear or loneliness, no confusion or doubt. But these sufferings can only be dealt with creatively when they are understood as wounds integral to our human condition. Therefore ministry is a very confronting service. It does not allow people to live with illusions of immortality and wholeness. It keeps reminding others that they are mortal and broken but also that, with the recognition of this condition, liberation starts.

Ministers cannot save anyone. They can only offer themselves as guides to fearful people. Yet, paradoxically, it is precisely in this guidance that the first signs of hope become visible. This is so because a shared pain is no longer paralyzing when understood as a way to liberation. When we become aware that we do not have to escape our pains, but that we can mobilize them into a common search for life, those very pains are transformed from expressions of despair into signs of hope.

Through this common search, hospitality becomes community as it creates a unity based on the shared confession of our basic brokenness and on a shared hope. This hope in turn leads us far beyond the boundaries of human togetherness to God, who calls as away from the land of slavery to the land of freedom. It belongs to the central insight of the Judeo-Christian tradition, that it is the call of God which forms the people of God.

A Christian community is therefore a healing community not because wounds are cured and pains are alleviated but because wounds and pains become openings or occasions for new vision. Mutual confession then becomes a mutual deepening of hope, and sharing weakness becomes a reminder to one and all of the coming strength.

When loneliness is among the chief wounds of the minister, hospitality can convert that wound into a source of healing. Concentration prevents ministers from burdening others with their pain and allows them to accept their wounds as helpful teachers of their own and their neighbors' condition. Community arises where the sharing of pain takes place, not as a stifling form of self-complaint but as a recognition of God's saving promises.

Conclusion

I started this chapter with the story of Rabbi Yoshua ben Levi, who asked Elijah, "When will the Messiah come?" There is an important conclusion to this story. When Elijah had explained to him how he could find the Messiah sitting among the poor at the gates of the city, the rabbi went to the Messiah and said to him:

> "Peace unto you, my master and teacher."
> The Messiah answered, "Peace unto you, son of Levi."

He asked, "When is the master coming?"

"Today," he answered.

Rabbi Yoshua returned to Elijah, who asked, "What did he tell you?"

"He indeed has deceived me, for he said 'Today I am coming' and he has not come."

Elijah said, "This is what he told you: 'Today if you would listen to His voice.'" (Ps 95:7)

Even when we know that we are called to be wounded healers, it is still very difficult to acknowledge that healing has to take place today. Because we are living in days when our wounds have become all too visible. Our loneliness and isolation have become so much a part of our daily experience that we cry out for a Liberator who will take us away from our misery and bring us justice and peace.

To announce, however, that the Liberator is sitting among the poor and that the wounds are signs of hope and that today is the day of liberation is a step very few can take. But this is exactly the announcement of the wounded healer: "The Messiah is coming—not tomorrow, but today, not next year, but this year, not after all our misery is passed, but in the middle of it, not in another place but right here where we are standing."

And with a challenging confrontation the wounded healer says:

> If only you would listen to him today!
> Do not harden your hearts as at Meribah,
> as at the time of Massah in the desert,
> when your ancestors challenged me,
> put me to the test, and saw what I could do!
>
> (Ps 95:7–9)

If we listen to the voice and believe that ministry is a sign of hope, because it makes visible the first rays of light of the coming Messiah, we can make ourselves and others understand that we already carry in us the source of our own search. Thus ministry can indeed be a witness to the living truth that the wound, which causes us to suffer now, will be revealed to us later as the place where God intimated the new creation.

CONCLUSION

∎

A Forward Thrust

IN THE LAST CHAPTER of this book I described hospitality as a central attitude of ministers who want to make their own wounded condition available to others as a source of healing. Hopefully the implications of this attitude have become visible through the different guests for whom ministers are called to be receptive hosts. Mr. Harrison, the old farmer, lost in the impersonal milieu of the hospital, afraid to die and afraid to live; the members of the inward, fatherless, and convulsive generation; and those searching for new modes of immortality in the middle of a fragmented and dislocated existence—they are all asking for free space in which they can move without fear and discover new directions.

When the imitation of Christ means not to live a life like Jesus, but to live your life as authentically as Jesus lived his, then there are many ways and forms in which people can be Christians. Ministers are the ones who can make this search for authenticity possible, not by standing on the side as neutral screens or impartial observers, but as articulate witnesses of Christ, who put their own search at the disposal of others. This hospitality requires that ministers know where they stand and whom they stand for, but it also requires that they allow others to enter their lives, come close, and ask how their lives connect.

Nobody can predict where this will lead us, because every time hosts allow themselves to be influenced by their guests they take a risk. But it is exactly in common searches and shared risks that new ideas are born, that new visions reveal themselves, and that new roads become visible.

We do not know where we will be two, ten, or twenty years from now. What we can know, however, is that we all suffer and that a sharing of suffering can make us move forward.

Minister are called to make this forward thrust credible to their many guests, so that they do not stay but have a growing desire to move on, in the conviction that the full liberation of humanity and our world is still to come.

NOTES

Introduction

1. Antonio Porchia, in *Voices* (Chicago, 1969).

1. Ministry in a Dislocated World

1. *Tales of Ancient India,* trans. by J. A. B. van Buitenen (New York: Bantam Books, 1961), pp. 50–51.
2. Robert Jay Lifton, *History and Human Survival* (New York: Random House, 1970), p. 318.
3. Robert Jay Lifton, *Boundaries* (New York: Random House, 1970), p. 98.
4. Quotation from Lifton, *History and Human Survival,* p. 318.
5. Lifton, *Boundaries,* p. 22.
6. Lifton, *History and Human Survival,* p. 330.
7. See Carl Rogers, *On Becoming a Person* (Boston: Houghton Mifflin, 1961), p. 26.

2. Ministry for a Rootless Generation

1. Jeffrey K. Hadden, in *Psychology Today,* Oct. 1969.
2. Portions of the lyrics from "Epitaph." Words and music by Robert Fripp, Ian McDonald, Greg Lake, Michael Giles and Peter Sinfield © Copyright 1969 and 1971 Enthoven Gaydon & Co., London, England. TRO-TOTAL MUSIC, INC., New York. Used by permission.
3. Portions of the lyrics from "I Talk to the Wind." Words and music by Ian McDonald and Peter Sinfield. © Copyright 1969 Enthoven Gaydon & Co., London, England. TRO-TOTAL MUSIC, INC., New York. Used by permission.
4. Portions of the lyrics from "Epitaph." Words and music by Robert Fripp, Ian McDonald, Greg Lake, Michael Giles and Peter Sinfield. © Copyright 1969 and 1971 Enthoven Gaydon & Co., London, England. TRO-TOTAL MUSIC, INC., New York. Used by permission.
5. David Riesman, in *Psychology Today,* Oct. 1969.

6. Ibid.

3. Ministry to a Hopeless Individual

1. See Alexander Berkman, *Prison Memoirs of an Anarchist* (New York: Schocken Books, 1970).
2. See George Jackson, *Soledad Brother: The Prison Letters of George Jackson* (New York: Coward-McCann, 1970).
3. Seward Hiltner, *Counselor on Counseling* (Nashville: Abingdon Press, 1950).
4. Carl Rogers, *On Becoming a Person* (Boston: Houghton Mifflin, 1961), p. 26.

4. Ministry by Lonely Ministers

1. Taken from the tractate Sanhedrin.
2. See James Hillman, *Insearch* (New York: Charles Scribner's Sons, 1967), p. 18.
3. Ibid., p. 31.

REACHING OUT

The Three Movements

of the Spiritual Life

∎

To my Mother and Father
with Love and Affection

ACKNOWLEDGMENTS

∎

THE FIRST PLANS for this book developed during a short, lively seminar on Christian Spirituality at the Yale Divinity School. Its last pages were written two and a half years later during a long, quiet retreat at the Trappist Abbey of the Genesee. Although this book is closer to me than anything I have written and tries to articulate my most personal thoughts and feelings about being a Christian, it definitely is the book that needed and received the most help.

Without the sincere interest, the critical response, and the original contributions of many students, I would never have been able to distinguish between what is personal and what is private, between what is universal and what is "just me."

I am grateful to Gary Cash for his careful assistance in helping me integrate in this text many ideas that were expressed by students as a response to our first seminar. I also am very thankful to Ellie Drury for encouraging me to say what I had to say directly and straightforwardly, and to Mrs. James Angell for helping me say it in correct English.

I owe a special word of thanks to John J. Delaney, Dorothy Holman, and John Eudes Bamberger for their invaluable editorial suggestions and to Pat Murray Kelly for her generous and skillful assistance in the typing and retyping of the manuscript.

To my mother and father, who created the space where I could hear and follow God's call, I dedicate this book with love and affection.

Abbey of the Genesee
Piffard, New York

CONTENTS

■

PREFACE

∎

THIS BOOK IS A RESPONSE to the question: "What does it mean to live a life in the Spirit of Jesus Christ?" Therefore, it is a personal book, a book born out of struggles which in the first place were and still are my own. But during the years it became more and more clear that by deepening these struggles, by following them to their roots, I was touching a level where they could be shared. This book does not offer answers or solutions but is written in the conviction that the quest for an authentic Christian spirituality is worth the effort and the pain, since in the midst of this quest we can find signs offering hope, courage, and confidence.

During the last few years I have read many studies about spirituality and the spiritual life; I have listened to many lectures, spoken with many spiritual guides, and visited many religious communities. I have learned much, but the time has come to realize that neither parents nor teachers nor counselors can do much more than offer a free and friendly place where one has to discover one's own lonely way. Maybe my own deep-rooted fear of being on my own and alone kept me going from person to person, book to book, and school to school, anxiously avoiding the pain of accepting the responsibility for my own life. All that is quite possible, but more important is that the time seems to have come when I can no longer stand back with the remark "Some say . . . others say" but have to respond to the question, "But what do you say?" (see Mk 8:27–30).

The question about the spiritual life is a very challenging question. It touches the core of life. It forces you to take nothing for granted—neither good nor evil, neither life nor death, neither human beings nor God. That is why this question, while intimately my own, is also the question that asks for so much guidance. That is why the decisions that are most personal ask for the greatest support. That is why, even after many years of education and formation, even after the good advice and counsel of many, I can still

179

say with Dante, "In the middle of the way of our life I find myself in a dark wood."[1] This experience is frightful as well as exhilarating because it is the great experience of being alone, alone in the world, alone before God.

I wanted to write this book because it is my growing conviction that my life belongs to others just as much as it belongs to me and that what is experienced as most unique often proves to be most solidly embedded in the common condition of being human.

One way to bring all that is written in the following pages together is to say that the spiritual life is a reaching out to our innermost self, to our fellow human beings, and to our God. "Reaching out" indeed expresses best the mood and the intention of this book. In the midst of a turbulent, often chaotic, life we are called to reach out, with courageous honesty to our innermost self, with relentless care to our fellow human beings, and with increasing prayer to our God. To do that, however, we have to face and explore directly our inner restlessness, our mixed feelings toward others, and our deep-seated suspicions about the absence of God.

For a long time I have been hesitant to write this book, which has such a personal background. How can I tell others about reaching out while I find myself so often caught in my own passions and weaknesses? I found some consolation and encouragement in the words of one of the most stern ascetics, the seventh-century John of the Ladder, who lived for forty years a solitary life at Mount Sinai. In his chapter on discernment, step 26 of his spiritual ladder, he writes:

> If some are still dominated by their former bad habits, and yet can teach
> by mere words, let them teach. . . . For perhaps, being put to shame by
> their own words, they will eventually begin to practice what they teach.[2]

These words seem sufficient to overcome my apprehensions and to make me free to describe the great human call to reach out to God and to those created in God's image and likeness.

INTRODUCTION

■

IN A SOCIETY that gives much value to development, progress, and achievement, the spiritual life becomes quite easily subject to concerns expressed in questions such as "How far advanced am I?"—"Have I matured since I started on the spiritual path?"—"On what level am I and how do I move to the next one?"—"When will I reach the moment of union with God and the experience of illumination or enlightenment?" Although none of these questions as such is meaningless, they can become dangerous against the background of a success-oriented society. Many great saints have described their religious experiences, and many lesser saints have systematized them into different phases, levels, or stages. These distinctions can be helpful for those who write books and for those who use them to instruct, but it is of great importance that we leave the world of measurements behind when we speak about the life of the Spirit. A personal reflection can illustrate this:

> When after many years of adult life I ask myself, "Where am I as a Christian?" there are just as many reasons for pessimism as for optimism. Many of the real struggles of twenty years ago are still very much alive. I am still searching for inner peace, for creative relationships with others, and for the experience of God and neither I nor anyone else has any way of knowing if the small psychological changes during the past years have made me a more or a less spiritual man.

We may say, however, one thing: In the middle of all our worries and concerns, often disturbingly similar over the years, we can become more aware of the different poles between which our lives vacillate and are held in tension. These poles offer the context in which we can speak about the spiritual life, because they can be recognized by anyone who is striving to live a life in the Spirit of Jesus Christ.

The first polarity deals with our relationship to ourselves. It is the polarity between loneliness and solitude. The second polarity forms the basis of our relationship to others. This is the polarity between hostility and hospitality. The third, final, and most important polarity structures our relationship with God. This is the polarity between illusion and prayer. During our lives we become more aware not only of our crying loneliness but also of our real desire for a solitude of heart; we come to the painful realization not only of our cruel hostilities but also of our hope to receive our fellow humans with unconditional hospitality; and underneath all of this we discover not only the endless illusions which make us act as if we are masters of our fate but also the precarious gift of prayer hidden in the depth of our innermost self.

Thus, the spiritual life is that constant movement between the poles of loneliness and solitude, hostility and hospitality, illusion and prayer. The more we come to the painful confession of our loneliness, hostilities, and illusions, the more we are able to see solitude, hospitality, and prayer as part of the vision of our lives. Although after many years of living we often feel more lonely, hostile, and filled with illusions than when we had hardly a past to reflect upon, we also know better than before that all these pains have deepened and sharpened our urge to reach out to a solitary, hospitable, and prayerful mode of existence.

And so, writing about the spiritual life is like making prints from negatives. Maybe it is exactly the experience of loneliness that allows us to describe the first tentative lines of solitude. Maybe it is precisely the shocking confrontation with our hostile self that gives us words to speak about hospitality as a real option, and maybe we will never find the courage to speak about prayer as a human vocation without the disturbing discovery of our own illusions. Often it is the dark forest that makes us speak about the open field. Frequently prison makes us think about freedom, hunger helps us to appreciate food, and war gives us words for peace. Not seldom are our visions of the future born out of the sufferings of the present and our hope for others out of our own despair. Only few "happy endings" make us happy, but often someone's careful and honest articulation of the ambiguities, uncertainties, and painful conditions of life gives us new hope. The paradox is indeed that new life is born out of the pains of the old.

The life of Jesus has made it very clear to us that the spiritual life does not allow bypasses. Bypassing loneliness, hostility, or illusion will never lead us to solitude, hospitality, and prayer. We will never know for sure if we will fully realize the new life that we can discover in the midst of the old. Maybe we will die lonely and hostile, taking our illusions with us to the grave. Many seem to do so. But when Jesus asks us to take up our cross and follow him (Mk 8:34) we are invited to reach out far beyond our broken and sinful condition and give shape to a life that intimates the great things that are prepared for us.

Because of the conviction that to live a spiritual life means first of all to come to the awareness of the inner polarities between which we are held in tension, this book is divided into three parts, each one representing a different movement of the spiritual life. The first movement, from loneliness to solitude, focuses primarily on the spiritual life as it relates to the experience of our own selves. The second movement, from hostility to hospitality, deals with the spiritual life as a life for others. The third and final movement, from illusion to prayer, offers some tentative formulations of that most precious and mysterious relationship which is the source of all spiritual life, our relationship to God.

It hardly needs to be stressed that these movements are not clearly separated. Certain themes recur in the different movements in various tonalities and often flow into one another as the movements of a symphony. But hopefully the distinctions will help us better to recognize the different elements of the spiritual life and so encourage us to reach out to our innermost self, our fellow human beings, and our God.

REACHING OUT
TO OUR
INNERMOST SELF

.

The First Movement:
From Loneliness to Solitude

1

A SUFFOCATING LONELINESS

■

Between Competition and Togetherness

IT IS FAR FROM EASY to enter into the painful experience of loneliness. We like to stay away from it. Still it is an experience that enters into everyone's life at some point. You might have felt it as a little child when your classmates laughed at you because you were cross-eyed or as a teenager when you were the last one chosen on the baseball team. You might have felt it when you were homesick in a boarding school or angry about nonsense rules which you could not change. You might have felt it as a young adult in a university where everyone talked about grades but where a good friend was hard to find, or in an action group where nobody paid any attention to your suggestions. You might have felt it as a teacher when students did not respond to your carefully prepared lectures or as a preacher when people were dozing during your well-intentioned sermons. And you still might feel it day after day during staff meetings, conferences, counseling sessions, during long office hours or monotonous manual labor, or just when you are by yourself staring away from a book that cannot keep your attention. Practically every human being can recall similar or much more dramatic situations in which he or she has experienced that strange inner gnawing, that mental hunger, that unsettling unrest that makes us say, "I feel lonely."

Loneliness is one of the most universal human experiences, but our contemporary Western society has heightened the awareness of our loneliness to an unusual degree.

During a recent visit to New York City, I wrote the following note to myself:

Sitting in the subway, I am surrounded by silent people hidden behind their newspapers or staring away in the world of their own fantasies.

Nobody speaks with a stranger, and a patroling policeman keeps reminding me that people are not out to help each other. But when my eyes wander over the walls of the train covered with invitations to buy more or new products, I see young, beautiful people enjoying each other in a gentle embrace, playful men and women smiling at each other in fast sailboats, proud explorers on horseback encouraging each other to take brave risks, fearless children dancing on a sunny beach, and charming girls always ready to serve me in airplanes and ocean liners. While the subway train runs from one dark tunnel into the other and I am nervously aware where I keep my money, the words and images decorating my fearful world speak about love, gentleness, tenderness, and about a joyful togetherness of spontaneous people.

The contemporary society in which we find ourselves makes us acutely aware of our loneliness. We increasingly realize that we are living in a world where even the most intimate relationships have become part of competition and rivalry.

Pornography seems one of the logical results. It is intimacy for sale. In the many "porno shops" hundreds of lonely young and old men, full of fear that anyone will recognize them, gaze silently at the pictures of nude girls drawing their minds into intimate, close rooms where some stranger will melt away their loneliness. The streets meanwhile shout about the cruel struggle for survival and even the porno corners cannot silence that noise, certainly not when the shop owners keep reminding their customers that they should buy instead of "just looking."

Loneliness is one of the most universal sources of human suffering today. Psychiatrists and clinical psychologists speak about it as the most frequently expressed compliant and the root not only of an increasing number of suicides but also of alcoholism, drug use, different psychosomatic symptoms—such as headaches, stomachaches, and low-back pains—and of a large number of traffic accidents. Children, adolescents, adults, and old people are in growing degree exposed to the contagious disease of loneliness in a world in which a competitive individualism tries to reconcile itself with a culture that speaks about togetherness, unity, and community as the ideals to strive for.

Why is it that many parties and friendly get-togethers leave us so empty and sad? Maybe even there the deep-seated and often unconscious competition between people prevents them from revealing themselves to each other and from establishing relationships that last longer than the party itself. Where we are always welcome, our absence won't matter that much either, and when everyone can come, nobody will be particularly missed. Usually there is food enough and people enough willing to eat it, but often it seems that the food has lost the power to create community and not seldom do we leave the party more aware of our loneliness than when we came.

The language we use suggests anything but loneliness. "Please come in, it is so good to see you. . . . Let me introduce you to this very special friend of mine, who will love to meet you. . . . I have heard so much about you and I can't say how pleased I am to see you now in person. . . . What you are saying is most interesting, I wish more people could hear that. . . . It was so great to talk to you and to have a chance to visit with you. . . . I dearly hope we will meet again. Know that you are always welcome and don't hesitate to bring a friend. . . . Come back soon." It is a language that reveals the desire to be close and receptive but that in our society sadly fails to heal the pains of our loneliness, because the real pain is felt where we can hardly allow anyone to enter.

The roots of loneliness are very deep and cannot be touched by optimistic advertisements, substitute love images, or social togetherness. They find their food in the suspicion that there is no one who cares and offers love without conditions, and no place where we can be vulnerable without being used. The many small rejections of every day—a sarcastic smile, a flippant remark, a brisk denial, or a bitter silence—may all be quite innocent and would hardly be worth our attention if they did not constantly arouse our basic human fear of being left totally alone with "darkness . . . [as our] one companion left" (Ps 88).

The Avoidance of the Painful Void

It is this most basic human loneliness that threatens us and is so hard to face. Too often we will do everything possible to avoid confrontation with the experience of being alone, and sometimes we are able to create the most ingenious devices to prevent ourselves from being reminded of this condition. Our culture has become quite sophisticated in the avoidance of pain, not only our physical pain but our emotional and mental pain as well. We not only bury our dead as if they were still alive but also bury our pains as if they were not really there. We have become so used to this state of anesthesia that we panic when there is nothing or nobody left to distract us. When we have no project to finish, no friend to visit, no book to read, no television to watch, or no record to play, and when we are left all alone by ourselves we are brought so close to the revelation of our basic human aloneness and are so afraid of experiencing an all-pervasive sense of loneliness that we will do anything to get busy again and continue the game which makes us believe that everything is fine after all. John Lennon says: "Feel your own pain," but how hard that is!

In 1973 the Educational Television Network showed a series of life portraits of a family in Santa Barbara, California. This series, which was produced under the name "An American Family," offered an honest and candid portrayal of the day-to-day life of Mr. and Mrs. Loud and their five children. Although the revelations about this "average family," which included the divorce of the parents and the homosexual life of the oldest son, shocked many viewers, a detailed film analysis of any family probably would have been as shocking as this one.

The film, which was made with the full permission and knowledge of all the members of the family, not only unmasked the illusion that this family could be presented as an example to the American people but also showed in detail our tendency to avoid the experience of pain at all costs. Painful issues remained unmentioned and embarrassing situations were simply denied. Pat, the wife and mother in the family, expressed this attitude best when she said, "I don't like things that make me feel uncomfortable." The consequences of this pain avoidance, however, were well expressed by her eighteen-year-old son when he said, "You see seven lonely people trying desperately to love each other—and not succeeding."[1]

It is not very difficult to see that the Loud family is indeed no exception and in many respects "average" in a society growingly populated with lonely people desperately trying to love each other without succeeding. Is this not in large part due to our inability to face the pain of our loneliness? By running away from our loneliness and by trying to distract ourselves with people and special experiences, we do not realistically deal with our human predicament. We are in danger of becoming unhappy people suffering from many unsatisfied cravings and tortured by desires and expectations that never can be fulfilled. Does not all creativity ask for a certain encounter with our loneliness, and does not the fear of this encounter severely limit our possible self-expression?

> When I have to write an article and face a white empty sheet of paper I nearly have to tie myself to the chair to keep from consulting one more book before putting my own words on paper. When, after a busy day, I am alone and free I have to fight the urge to make one more phone call, one more trip to the mailbox, or one more visit to friends who will entertain me for the last few hours of the day. And when I think about

the busy day I sometimes wonder if the educational enterprise so filled with lectures, seminars, conferences, requirements to make up and to fulfill, papers to write and to read, examinations to undergo and to go to has, in fact, not become one big distraction—once in a while entertaining, but mostly preventing me from facing my lonely self, which should be my first source of search and research.

The superficial life to which this leads was vividly portrayed by Henry David Thoreau when he wrote:

> When our life ceases to be inward and private, conversation degenerates into mere gossip. We rarely meet a man who can tell us any news which he has not read in a newspaper, or been told by his neighbor; and, for the most part, the only difference between us and our fellow is that he has seen the newspaper, or been out to tea, and we have not. In proportion as our inward life fails, we go more constantly and desperately to the post office. You may depend on it, that the poor fellow who walks away with the greatest number of letters proud of his extensive correspondence has not heard from himself this long while.[2]

The first task of any school should be to protect its privilege of offering free time—the Latin word *schola* means free time—to understand ourselves and our world a little better. It is a hard struggle to keep free time truly free and to prevent education from degenerating into just another form of competition and rivalry.

The problem, however, is that we not only want our freedom but also fear it. It is this fear that makes us so intolerant toward our own loneliness and makes us grab prematurely for what seem to be "final solutions."

The Danger of the Final Solution

There is much mental suffering in our world. But some of it is suffering for the wrong reason because it is born out of the false expectation that we are called to take each other's loneliness away. When our loneliness drives us away from ourselves into the arms of our companions in life, we are, in fact, driving ourselves into excruciating relationships, tiring friendships, and suffocating embraces. To wait for moments or places where no pain exists, no separation is felt, and where all human restlessness has turned into inner peace is to wait for a dreamworld. No friend or lover, no husband or wife, no community or commune will be able to put to rest our deepest cravings for unity and wholeness. And by burdening others with these divine expectations, of which we ourselves are often only partially aware, we might inhibit the expression of free friendship and love and evoke instead feelings of inadequacy and weakness.

Friendship and love cannot develop in the form of an anxious clinging to each other. They ask for gentle, fearless space in which we can move to and from each other. As long as our loneliness brings us together with the hope that together we no longer will be alone, we castigate each other with our unfulfilled and unrealistic desires for oneness, inner tranquility, and the uninterrupted experience of communion.

It is sad to see how people suffering from loneliness, often deepened by the lack of affection in their intimate family circle, search for a final solution for their pains and look at a new friend, a new lover, or a new community with Messianic expectations. Although their minds know about their self-deceit, their hearts keep saying, "Maybe this time I have found what I have knowingly or unknowingly been searching for." It is indeed amazing at first sight that men and women who have had such distressing relationships with their parents, brothers, or sisters can throw themselves blindly into relationships with far-reaching consequences in the hope that from now on things will be totally different.

But we might wonder if the many conflicts and quarrels, the many accusations and recriminations, the many moments of expressed and repressed anger and of confessed or unconfessed jealousies, which are so often part of these rushed-into relationships, do not find their roots in the false claim that the one has to take the other's loneliness away. Indeed, it seems that the desire for "final solutions" often forms the basis for the destructive violence that enters into the intimacy of human encounters. Mostly this violence is a violence of thoughts, violating the mind with suspicion, inner gossip, or revengeful fantasies. Sometimes it is a violence of words disturbing the peace with reproaches and complaints, and once in a while it takes the dangerous form of harmful actions. Violence in human relationship is so utterly destructive because it not only harms the other but also drives the self into a vicious circle asking for more and more when less and less is received.

In a time with strong emphasis on interpersonal sensitivity, in which we are encouraged to explore our communicative capacities and experiment with many forms of physical, mental, and emotional contact, we are sometimes tempted to believe that our feelings of loneliness and sadness are only signs of lack of mutual openness. Sometimes this is true, and many sensitivity centers make invaluable contributions to broadening the range of human interactions. But real openness to each other also means a real closedness, because only one who can hold a secret can safely share his or her knowledge. When we do not protect with great care our own inner mystery, we will never be able to form community. It is this inner mystery that attracts us to each other and allows us to establish friendship and develop lasting relationships of love. An intimate relationship between people asks not only for mutual openness but also for mutual respectful protection of each other's uniqueness.

Together, Yet Not Too Near

There is a false form of honesty that suggests that nothing should remain hidden and that everything should be said, expressed, and communicated. This honesty can be very harmful, and if it does not harm, it at least makes the relationship flat, superficial, empty, and often very boring. When we try to shake off our loneliness by creating a milieu without limiting boundaries, we may become entangled in a stagnating closeness. It is our vocation to prevent the harmful exposure of our inner sanctuary, not only for our own protection but also as a service to our fellow human beings with whom we want to enter in a creative communion.

Just as words lose their power when they are not born out of silence, so openness loses its meaning when there is no ability to be closed. Our world is full of empty chatter, easy confessions, hollow talk, senseless compliments, poor praise, and boring confidentialities. Not a few magazines become wealthy by suggesting that they are able to furnish us with the most secret and intimate details of the lives of people we always wanted to know more about. In fact, they present us with the most boring trivialities and the most supercilious idiosyncrasies of people whose lives are already flattened out by morbid exhibitionism.

The American way of life tends to be suspicious toward closedness.

> When I came to this country for the first time, I was struck by the open-door lifestyle. In schools, institutes, and office buildings everyone worked with open doors. I could see the secretaries typing behind their machines, the teachers teaching behind their lecterns, the administrators administering behind their desks, and the occasional readers reading behind their books. It seemed as if everyone was saying to me, "Do not hesitate to walk in and interrupt at any time," and most conversations had the same

open quality—giving me the impression that people had no secrets and were ready for any question ranging from their financial status to their sex life.

It is clear that most of these are first impressions and that second and third impressions reveal quickly that there is less openness than suggested. But still, closed doors are not popular, and it needs special effort to establish boundaries that protect the mystery of our lives. Certainly in a period of history in which we have become so acutely aware of our alienation in its different manifestations, it has become difficult to unmask the illusion that the final solution for our experience of loneliness is to be found in human togetherness.

It is easy to see how many marriages are suffering from this illusion. Often they are started with the hope of a union that can dispel all painful feelings of "not belonging" and continue with the desperate struggle to reach a perfect physical and psychological harmony. Many people find it very hard to appreciate a certain closedness in a marriage and do not know how to create the boundaries that allow intimacy to become an always new and surprising discovery of each other. Still, the desire for protective boundaries by which man and woman do not have to cling to each other, but can move graciously in and out of each other's life circle, is clear from the many times that Kahlil Gibran's words are quoted at a wedding ceremony:

> Sing and dance together and be joyous,
> but let each one of you be alone.
> Even as the strings of a lute are alone
> though they quiver with the same music.
> Stand together yet not too near together
> For the pillars of the temple stand apart,
> and the oak tree and the cypress
> grow not in each other's shadow.[3]

From Desert to Garden

But what then can we do with our essential aloneness, which so often breaks into our consciousness as the experience of a desperate sense of loneliness? What does it mean to say that neither friendship nor love, neither marriage nor community can take that loneliness away? Sometimes illusions are more livable than realities, and why not follow our desire to cry out in loneliness and search for someone whom we can embrace and in whose arms our tense bodies and minds can find a moment of deep rest and enjoy the momentary experience of being understood and accepted? These are hard questions because they come forth out of our wounded hearts, but they have to be listened to even when they lead to a difficult road.

This difficult road is the road of conversion, the conversion from loneliness into solitude. Instead of running away from our loneliness and trying to forget or deny it, we have to protect it and turn it into a fruitful solitude. To live a spiritual life we must first find the courage to enter into the desert of our loneliness and to change it by gentle and persistent efforts into a garden of solitude. This requires not only courage but also a strong faith. As hard as it is to believe that the dry, desolate desert can yield endless varieties of flowers, it is equally hard to imagine that our loneliness is hiding unknown beauty. The movement from loneliness to solitude, however, is the beginning of any spiritual life because it is the movement from the restless senses to the restful spirit, from the outward-reaching cravings to the inward-reaching search, from the fearful clinging to the fearless play.

A young student reflecting on his own experience wrote recently:

> When loneliness is haunting me with its possibility of being a threshold instead of a dead end, a new creation instead of a grave, a meeting place instead of an abyss, then time loses its desperate clutch on me. Then I no longer have to live in a frenzy of activity, overwhelmed and afraid for the missed opportunity.

It is far from easy to believe that this is true. Often we go to good men and women with our problems in the secret hope that they will take our burden away from us and free us from our loneliness. Frequently the temporary relief they offer only leads to a stronger recurrence of the same pains when we are again by ourselves. But sometimes we meet and hear that exceptional person who says: "Do not run, but be quiet and silent. Listen attentively to your own struggle. The answer to your question is hidden in your own heart."

In the beautiful book *Zen Flesh, Zen Bones* we find the story of such an encounter.

> Daiju visited the master Baso in China. Baso asked: "What do you seek?"
> "Enlightenment," replied Daiju.

"You have your own treasure house. Why do you search outside?" Baso asked.

Daiju inquired: "Where is my treasure house?"

Baso answered: "What you are asking *is* your treasure house."

Daiju was enlightened! Ever after he urged his friends: "Open your own treasure house and use those treasures."[4]

The real spiritual guide is the one who, instead of advising us what to do or to whom to go, offers us a chance to stay alone and take the risk of entering into our own experience. That person makes us see that pouring little bits of water on our dry land does not help, but that we will find a living well if we reach deep enough under the surface of our complaints.

A friend once wrote: "Learning to weep, learning to keep vigil, learning to wait for the dawn. Perhaps this is what it means to be human." It is hard to really believe this because we constantly find ourselves clinging to people, books, events, experiences, projects, and plans, secretly hoping that this time it will be different. We keep experimenting with many types of anesthetics, we keep finding "psychic numbing" more agreeable than the sharpening of our inner sensitivities. But . . . we can at least remind ourselves of our self-deceit and confess at times our morbid predilection for dead-end streets.

The few times, however, that we do obey our severe masters and listen carefully to our restless hearts, we may start to sense that in the midst of our sadness there is joy, that in the midst of our fears there is peace, that in the midst of our greediness there is the possibility of compassion, and that indeed in the midst of our irking loneliness we can find the beginnings of a quiet solitude.

2

A RECEPTIVE
SOLITUDE

■

Solitude of Heart

THE WORD SOLITUDE can be misleading. It suggests being by yourself in an isolated place. When we think about solitaries, our minds easily evoke images of monks or hermits who live in remote places secluded from the noise of the busy world. In fact, the words "solitude" and "solitary" are derived from the Latin word *solus,* which means alone, and during the ages many men and women who wanted to live a spiritual life withdrew to remote places—deserts, mountains, or deep forests—to live as recluses.

It is probably difficult, if not impossible, to move from loneliness to solitude without any form of withdrawal from a distracting world, and therefore it is understandable that those who seriously try to develop their spiritual life are attracted to places and situations where they can be alone, sometimes for a limited period of time, sometimes more or less permanently. But the solitude that really counts is the solitude of heart; it is an inner quality or attitude that does not depend on physical isolation. On occasion this isolation is necessary to develop this solitude of heart, but it would be sad if we considered this essential aspect of the spiritual life as a privilege of monks and hermits.

It seems more important than ever to stress that solitude is one of the human capacities that can exist, be maintained and developed in the center of a big city, in the middle of a large crowd, and in the context of a very active and productive life. A man or woman who has developed this solitude of heart is no longer pulled apart by the most divergent stimuli of the surrounding world but is able to perceive and understand this world from a quiet inner center.

By attentive living we can learn the difference between being present in loneliness and being present in solitude. When you are alone in an office, a house, or an empty waiting room, you can suffer from restless loneliness but also enjoy a quiet solitude. When you are teaching in a classroom, listening to a lecture, watching a movie, or chatting at a "happy hour," you can have the unhappy feeling of loneliness but also the deep contentment of someone who speaks, listens, and watches from a tranquil center of solitude. It is not too difficult to distinguish between the restless and the restful, between the driven and the free, between the lonely and the solitary in our surroundings. When we live with a solitude of heart, we can listen with attention to the words and the worlds of others, but when we are driven by loneliness, we tend to select just those remarks and events that bring immediate satisfaction to our own craving needs.

Our world, however, is not divided between lonely people and solitaries. We constantly fluctuate between these poles and differ from hour to hour, day to day, week to week, and year to year. We must confess that we have only a very limited influence on this fluctuation. Too many known and unknown factors play roles in the balance of our inner life. But when we are able to recognize the poles between which we move and develop a sensitivity for this inner field of tension, then we no longer have to feel lost and can begin to discern the direction in which we want to go.

The Beginning of the Spiritual Life

The development of this inner sensitivity is the beginning of a spiritual life. It seems that the emphasis on interpersonal sensitivity has at times made us forget to develop the sensitivity that helps us to listen to our own inner voices. Sometimes one wonders if the fact that so many people ask support, advice, and counsel from so many other people is not, in large part, due to their having lost contact with their innermost self. They ask: Should I go to school or look for a job, should I become a doctor or a lawyer, should I marry or remain single, should I leave my position or stay where I am, should I go into the military or refuse to go to war, should I obey my superior or follow my own inclination, should I live a poor life or gain more money for the costly education of my children? There are not enough counselors in the world to help with all these hard questions, and sometimes one feels as if one half of the world is asking advice of the other half while both sides are sitting in the same darkness.

On the other hand, when our insecurity does not lead us to others for help, how often does it lead us against others in self-defense? Sometimes it seems that gossip, condemnation of other people's behavior, and outright attacks on their life choices are signs more of our own self-doubt than of our solidly grounded convictions.

Maybe the most important advice to all searching people is the advice that Rainer Maria Rilke gave to the young man who asked him if he should become a poet. Rilke said:

> You ask whether your verses are good. You ask me. You have asked others before. You send them to magazines. You compare them with other poems, and you are disturbed when certain editors reject your efforts. Now . . . I beg you to give up all that. You are looking outward and that above all you should not do now. Nobody can counsel and help you, nobody. There is only one single way. Go into yourself. Search for the reason that bids you to write; find out whether it is spreading out its roots in the deepest places of your heart, acknowledge to yourself whether you would have to die if it were denied you to write. This above all—ask yourself in the stillest hour of your night: *must* I write? Delve into yourself for a deep answer. And if this should be affirmative, if you may meet this earnest question with a strong and simple *"I must,"* then build your life according to this necessity; your life even into its most indifferent and slightest hour must be a sign of this urge and a testimony to it.[1]

To Live the Question

By slowly converting our loneliness into a deep solitude, we create that precious space where we can discover the voice telling us about our inner necessity—that is, our vocation. Unless our questions, problems, and concerns are tested and matured in solitude, it is not realistic to expect answers that are really our own. How many people can claim their ideas, opinions, and viewpoints as their own? Sometimes intellectual conversations boil down to the capacity to quote the right authority at the right time. Even the most intimate concerns, such as concerns about the meaning and value of life and death, can become victims of the fashion of the time. Frequently, we are restlessly looking for answers, going from door to door, from book to book, or from school to school, without having really listened carefully and attentively to the questions. Rilke said to the young poet:

> I want to beg you as much as I can . . . to be patient toward all that is unsolved in your heart and to try to love the questions themselves. . . .

Do not now seek answers which cannot be given you because you would not be able to live them. And the point is to live everything. *Live* the questions now. Perhaps you will then gradually, without noticing it, live along some distant day into the answer . . . take whatever comes with great trust, and if only it comes out of your own will, out of some need of your innermost being, take it upon yourself and hate nothing.[2]

This is a very difficult task, because in our world we are constantly pulled away from our innermost self and encouraged to look for answers instead of listening to the questions. A lonely person has no inner time nor inner rest to wait and listen. He or she wants answers and wants them here and now. But in solitude we can pay attention to our inner self. This has nothing to do with egocentrism or unhealthy introspection because, in the words of Rilke, "what is going on in your innermost being is worthy of your whole love."[3] In solitude we can become present to ourselves. There we can live, as Anne Morrow Lindbergh says, "like a child or a saint in the immediacy of here and now." There "every day, every act is an island, washed by time and space and has an island's completion."[4] There we also can become present to others by reaching out to them, not greedy for attention and affection but offering our own selves to help build a community of love.

Solitude does not pull us away from our fellow human beings but instead makes real fellowship possible. Few people have expressed this better than the Trappist monk Thomas Merton, who spent the last years of his life living as a hermit but whose contemplative solitude brought him into very intimate contact with others. On January 12, 1950, he wrote in his diary:

It is in deep solitude that I find the gentleness with which I can truly love my brothers. The more solitary I am, the more affection I have for them. It is pure affection and filled with reverence for the solitude of others.[5]

As his life grew in spiritual maturity, Merton came to see with a penetrating clarity that solitude did not separate him from his contemporaries but instead brought him into a deep communion with them. How powerful this insight was for Merton himself is evident from the moving passage he wrote after a short visit to Louisville, where he had watched the people in a busy shopping district. He wrote:

Though "out of the world" we [monks] are in the same world as everybody else, the world of the bomb, the world of race hatred, the world of technology, the world of mass media, big business, revolution, and all the rest. We take a different attitude to all these things, for we belong to God. Yet so does everybody else belong to God. . . . This sense of liberation from an illusory difference was such a relief and such a joy to me that I almost laughed out loud. And I suppose my happiness could have taken form in these words: "Thank God, thank God that I *am* like other men, that I am only a man among others." . . . It is a glorious destiny to be a member of the human race, though it is a race dedicated to many absurdities and one which makes many terrible mistakes: yet, with all that, God Himself gloried in becoming a member of the human race! To think that such a commonplace realization should suddenly seem like news that one holds the winning ticket in a cosmic sweepstake.

I have the immense joy of being *man,* a member of a race in which God Himself became incarnate. As if the sorrows and stupidities of the human condition could overwhelm me, now I realize what we all are. And if only everybody could realize this! But it cannot be explained. There is no way of telling people that they are walking around shining like the sun.

This changes nothing in the sense and value of my solitude, for it is in fact the function of solitude to make one realize such things with a clarity that would be impossible to anyone completely immersed in the other cares, the other illusions, and all the automatisms of a highly collective existence. My solitude, however, is not my own, for I see now how much it belongs to them—and that I have a responsibility for it in their regard, not just in my own. It is because I am one with them that I owe it to them to be alone, and when I am alone, they are not "they" but my own self. There are not strangers![6]

His own personal experience taught Merton that solitude not only deepens our affection for others but also is the place where real community becomes possible. Although Merton himself lived as a monk first in a monastic community and later in a hermitage, it is clear from this and other writers that what really counts for him is not the physical solitude but the solitude of heart.

Without the solitude of heart, the intimacy of friendship, marriage, and community life cannot be creative. Without the solitude of heart, our relationships with others easily become needy and greedy, sticky and clinging, dependent and sentimental, exploitative and parasitic, because without the solitude of heart we cannot experience the others as different from ourselves but only as people who can be used for the fulfillment of our own, often hidden, needs.

The mystery of love is that it protects and respects the aloneness of the other and creates the free space where they can convert their loneliness into a solitude that can be shared. In this solitude we can strengthen each other by mutual respect, by careful consideration of each other's individuality, by an obedient distance from each other's privacy, and by a reverent understanding of the sacredness of the human heart. In this solitude we encourage each other to enter into the silence of our innermost being and discover there the voice that calls us beyond the limits of human togetherness to a new communion. In this solitude we can slowly become aware of a presence of the One who embraces friends and lovers and offers us the freedom to love each other, because God loved us first (see 1 Jn 4:19).

Holy Ground

All this might sound like a new sort of romanticism, but our own very concrete experiences and observations will help us to recognize this as realism. Often we must confess that the experience of our loneliness is stronger than that of our solitude and that our words about solitude are spoken out of the painful silence of loneliness. But there are happy moments of direct knowing, affirming our hopes and encouraging us in our search for that deep solitude where we can sense an inner unity and live in union with our fellow human beings and our God.

I vividly remember the day on which a man who had been a student in one of my courses came back to the school and entered my room with the disarming remark "I have no problems this time, no questions to ask you. I do not need counsel or advice, but I simply want to celebrate some time with you."

We sat on the ground facing each other and talked a little about what life had been for us in the last year, about our work, our common friends, and about the restlessness of our hearts. Then slowly as the minutes passed by we became silent. Not an embarrassing silence but a silence that could bring us closer together than the many small and big events of the last year. We would hear a few cars pass and the noise of someone who was emptying a trash can somewhere. But that did not hurt. The silence which grew between us was warm, gentle, and vibrant. Once in a while we looked at each other with the beginning of a smile pushing away the last remnants of fear and suspicion.

It seemed that while the silence grew deeper around us we became more and more aware of a presence embracing both of us. Then he said, "It is good to be here," and I said, "Yes, it is good to be together again," and after that we were silent again for a long period. And as a deep peace filled the empty space between us he said hesitantly, "When I look at you it is as if I am in the presence of Christ."

I did not feel startled, surprised, or in need of protesting, but I could only say, "It is the Christ in you who recognizes the Christ in me." "Yes," he said. "He indeed is in our midst," and then he spoke the words which entered into my soul as the most healing words I had heard in many years, "From now on, wherever you go, or wherever I go, all the ground between us will be holy ground." And when he left I knew that he had revealed to me what community really means.

Community as an Inner Quality

This experience explains what Rainer Marie Rilke meant when he said, "Love . . . consists in this, that two solitudes protect and border and salute each other"[7] and what Anne Morrow Lindbergh had in mind when she wrote, "I feel we are all islands in a common sea."[8] It made me see that the togetherness of friends and lovers can become moments in which we can enter into a common solitude which is not restricted by time and place.

Don't we often dream about being together with friends without realizing that our dreams are searching for much more than any factual reunion will ever be able to realize? But slowly we can become aware of the possibility of making our human encounters into moments by which our solitude grows and expands itself to embrace more and more people into the community of our life. It indeed is possible for all those with whom we stayed for a long time or for only a moment to become members of that community since, by their encounter in love, all the ground between them and us has indeed become holy ground, and those who leave can stay in the hospitable solitude of our hearts. Friendship is one of the most precious gifts of life, but physical proximity can be the way as well as in the way of its full realization.

A few times in my life I had the seemingly strange sensation that I felt closer to my friends in their absence than in their presence. When they were gone, I had a strong desire to meet them again but I could not avoid a certain emotion of disappointment when the meeting was realized. Our physical presence to each other prevented us from a full encounter. As if we sensed that we were more for each other than we could express. As if our individual concrete characters started functioning as a wall behind which we kept our deepest personal selves hidden. The distance created by a temporary absence helped me to see beyond their characters and revealed to me their greatness and beauty as persons which formed the basis of our love.

Kahlil Gibran wrote:

> When you part from your friend, you grieve not: For that which you love most in him may be clearer in his absence, as the mountain to the climber is clearer from the plain.[9]

Living together with friends is an exceptional joy, but our lives will be sad if that becomes the aim of our strivings. Having a harmonious team working in unity of heart and mind is a gift from heaven, but if our own sense of worth depends on that situation we are sad people. Letters of friends are good to receive, but we should be able to live happily without them. Visits are gifts to be valued, but without them we should not fall into the temptation of a brooding mood. Phone calls, "just to say hello," can fill us with gratitude, but when we expect them as a necessary way to sedate our fear of being left alone, we are becoming the easy victims of our self-complaints. We are always in search of a community that can offer us a sense of belonging, but it is important to realize that being together in one place, one house, one city, or one country is only secondary to the fulfillment of our legitimate desire.

Friendship and community are, first of all, inner qualities allowing human togetherness to be the playful expression of a much larger reality. They can never be claimed, planned, or organized, but in our innermost self the place can be formed where they can be received as gifts.

This inner sense of friendship and community sets us free to live a "worldly" life even in the seclusion of a room, since no one should be excluded from our solitude. But it also allows us to travel light vast distances because for those who share their solitude without fear, all the ground between people has become holy ground.

So our loneliness can grow into solitude. There are days, weeks, and maybe months and years during which we are so overwhelmed by our sense of loneliness that we can hardly believe that the solitude of heart is within our horizon. But when we have once sensed what this solitude can mean, we will never stop searching for it. Once we have tasted this solitude a new life becomes possible, in which we can become detached from false ties and attached to God and each other in a surprisingly new way.

3

A CREATIVE RESPONSE

∎

Reactionary Lifestyle

THE MOVEMENT FROM LONELINESS to solitude is not a movement of a growing withdrawal but is instead a movement toward a deeper engagement in the burning issues of our time. The movement from loneliness to solitude can make it possible to convert slowly our fearful reactions into a loving response.

As long as we are trying to run away from our loneliness we are constantly looking for distractions with the inexhaustible need to be entertained and kept busy. We become the passive victims of a world asking for our idolizing attention. We become dependent on the shifting chain of events leading us into quick changes of mood, capricious behavior, and, at times, vengeful violence. Then our lives become spastic and often destructive sequences of actions and reactions pulling us away from our inner selves.

It is not so difficult to see how "reactionary" we tend to be: that is, how often our lives become series of nervous and often anxious reactions to the stimuli of our surroundings. We often are very, very busy, and usually very tired as a result, but we should ask ourselves how much of our reading and talking, visiting and lobbying, lecturing and writing, is more part of an impulsive reaction to the changing demands of our surroundings than an action that was born out of our own center.

We probably shall never reach the moment of a "pure action," and it even can be questioned how realistic or healthy it is to make that our goal. But it seems of great importance to know with an experiential knowledge the difference between an action that is triggered by a change in the surrounding scene and an action that has ripened in our hearts through careful listening to the world in which we live.

The movement from loneliness to solitude should lead to a gradual conversion from an anxious reaction to a loving response. Loneliness leads to

205

quick, often spastic, reactions which make us prisoners of our constantly changing world. But in solitude of heart we can listen to the events of the hour, the day, and the year and slowly "formulate," give form to, a response that is really our own. In solitude we can pay careful attention to the world and search for an honest response.

Alertness in Solitude

> Not too long ago a priest told me that he canceled his subscription to *The New York Times* because he felt that the endless stories about war, crime, power games, and political manipulation only disturbed his mind and heart and prevented him from meditation and prayer.

That is a sad story because it suggests that only by denying the world can you live in it, that only by surrounding yourself with an artificial, self-induced quietude can you live a spiritual life. A real spiritual life does exactly the opposite: it makes us so alert and aware of the world around us that all that is and happens becomes part of our contemplation and meditation and invites us to a free and fearless response.

It is this alertness in solitude that can change our lives indeed. It makes all the difference in the world how we look at and relate to our own histories, through which the world speaks to us.

> When I look back at the last twenty years, I see that I find myself in a place and situation I had not even dreamt of when I, together with twenty-eight classmates, prostrated myself on the floor of a Dutch cathedral on the day of my ordination. I had hardly heard about Martin Luther King and racial problems, nor did I know the names of John F. Kennedy and Dag Hammarskjöld. I had seen the old, fat Cardinal Roncalli on a pilgrimage to Padua and thought of him as an example of clerical decadency. I had read wild books about political intrigues in the Kremlin and felt happy that such things were impossible in the free world. I had heard more than I could bear about the Jewish concentration camps but realized that they belonged to a world of the older generation and were incompatible with my own. And now, only a few years later, my mind and heart are full of memories and facts that have molded me into a quite different person than I ever expected to be. Now, while able to see the end of my life cycle as well as its beginning, I realize that I have only one life to live and that it will be a life covering a period of history of which I not only

am a part but also helped to shape. Now I see that I cannot just point to Dallas, Vietnam, My Lai, and Watergate as the explanation of why my life was different than I had foreseen, but I have to search for the roots of these names in the center of my own solitude.

In our solitude, our history no longer can remain a random collection of disconnected incidents and accidents but has to become a constant call for the change of heart and mind. There we can break through the fatalistic chain of cause and effect and listen with our inner senses to the deeper meaning of the actualities of everyday life. There the world no longer is diabolic, dividing us into "fors" and "againsts" but becomes symbolic, asking us to unite and reunite the outer with the inner events. There the killing of a president, the success of a moon shot, the destruction of cities by cruel bombing, and the disintegration of a government by the lust for power, as well as the many personal disappointments and pains, no longer can be seen as unavoidable concomitants of our life but all become urgent invitations to a response; that is, a personal engagement.

Molding Interruptions

While visiting the University of Notre Dame, where I had been a teacher for a few years, I met an older, experienced professor who had spent most of his life there. And as we strolled over the beautiful campus, he said with a certain melancholy in his voice, "You know, . . . my whole life I have been complaining that my work was constantly interrupted, until I discovered that my interruptions were my work."

Don't we often look at the many events of our lives as big or small interruptions, interrupting many of our plans, projects, and life schemes? Don't we feel an inner protest when a student interrupts our reading, bad weather our summer, illness our well-scheduled plans, the death of a dear friend our peaceful state of mind, a cruel war our ideas about the goodness of humanity, and the many harsh realities of life our good dreams about it? And doesn't this unending row of interruptions build in our hearts feelings of anger, frustration, and even revenge, so much so that at times we see the real possibility that growing old can become synonymous with growing bitter?

But what if our interruptions are in fact our opportunities, if they are challenges to an inner response by which growth takes place and through which we come to the fullness of being? What if the events of our histories are molding us as a sculptor molds clay, and if it is only in a careful obedience to these molding hands that we can discover our real vocation and become mature people? What if all the unexpected interruptions are in fact the invitations to give up old-fashioned and outmoded styles of living and are opening up new, unexplored areas of experience? And finally: What if our histories do not prove to be blind, impersonal sequences of events over which we have no control but rather reveal to us a guiding hand pointing to a personal encounter in which all our hopes and aspirations will reach their fulfillment?

Then our lives would indeed be different lives because then fate becomes opportunity, wounds a warning, and paralysis an invitation to search for deeper sources of vitality. Then we can look for hope in the middle of crying cities, burning hospitals, and desperate parents and children. Then we can cast off the temptation of despair and speak about the fertile tree while witnessing the dying of the seed. Then indeed we can break out of the prison of an anonymous series of events and listen to the God of history, who speaks to us in the center of our solitude and respond to God's ever new call for conversion.

A Contrite Heart

It is tragic to see how the religious sentiment of the West has become so individualized that concepts such as "a contrite heart" have come to refer only to personal experiences of guilt and the willingness to do penance for it. The awareness of our impurity in thoughts, words, and deeds can indeed put us in a remorseful mood and create in us the hope for a forgiving gesture. But if the catastrophic events of our days, the wars, mass murders, unbridled violence, crowded prisons, torture chambers, the hunger and illness of millions of people, and the unnameable misery of a major part of the human race are safely kept outside the solitude of our hearts, our contrition remains no more than a pious emotion.

The newspaper of the day on which this is written shows a picture of three Portuguese soldiers, two of whom are pulling out the arms of a naked prisoner while the third cuts off his head. That same paper reports that a Dallas policeman killed a twelve-year-old handcuffed boy while interrogating him in a patrol car, and that a Japanese 747 Jumbo Jet with 122 passengers was hijacked and flown to an unknown destination. It also reveals that the U.S. Air Force dropped $145 million worth of bombs on Cambodia during a period in which the president declared publicly that the neutrality of that country was fully respected. It gives a gruesome description of the electric torture techniques used in Greece and Turkey. All of these "news" items are simply mentioned as secondary items whereas the headlines speak about break-ins, lies, and the use of huge sums of money by the highest officials in the government, an event described as the greatest tragedy in the history of this country. And today's newspaper is not different from yesterday's and is not likely to differ much from tomorrow's.

Shouldn't that crush our hearts and make us bow our heads in an endless sorrow? Shouldn't that bring all human beings who believe that life is worth living together in a common contrition and a public penance? Shouldn't that bring us finally to a confession that we as a people have sinned and need forgiveness and healing? Shouldn't this be enough to force us to break out of our individual pious shells and stretch out our arms with the words:

> From the depths I call to you, Yahweh:
>> Lord, hear my cry.
> Listen attentively
>> to the sound of my pleading!
>
> If you kept a record of our sins,
>> Lord, who could stand their ground?
> But with you is forgiveness,
>> that you may be revered.
>
> I rely, my whole being relies,
>> Yahweh, on your promise.
> My whole being hopes in the Lord,
>> more than watchmen for daybreak;
>> let Israel hope in Yahweh.
>
> For with Yahweh is faithful love,
>> with him generous ransom;
> and he will ransom Israel
>> from all its sins.
> (Ps 130)

The Burden of Reality

Can we carry the burden of reality? How can we remain open to all human tragedies and aware of the vast ocean of human suffering without becoming mentally paralyzed and depressed? How can we live healthy and creative lives when we are constantly reminded of the fate of the millions who are poor, sick, hungry, and persecuted? How can we even smile when we keep being confronted by pictures of tortures and executions?

I do not know the answers to these questions. There are people in our midst who have allowed the pain of the world to enter so deeply into their hearts that it has become their vocation to remind us constantly, mostly against our will, of the sins of this world. There are even a few saints who have become so much a part of the human condition and have identified themselves to such a degree with the misery of their fellow human beings that they refuse happiness for themselves as long as there are suffering people in this world. Although they irritate us and although we would like to dispose of them by labeling them masochists or doomsday prophets, they are indispensable reminders that no lasting healing will ever take place without a solidarity of heart. These few "extremists" or "fanatics" force us to ask ourselves how many games we play with ourselves and how many walls we keep erecting to prevent ourselves from knowing and feeling the burden of human solidarity.

Maybe, for the time being, we have to accept the many fluctuations between knowing and not knowing, seeing and not seeing, feeling and not feeling, between days in which the whole world seems like a rose garden and days in which our hearts seem tied to a millstone, between moments of ecstatic joy and moments of gloomy depression, between the humble confession that the newspaper holds more than our souls can bear and the realization that it is only through facing up to the reality of our world that we can grow into our own responsibility. Maybe we have to be tolerant toward our own avoidances and denials in the conviction that we cannot force ourselves to face what we are not ready to respond to and in the hope that in one future day we will have the courage and strength to open our eyes fully and see without being destroyed.

All this might be the case as long as we remember that there is no hope in denial or avoidance, neither for ourselves nor for anyone else, and that new life can only be born out of the seed planted in crushed soil. Indeed God, our Lord, "will not scorn this crushed and broken heart" (Ps 51:17).

What keeps us from opening ourselves to the reality of the world? Could it be that we cannot accept our powerlessness and are only willing to see those wounds that we can heal? Could it be that we do not want to give up our illusion that we are sovereigns over our world and, therefore create our own Disneyland, where we can make ourselves believe that all events of life are safely under control? Could it be that our blindness and deafness are signs of our own resistance to acknowledging that we are not the Rulers of the Universe? It is hard to allow these questions to go beyond the level of rhetoric and to really sense in our innermost self how much we resent our powerlessness.

Protest out of Solitude

But life can teach us that although the events of the day are out of our hands, they should never be out of our hearts, that instead of becoming bitter our lives can yield to the wisdom that only from the heart can a creative response come forth. When the answer to our world hangs between our minds and our hands, it remains weak and superficial. When our protests against war, segregation, and social injustice do not reach beyond the level of reaction, then our indignation becomes self-righteous, our hope for a better world degenerates into a desire for quick results, and our generosity is soon exhausted by disappointments. Only when our mind has descended into our heart can we expect a lasting response to well up from our inner-most self.

Many of those who worked hard for civil rights and were very active in the peace movement of the sixties have grown tired and often cynical. When they discovered that the situation was out of their hands, that little could be done, that no visible changes took place, they lost their vitality and fell back on their wounded selves, escaped into a world of dreams and fantasies, or joined spitefully the crowd they had been protesting against. It is, there-fore, not surprising to find many of the old activists struggling with their frustrations in psychotherapy, denying them by drugs, or trying to alleviate them in the context of new cults.

If any criticism can be made of the sixties, it is not that protest was meaningless but that it was not deep enough, in the sense that it was not rooted in the solitude of heart. When only our minds and hands work together we quickly become dependent on the results of our actions and tend to give up when they do not materialize. In the solitude of heart we can truly listen to the pains of the world because there we can recognize them not as strange and unfamiliar pains but as pains that are indeed our own. There we can see that what is most universal is most personal and that indeed nothing human is strange to us. There we can feel that the cruel reality of history is indeed the reality of the human heart, our own included, and that to protest asks, first of all, for a confession of our own participation in the human condition. There we can indeed respond.

It would be paralyzing to proclaim that we, as individuals, are responsible for all human suffering, but it is a liberating message to say that we are called to respond to it. Because out of an inner solidarity with our fellow humans the first attempts to alleviate these pains can come forth.

Compassion

It is this inner solidarity which prevents self-righteousness and makes compassion possible. Thomas Merton, the monk, expressed this well when he wrote:

> Once God has called you to solitude, everything you touch leads you further into solitude. Everything that affects you builds you into a hermit, as long as you do not insist on doing the work yourself and building your own kind of hermitage. What is my new desert? The name of it is compassion. There is no wilderness so terrible, so beautiful, so arid and so fruitful as the wilderness of compassion. It is the only desert that shall truly flourish like the lily. It shall become a pool, it shall bud forth and blossom and rejoice with joy. It is in the desert of compassion that the thirsty land turns into springs of water, that the poor possess all things.[1]

The paradox of Merton's life indeed is that his withdrawal from the world brought him into closer contact with it. The more he was able to convert his restless loneliness into a solitude of heart, the more he could discover the pains of his world in his own inner center and respond to them. His compassionate solidarity with the human struggle made him a spokesman for many who, although lacking his talent for writing, shared his solitude. How much Merton became aware of his responsibilities in solitude became clear when he wrote:

> That I should have been born in 1915, that I should be the contemporary of Auschwitz, Hiroshima, Viet Nam and the Watts riots are things about which I was not first consulted. Yet they are also events in which, whether I like it or not, I am deeply and personally involved.[2]

And not without a touch of sarcasm he added:

> It has become transparently obvious that mere automatic "rejection of the world" and "contempt for the world" is in fact not a choice but the

evasion of a choice. The man who pretends that he can turn his back on Auschwitz, or Viet Nam and act as if they were not there is simply bluffing. I think that this is getting to be generally admitted, even by monks.[3]

Compassion born in solitude makes us very much aware of own historicity. We are called to respond not to generalities but to the concrete facts with which we are confronted day after day. Compassionate people can no longer look at these manifestations of evil and death as disturbing interruptions of their life plans but rather have to confront them as opportunities for the conversion of themselves and their fellow human beings. Every time in history that men and women have been able to respond to the events of their world as occasions to change their hearts, an inexhaustible source of generosity and new life has been opened, offering hope far beyond the limits of human prediction.

Solidarity in Pain

When we think about the people who have given us hope and have increased the strength of our souls, we might discover that they were not the advice givers, warners, or moralists but the few who were able to articulate in words and actions the human condition in which we participate and who encouraged us to face the realities of life. Preachers who reduce mysteries to problems and offer Band-Aid-type solutions are depressing because they avoid the compassionate solidarity out of which healing comes forth. But Tolstoy's description of the complex emotions of Anna Karenina, driving her to suicide, and Graham Greene's presentation of the burned-out case of the Belgian architect Querry, whose search for meaning leads him to his death in the African jungle, can give us a new sense of hope. Not because of any solution they offered but because of the courage to enter so deeply into human suffering and speak from there.

Neither Kierkegaard nor Sartre nor Camus nor Hammarskjöld nor Solzhenitsyn has offered solutions, but many who read their words find new strength to pursue their own personal search. Those who do not run away from our pains but touch them with compassion bring healing and new strength. The paradox indeed is that the beginning of healing is in solidarity with the pain. In our solution-oriented society it is more important than ever to realize that wanting to alleviate pain without sharing it is like wanting to save a child from a burning house without the risk of being hurt. It is in solitude that this compassionate solidarity takes its shape.

The movement from loneliness to solitude, therefore, is not a growing withdrawal from, but rather a movement toward, a deeper engagement in the burning issues of our time. The movement from loneliness to solitude is a movement which allows us to perceive interruptions as occasions for a conversion of heart, which makes our responsibilities a vocation instead of a burden, and which creates the inner space where a compassionate solidarity with our fellow human beings becomes possible. The movement from loneliness to solitude is a movement by which we reach out to our innermost being to find there our great healing powers, not as a unique property to be defended but as a gift to be shared with all human beings. And so, the movement from loneliness to solitude leads us spontaneously to the movement from hostility to hospitality. It is this second movement that can encourage us to reach out creatively to the many whom we meet on our way.

REACHING OUT
TO OUR FELLOW
HUMAN BEINGS

·

The Second Movement: From Hostility to
Hospitality

4

CREATING SPACE
FOR STRANGERS

∎

Living in a World of Strangers

THE FIRST CHARACTERISTIC of the spiritual life is the continuing movement from loneliness to solitude. Its second equally important characteristic is the movement by which our hostilities can be converted into hospitality. It is there that our changing relationship to ourselves can be brought to fruition in an ever-changing relationship to our fellow human beings. It is there that our reaching out to our innermost being can lead to a reaching out to the many strangers whom we meet on our way through life.

In our world full of strangers, estranged from their own past, culture, and country, from their neighbors, friends, and family, from their deepest self and their God, we witness a painful search for a hospitable place where life can be lived without fear and where community can be found. Although many, we might even say most, strangers in this world become easily the victims of a fearful hostility, it is possible for men and women and obligatory for Christians to offer an open and hospitable space where strangers can cast off their strangeness and become our fellow human beings.

The movement from hostility to hospitality is full of difficulties. Our society seems to be increasingly full of fearful, defensive, aggressive people anxiously clinging to their property and inclined to look at their surrounding world with suspicion, always expecting an enemy to suddenly appear, intrude, and do harm. But still—that is our vocation: to convert the *hostis* into a *hospes,* the enemy into a guest, and to create the free and fearless space where brotherhood and sisterhood can be formed and fully experienced.

A Biblical Term

At first the word "hospitality" might evoke the image of soft, sweet kindness, tea parties, bland conversations, and a general atmosphere of coziness. Probably this has its good reasons since in our culture the concept of hospitality has lost much of its power and is often used in circles where we are more prone to expect a watered down piety than a serious search for an authentic Christian spirituality. But still, if there is any concept worth restoring to its original depth and evocative potential, it is the concept of hospitality. It is one of the richest biblical terms, which can deepen and broaden our insight in our relationships to our fellow human beings.

Stories in the Hebrew and the Christian Scriptures not only show how serious our obligation is to welcome the stranger in our home but also tell us that guests are carrying precious gifts with them, which they are eager to reveal to a receptive host. When Abraham received three strangers at Mamre and offered them water, bread, and a fine, tender calf, they revealed themselves to him as the Lord announcing that Sarah his wife would give birth to a son (Gn 18:1–15). When the widow of Zarephath offered food and shelter to Elijah, he revealed himself as a man of God offering her an abundance of oil and meal and raising her son from the dead (I Kgs 17:9–24). When the two travelers to Emmaus invited the stranger who had joined them on the road to stay with them for the night, he made himself known in the breaking of the bread as their Lord and Saviour (Lk 24:13–35).

When hostility is converted into hospitality then fearful strangers can become guests revealing to their hosts the promise they are carrying with them. Then, in fact, the distinction between host and guest proves to be artificial and evaporates in the recognition of the newfound unity.

Thus the biblical stories help us to realize not just that hospitality is an important virtue but even more that in the context of hospitality guest and host can reveal their most precious gifts and bring new life to each other.

During the last decades psychology has made great contributions to a new understanding of interpersonal relationships. Not only psychiatrists and clinical psychologists but also social workers, occupational therapists, ministers, priests, and many others working in the helping professions have made grateful use of these new insights in their work. But maybe some of us have become so impressed by these new findings that we have lost sight of the great wealth contained and preserved in such ancient concepts as hospitality. Maybe the concept of hospitality can offer a new dimension to our understanding of a healing relationship and the formation of a re-creative community in a world so visibly suffering from alienation and estrangement.

The term "hospitality," therefore, should not be limited to its literal sense of receiving a stranger in our house—although it is important never to forget or neglect that!—but should be seen as a fundamental attitude toward our fellow human beings, which can be expressed in a great variety of ways.

Ambivalence Toward the Stranger

Although it belongs to the core of a Christian spirituality to reach out to strangers and invite them into our lives, it is important to realize clearly that our spontaneous feelings toward strangers are quite ambivalent. It does not require much social analysis to recognize how many forms of hostility, usually pervaded with fear and anxiety, prevent us from inviting people into our world.

To fully appreciate what hospitality can mean, we possibly have to become first strangers ourselves. A student wrote:

> I left Nice one day with little money and stuck out my thumb. For five days I went wherever the wind blew me. I ran out of money and had to depend on the kindness of others. I learned what it is to be humble, thankful for a meal, a ride, and totally at the mercy of chance.

We can say that during the last years strangers have become more and more subject to hostility than to hospitality. In fact, we have protected our apartments with dogs and double locks, our buildings with vigilant door attendants, our roads with anti-hitchhike signs, our subways with security guards, our airports with safety officials, our cities with armed police, and our country with an omnipresent military. Although we might want to show sympathy for the poor, the lonely, the homeless, and the rejected, our feelings toward a stranger knocking on our door and asking for food and shelter are ambivalent at the least. In general we do not expect much from strangers. We say to each other: "You better hide your money, lock your door, and chain your bike." People who are unfamiliar, speak another language, have another color, wear a different type of clothes, and live a lifestyle different from ours make us afraid and even hostile. Frequently we return home from vacation with that gnawing suspicion that some stranger might have broken into our home and discovered the closet where we have hidden our "valuables."

In our world the assumption is that strangers are a potential danger and that it is up to them to disprove it. When we travel we keep a careful eye on our luggage; when we walk the streets we are aware of where we keep our money; and when we walk at night in a dark park our whole bodies are tense with fear of an attack. Our hearts might desire to help others: to feed the hungry, visit the prisoners, and offer a shelter to travelers; but meanwhile we have surrounded ourselves with a wall of fear and hostile feelings, instinctively avoiding people and places where we might be reminded of our good intentions.

It really does not have to be so dramatic. Fear and hostility are not limited to our encounters with burglars, drug addicts, or strangely behaving types. In a world so pervaded with competition, even those who are very close to each other, such as classmates, teammates, co-actors in a play, colleagues in work, can become infected by fear and hostility when they experience each other as threats to their intellectual or professional safety.

Many places that are created to bring people closer together and help them form a peaceful community have degenerated into mental battlefields. Students in classrooms, teachers in faculty meetings, staff members in hospitals, and co-workers in projects often find themselves paralyzed by mutual hostility, unable to realize their purposes because of fear, suspicion, and even blatant aggression. Sometimes institutions explicitly created to offer free time and free space to develop the most precious human potentials have become so dominated by hostile defensiveness that some of the best ideas and some of the most valuable feelings remain unexpressed. Grades, exams, selective systems, promotion chances, and desires for awards often block the manifestation of the best that we can produce.

The Recognition of Backstage Hostility

Recently an actor told me stories about his professional world which seemed symbolic of much of our contemporary situation. While rehearsing the most moving scenes of love, tenderness, and intimate relationships, the actors were so jealous of each other and so full of apprehension about their chances to "make it" that the backstage scene was one of hatred, harshness, and mutual suspicion. Those who kissed each other on the stage were tempted to hit each other behind it, and those who portrayed the most profound human emotions of love in the footlights displayed the most trivial and hostile rivalries as soon as the footlights had dimmed.

Much of our world is similar to the acting stage on which peace, justice, and love are portrayed by actors who cripple each other by mutual hostilities. Aren't there many doctors, priests, lawyers, social workers, psychologists, and counselors who started their studies and work with a great desire to be of service but find themselves soon victimized by the intense rivalries and hostilities in their own personal as well as professional circles? Many ministers and priests who announce peace and love from the pulpit cannot find much of it in their own rectories around their own tables. Many social workers trying to heal family conflicts struggle with the same at home. And how many of us don't feel an inner apprehension when we hear our own pains in the stories of those who ask our help?

But maybe it is exactly this paradox that can give us our healing power. When we have seen and acknowledged our own hostilities and fears without hesitation, it is more likely that we also will be able to sense from within the other pole toward which we want to lead not only ourselves but our neighbors as well. The act on the stages of our lives will probably always look better than what goes on behind the curtains, but as long as we are willing to face the contrast and struggle to minimize it the tension can keep us humble by allowing us to offer our service to others, without being whole ourselves.

Creating a Free and Friendly Space

When we have become sensitive to the painful contours of our hostility we can start identifying the lines of its opposite, toward which we are called to move: hospitality. The German word for hospitality is *Gastfreundschaft,* which means friendship for the guest. The Dutch use the word *gastvrijheid,* which means the freedom of the guest. Although this might reflect that the Dutch people find freedom more important than friendship, it definitely shows that hospitality wants to offer friendship without binding guests and freedom without leaving them alone.

Hospitality, therefore, means primarily the creation of a free space where the stranger can enter and become a friend instead of an enemy. Hospitality is not to change people but to offer them space where change can take place. It is not to bring men and women over to our side but to offer freedom not disturbed by dividing lines. It is not to lead our neighbor into a corner where there are no alternatives left but to open a wide spectrum of options for choice and commitment. It is not an educated intimidation with good books, good stories, and good works but the liberation of fearful hearts so that words can find roots and bear ample fruit. It is not a method of making our God and our way into the criteria of happiness but the opening of an opportunity to others to find their God and their way.

The paradox of hospitality is that it wants to create emptiness, not a fearful emptiness, but a friendly emptiness where strangers can enter and discover themselves as created free; free to sing their own songs, speak their own languages, dance their own dances; free also to leave and follow their own vocations. Hospitality is not a subtle invitation to adopt the lifestyle of the host but the gift of a chance for guests to find their own.

Henry David Thoreau gave a good example of this attitude when he wrote:

> I would not have anyone adopt *my* mode of living on any account; for, beside that before he has fairly learned it I may have found out another for myself, I desire that there may be as many different persons in the world as possible; but I would have each one be very careful to find out and pursue *his own* way, and not his father's or his mother's or his neighbor's instead.[1]

Creating space for the other is far from an easy task. It requires hard concentration and articulate work. It is like the task of a police officer trying to create some space in a mob of panic-driven people for an ambulance to reach the center of the accident. Indeed, more often than not rivalry and competition, desire for power and immediate results, impatience and frustration, and, most of all, plain fear make their forceful demands and tend to fill every possible empty corner of our lives.

Empty space tends to create fear. As long as our minds, hearts, and hands are occupied we can avoid confronting the painful questions, to which we never gave much attention and which we do not want to surface. "Being busy" has become a status symbol, and most people continue encouraging each other to keep their bodies and minds in constant motion. From a distance, it appears that we try to keep each other filled with words and actions, without tolerance for a moment of silence. Hosts often feel that they have to talk all the time to their guests and entertain them with things to do, places to see, and people to visit. But by filling up every empty corner and occupying every empty time their hospitality becomes more oppressing than revealing.

Occupied and Preoccupied Space

Occupation and not empty space is what most of us are looking for. When we are not occupied we become restless. We even become fearful when we do not know what we will do the next hour, the next day, or the next year. Then occupation is called a blessing and emptiness a curse. Many telephone conversations start with the words "I know you are busy, but . . . ," and we would confuse the speaker and even harm our reputation were we to say, "Oh no, I am completely free, today, tomorrow, and the whole week." Our client might well lost interest in a person who has so little to do.

Being busy, active, and on the move has nearly become part of our constitution. When we are asked to sit in a chair without a paper to read, a radio to listen to, a television to watch, without a visitor or a phone, we are inclined to become so restless and tense that we welcome anything that will distract us again.

This explains why silence is such a difficult task. Many people who say how much they desire silence, rest, quietude would find it nearly impossible to bear the stillness of a monastery. When all the movements around them have stopped, when nobody asks them a question, seeks advice, or even offers a helping hand, when there is no music or newspaper they quite often experience such an inner restlessness that they will grab any opportunity to become involved again. The first weeks or even months in a contemplative monastery, therefore, are not always as restful as they might seem, and it is indeed not surprising that vacations are more often spent on busy beaches and camping grounds, and around entertainment centers than in the silence of monasteries.

All this shows that preoccupation is in fact a greater stumbling block than occupation. We are so afraid of open spaces and empty places that we occupy them with our minds even before we are there. Our worries and concerns are expressions of our inability to leave unresolved questions unresolved and open-ended situations open-ended. They make us grab any possible solution and answer that seems to fit the occasion. They reveal our intolerance of the incomprehensibility of people and events and make us look for labels or classifications to fill the emptiness with self-created illusions.

We indeed have become very preoccupied people, afraid of unnameable emptiness and silent solitude. In fact, our preoccupations prevent our having new experiences and keep us hanging on to the familiar ways. Preoccupations are our fearful ways of keeping things the same, and it often seems that we prefer a bad certainty to a good uncertainty. Our preoccupations help us to maintain the personal worlds we have created over the years and block the way to revolutionary change. Our fears, uncertainties, and hostilities make us fill our inner world with ideas, opinions, judgments, and values to which we cling as to precious property. Instead of facing the challenge of new worlds opening themselves for us, and struggling in the open field, we hide behind the walls of our concerns, holding on to the familiar life items we have collected in the past.

The conservative power of our preoccupation is very convincingly expressed by Don Juan, the Yaqui Indian, in one of his conversations with the anthropologist Carlos Castaneda. One day Carlos asked Don Juan how he could better live in accordance with the Indian's teaching. "You think and talk too much, you must stop talking to yourself," Don Juan answered. He explained that we maintain our worlds by our inner talk, and that we talk to ourselves until everything is as it should be, repeating our inner choices over and over, staying always on the same paths. If we would stop telling ourselves that the world is such and so, it would cease to be so! Don Juan didn't think that Carlos was ready for such a blow, but he advised his student to listen to the world and so allow changes to take place.[2]

Although this advice might sound bizarre to the ears of the "organization man," it should not be strange for someone who has taken to heart the words of Jesus Christ. Didn't he also say that our worries prevent us from letting the kingdom, that is, the new world, come? Don Juan is asking how we ever can expect something really new to happen to us if our hearts and minds are so full of our own concerns that we do not even listen to the sounds announcing a new reality. And Jesus says: "Do not worry; do not say, 'What are we to eat? What are we to drink? What are we to wear?" It is the gentiles who set their hearts on all these things. Your heavenly Father knows you need them all. Set your hearts on his kingdom first, and on God's saving justice, and all these other things will be given you as well. So do not worry about tomorrow: tomorrow will take care of itself" (Mt 6:31–34).

So we can see that creating space is far from easy in our occupied and preoccupied society. And still, if we expect any salvation, redemption, healing, and new life, the first thing we need is an open, receptive place where something can happen to us. Hospitality, therefore, is an extremely important attitude. We cannot change the world by a new plan, project, or idea. We cannot even change other people by our convictions, stories, advice, and proposals, but we can offer a space where people are encouraged to disarm themselves, to lay aside their occupations and preoccupations, and to listen with attention and care to the voices speaking in their own center. How important it is to become empty in order that we may learn is well illustrated in the following Zen story:

> Nan-in, a Japanese master during the Meiji era (1868–1912) received a university professor who came to inquire about Zen. Nan-in served tea.

He poured his visitor's cup full, and then kept pouring. The professor watched the overflow until he could no longer restrain himself. "It is overfull. No more will go in!" "Like this cup," Nan-in said, "you are full of your opinions and speculations. How can I show you Zen unless you first empty your cup?"[3]

To convert hostility into hospitality requires the creation of the friendly empty space where we can reach out to our fellow human beings and invite them to a new relationship. This conversion is an inner event that cannot be manipulated but must develop from within. Just as we cannot force a plant to grow but can take away the weeds and stones which prevent its development, so we cannot force anyone to such a personal and intimate change of heart, but we can offer the space where such a change can take place.

5

FORMS OF HOSPITALITY

.

The "Ins" and "Outs" of Our Relationships

THE MOVEMENT FROM HOSTILITY to hospitality is a movement that determines our relationship to other people. We probably will never be free from all our hostilities, and there may even be days and weeks in which our hostile feelings dominate our emotional lives to such a degree that the best thing we can do is to keep distance, speak little to others, and not write letters, except to ourselves. Sometimes events in our lives breed feelings of bitterness, jealousy, suspicion, and even desires for revenge, which need time to be healed. It is realistic to realize that although we hope to move toward hospitality, life is too complex to expect a one-way direction. But when we make ourselves aware of the hospitality we have enjoyed from others and are grateful for the few moments in which we can create some space ourselves, we may become more sensitive to our inner movements and be more able to affirm an open attitude toward our fellow human beings.

Looking at hospitality as the creation of a free and friendly space where we can reach out to strangers and invite them to become our friends, it is clear that this can take place on many levels and in many relationships. Although the word "stranger" suggests someone who belongs to another world than ours, speaks another language, and has different customs, it is important, first of all, to recognize the stranger in our own familiar circle. When we are able to be good hosts for the strangers in our midst we may find also ways to expand our hospitality to broader horizons. Therefore, it might be worthwhile to look carefully at three types of relationships that can be better understood from the perspective of hospitality: the relationship between parents and their children, the relationship between teachers and their students, and the relationship between professionals—such as doctors, nurses, social workers, psychologists, counselors, ministers, and priests—and their patients, clients, counselees, and parishioners.

In all three types of relationships we become involved at some point in our own histories. The complexity of life is exactly related to the fact that often we find ourselves involved in all three types of relationships at the same time and on both sides. While being fathers to our children, teachers to our students, and counselors to our counselees, we also remain children, students, and patients in other contexts. While trying to be good mothers, we often still have responsibilities as daughters; while teaching in the daytime, we might be sitting on the other side of the classroom in the evening; and while giving advice to others, we realize at times how badly we need it ourselves.

We all are children and parents, students and teachers, healers and in need of care. And so we move in and out of each other's worlds at different times in different ways. While the complexity of these many "ins" and "outs" has created a still-growing number of studies, research projects, books, and institutes, the concept of hospitality might bring a unifying dimension to all these interpersonal relationships. It might help us see how they all stand together under the great commandment: "You must love your neighbour as yourself" (Mk 12:31).

Parents and Children

It may sound strange to speak of the relationship between parents and children in terms of hospitality. But it belongs to the center of the Christian message that children are not properties to own and rule over but gifts to cherish and care for. Our children are our most important guests, who enter into our homes, ask for careful attention, stay for a while, and then leave to follow their own way. Children are strangers whom we have to get to know. They have their own styles, their own rhythms, and their own capacities for good and evil. They cannot be explained by looking at their parents. It is, therefore, not surprising to hear parents say about their children, "They are all different, none is like the other and they keep surprising and amazing us." Fathers and mothers, more than their families and friends, are often aware how their children differ from their parents and each other.

Children carry a promise with them, a hidden treasure that has to be led into the open through education (*e* = out; *ducere* = to lead) in a hospitable home. It takes much time and patience to make the little stranger feel at home, and it is realistic to say that parents have to learn to love their children. Sometimes a father or mother will be honest and free enough to say that he or she looked at the new baby as at a stranger without feeling any special affection, not because the child was unwanted but because love is not an automatic reaction. It comes forth out of a relationship, which has to grow and deepen. We can even say that the love between parents and children develops and matures to the degree that they can reach out to each other and discover each other as fellow human beings, who have much to share and whose differences in age, talents, and behavior are much less important than their common humanity.

What parents can offer is a home, a place that is receptive but also has the safe boundaries within which their children can develop and discover what is helpful and what is harmful. There their children can ask questions without fear and can experiment with life without taking the risk of rejection. There they can be encouraged to listen to their own inner selves and to develop the freedom that gives them the courage to leave the home and travel on. The hospitable home indeed is the place where father, mother, and children can reveal their talents to each other, become present to each other as members of the same human family, and support each other in their common struggles to live and make live.

The awareness that children are guests can be a liberating awareness because many parents suffer from deep guilt feelings toward their children, thinking that they are responsible for everything their sons and daughters do. When they see their child living in ways they disapprove of, the parents may castigate themselves with the questions "What did we do wrong? What should we have done to prevent this behavior?" and they may wonder where they failed. But children are not properties we can control as a puppeteer controls her puppets, or train as a lion tamer trains his lions. They are guests we have to respond to, not possessions we are responsible for.

Many parents question the value of baptism of newborn babies. But one important aspect of early baptism is that when the parents bring their child to the church, they are reminded that the child is not their own private property but a gift of God given to a community that is much larger than the immediate family. In our culture it seems that all the responsibility for the child rests on the biological parents. The high-rise apartment buildings, in which families live in their small, isolated units and are often fearful of their neighbors, do indeed not offer the small child much more to depend on than his or her own parents.

> During a visit in Mexico, sitting on a bench in one of the village plazas, I saw how much larger the family of the children was. They were hugged, kissed, and carried around by aunts, uncles, friends, and neighbors, and it seemed that the whole community spending their evening playfully in

the plaza became father and mother for the little ones. Their affection, and their fearless movements made me aware that for them everyone was family.

The church is perhaps one of the few places left where we can meet people who are different than we are but with whom we can form a larger family. Taking our children out of the house and bringing them to the church for baptism is at least an important reminder of the larger community in which they are born and which can offer them a free space to grow to maturity without fear.

The difficult task of parenthood is to help children grow to the freedom that permits them to stand on their own feet, physically, mentally, and spiritually and to allow them to move away in their own direction. The temptation is, and always remains, to cling to our children, to use them for our own unfulfilled needs, and to hold on to them, suggesting in many direct and indirect ways that they owe us so much. It indeed is hard to see our children leave after many years of much love and much work to bring them to maturity, but when we keep reminding ourselves that they are just guests who have their own destinations, which we do not know or dictate, we might be more able to let them go in peace and with our blessing. A good host is able not only to receive guests with honor and offer them all the care they need but also to let them go when their time to leave has come.

Teachers and Students

Not only in the relationships between parents and their children but also in those between teachers and their students hospitality can be seen as a model for a creative interchange between people. If there is any area that needs a new spirit, a redemptive and liberating spirituality, it is the area of education, in which so many people spend their lives, or at least crucial parts of their lives, as students or teachers or both.

One of the greatest tragedies of our culture is that millions of young people spend many hours, days, weeks, and years listening to lectures, reading books, and writing papers with a constantly increasing resistance. This has become such a widespread phenomenon that teachers on all levels, from grade school to graduate school, are complimented and praised when they can get the attention of their students and motivate them to do their work. Practically every student perceives education as an endless row of obligations to be fulfilled. If there is any culture that has succeeded in killing the natural spontaneous curiosity of people and dulling the human desire to know, it is our technocratic society.

As teachers, we have even become insensitive to the ridiculous situation in which adult men and women feel that they "owe" us a paper of at least twenty pages. We have lost our sense of surprise when men and women who are taking courses about the questions of life and death anxiously ask us how much is "required." Instead of spending a number of free years searching for the value and meaning of our human existence with the help of others who expressed their own experiences in word or writing, most students are constantly trying to "earn" credits, degrees, and awards, willing to sacrifice even their own growth.

In such a climate it is not surprising that an enormous resistance to learning develops and that much real mental and emotional development is inhibited by an educational situation in which students perceive their teachers more as demanding bosses than as guides in their search for knowledge and understanding.

One of the greatest problems of education remains that solutions are offered without the existence of a question. It seems that the least-used source of formation and information is the experience of the students themselves. Sometimes teachers speak about love and hate, fear and joy, hope and despair while students make obedient notes or look out the window in boredom. This is understandable only when we realize that the students themselves have not had the opportunity to make their own experience of love and hate, fear and joy, hope and despair available to themselves and allow their real questions to be born from their personal source. But in a hostile climate nobody wants to become vulnerable and make it known to her- or himself, fellow students, or the teacher that some of the most central questions of life are still untouched.

Teaching, therefore, asks first of all the creation of a space where students and teachers can enter into a fearless communication with each other and allow their respective life experiences to be their primary and most valuable source of growth and maturation. It asks for a mutual trust in which those who teach and those who want to learn can become present to each other, not as opponents but as those who share in the same struggle and search for the same truth.

I remember a student presenting with great enthusiasm a summary of a book on Zen meditation while his own life experiences of restlessness, loneliness, and desire for solitude and quietude remained an unknown

book of knowledge to him. Just as words can become obstacles for communication, books can prevent self-knowledge.

Teaching situations in which students as well as teachers are deeply affected by fear of rejection, by doubt and insecurity about their own abilities,
and by an often-unexpressed anger toward each other are countereduca-
tional. Nobody will show his or her most precious talent to people who
evoke fear.

But is it possible to become hospitable to each other in a classroom? It is
far from easy since both teachers and students are part of a very demanding,
pushing, and often exploitative society, in which personal growth and development have become secondary to the ability to produce and earn not only
credits but a living. In such a production-oriented society even schools no
longer have the time or space where the questions about why we live and
love, work and die can be raised without fear of competition, rivalry, or
concerns about punishment or rewards.

And still teaching, from the point of view of a Christian spirituality,
means the commitment to provide the fearless space where such questions
can come to consciousness and can be responded to, not by prefabricated
answers but by an articulate encouragement to enter them seriously and
personally. When we look at teaching in terms of hospitality, we can say
that the teacher is called upon to create for the students a free and fearless
space where mental and emotional development can take place. When we
want to speak about the "spirituality of teachers," two aspects of their task
ask for special attention: revealing and affirming.

The hospitable teacher has to reveal to the students that they have something to offer. Many students have been for so many years on the receiving
side, and have become so deeply impregnated with the idea that there is still
a lot more to learn, that they have lost confidence in themselves and can
hardly imagine that they themselves have something to give, not only to
the ones who are less educated but to their fellow students and teachers
as well.

Therefore, teachers have first of all to reveal, to take away the veil covering many students' intellectual life, and help them see that their own life
experiences, their own insights and convictions, their own intuitions and
formulations are worth serious attention. Good hosts are the ones who
believe that their guests are carrying a promise they want to reveal to anyone
who shows genuine interest. It is so easy to impress students with books
they have not read, with terms they have not heard, or with situations with
which they are unfamiliar. It is much more difficult to be a receiver who

can help the students to distinguish carefully between the wheat and the weeds in their own lives and to show the beauty of the gifts they are carrying with them.

We will never believe that we have anything to give unless there is someone who is able to receive. Indeed, we discover our gifts in the eyes of the receiver. Teachers who can detach themselves from their need to impress and control, and who can allow themselves to become receptive to the news that their students carry with them, will find that it is in receptivity that gifts become visible.

What is revealed as good, worthwhile, or a new contribution needs to be affirmed. Affirmation, encouragement, and support are often much more important than criticism. The good host is the one who not only helps the guests to see that they have hidden talents but also is able to help them develop and deepen these talents so that they can continue their way on their own with a renewed self-confidence. Self-doubt is such a rampant disease in many schools that affirmation is more important than ever. Affirmation can mean many things. It can simply mean the expression of excitement and surprise or a word of thanks. It can mean recommendations of good books or referral to people with special talents. It often means just bringing the right persons together or setting apart time and place where more thinking can be done. But it always includes the inner conviction that a precious gift merits attention and continuing care.

Especially in religious education, revelation and affirmation are of great importance. The fact that so many students do not care for religious instruction is largely related to the fact that their own life experience is hardly touched. There are just as many ways to be a Christian as there are Christians, and it seems that more important than the imposition of any doctrine or precoded idea is to offer the students a place where they can reveal their great human potentials to love, to give, and to create, and where they can find the affirmation that gives them the courage to continue their search without fear.

Only when we have come in touch with our own life experiences and have learned to listen to our inner cravings for liberation and new life can we realize that Jesus did not just speak but reached out to us in our most personal needs. The Gospel doesn't just contain ideas worth remembering. It is a message responding to our individual human condition. The Church is not an institution forcing us to follow its rules. It is a community of people inviting us to still our hunger and thirst at its tables. Doctrines are not alien formulations which we must adhere to but the documentation of the most profound human experiences, which, transcending time and place, are handed over from generation to generation as a light in our darkness.

But what is the sense of speaking about light to people who do not sense their darkness? Why should we speak about the Way to someone who does not realize that there are many roads? How can anyone desire the truth when he or she doesn't even know that there are questions? It is not surprising that many find religious education boring, superfluous, and unnecessary, and that they complain that it creates fear instead of joy, mental imprisonment instead of spiritual freedom. But those who have been able to find a place of rest and inner solitude and have listened carefully to the questions arising from their own hearts will also recognize that words spoken in such a place are words not to hurt but to heal.

Thus, revelation and affirmation are two important aspects of the relationship between teachers and their students. Both aspects show that students are not just the poor, needy, ignorant beggars who come to the man or woman of knowledge but indeed like guests who honor the house with their visit and will not leave it without having made their own contribution. To look at teaching as a form of hospitality might free it from some of its unreal heaviness and bring some of its exhilarating moments back into perspective.

Just as parents are tempted to relate to their children as properties, teachers can develop a similar attitude toward their students. In fact, many teachers often become sad and depressed because of their possessive sense of responsibility. They feel unhappy or even guilty when students do not accept their ideas, advice, or suggestions, and often they suffer from a deep sense of inadequacy.

When we are teachers it is good, therefore, to realize that students cannot be molded into one special form of the good life but are only temporary visitors who have been in many rooms before they came into ours. Our relationship with our students is first of all a relationship in which we offer ourselves to our searching students, to help them develop some clarity in the many impressions of their minds and hearts and discover patterns of thoughts and feelings on which they can build their own lives. By a supportive presence we can offer the space with safe boundaries within which our students can give up their defensive stance and bend over their own life experience, with all its strong and weak sides, to find the beginnings of a plan worth following. As teachers we have to encourage our students to reflection which leads to vision—theirs, not ours.

It is, however, only realistic to say that many students have become so tired of the demands of the educational institutions they have to go through and so suspicious of anyone who expects something new that they can seldom respond to a really hospitable teacher and take the risk of trust—trust in the teacher and in themselves. On the other hand, it is also true that many highly motivated teachers have become so tired of trying to "reach" their students, and so exhausted by the demands put on them by the great, often anonymous, structures within which they have to work, that their hospitality quickly degenerates into defensiveness. Instead of revealing and affirming, they have found themselves demanding and policing, sometimes even exploding and taking revenge. It is, therefore, not so surprising that many schools are often more effective in producing bitter rivals than in forming receptive hosts.

Healers and Patients

Finally, all those who want to reach out to their fellow human beings in the context of one of the many helping professions, as doctors, social workers, counselors, ministers, or in many other capacities, have to keep reminding themselves that they do not own anyone who is in need of care. The great danger of the increasing professionalization of the different forms of healing is that they become ways of exercising power instead of offering service. It is easy to observe that many patients—that is, many people who suffer—view those who are helping them with fear and apprehension. Doctors, psychiatrists, psychologists, priests, ministers, nurses, social workers are often looked up to by those in need as if they were endowed with a mysterious power. Many patients accept that these professionals can say things that cannot be understood, do things that cannot be questioned, and often make decisions about their lives with no explanations. To witness the strange mixture of awe and fear on the faces of many patients, just look in at the many waiting rooms of the different healers. The poor are often most subject to these emotions, which only add to their already painful sufferings.

> While spending a summer in Bolivia, I discovered that practically all the baptisms I attended were baptisms of dead babies. I was horrified when I noticed that. But then I slowly realized that many people lived so far away from a priest that they hesitated to make the long walk—often more than five hours long—to the church, and did not have their children baptized. But when through illness, accidents, or lack of food the baby died, guilt feelings and fear became so intense that these same people were willing to carry the dead bodies over long distances to ask for

baptism before burial. The priests, caught between their conviction that baptism is for the living and not for the dead and their realization that a refusal to baptize only heightens fear and deepens sorrow, tried to help as best they could. But all this reveals how over the ages priests have become in the eyes of many of their own people distant, fearful, powerful men instead of intimate friends and trustworthy servants.

Even in our technically more advanced countries, rectories are seldom experienced as places where you are welcome at any time with any problem. Some people fear priests and ministers; others feel hostile or bitter toward them; many simply don't expect much real help from them; and only very few feel free to knock at their doors without uneasiness. In the eyes and feelings of many who suffer, church buildings are perceived more as houses of power than as houses of hospitality. This is true for other professions as well. How many leave hospitals healed of their physical illness but hurt in their feelings by the impersonal treatment they received; how many return from their consultations with psychiatrists, psychologists, social workers, or counselors increasingly irritated by the noncommittal attitude and professional distance they encounter?

But it is easy, too easy indeed, to point an accusing finger at the helping professions. Professionals themselves are often the first to recognize the problem of remaining open and receptive to their patients. In our society technocratic streamlining has depersonalized the interpersonal aspects of the healing professions to a high degree, and increasing demands often force healers to keep some emotional distance to prevent overinvolvement with their patients.

But still, even in these difficult circumstances, healers have to keep striving for a spirituality by which interpersonal violence can be prevented and by which the space can be created in which healer and patient can reach out to each other as fellow travelers sharing the same broken human condition.

From the point of view of a Christian spirituality, it is important to stress that every human being is called upon to be a healer. Although there are many professions asking for special, long and arduous training, we can never leave the task of healing to the specialist. In fact, the specialists can only retain their humanity in their work when they see their professions as a form of service which they carry out not instead of but as part of the whole people of God. We all are healers who can reach out to offer health, and we all are patients in constant need of help. Only this realization can keep professionals from becoming distant technicians and those in need of care from feeling used or manipulated.

The danger of specialization, therefore, is probably not so much with the specialists as with the nonspecialists, who tend to underestimate their own human potentials and quickly make a referral to those who have titles, thereby leaving their creative power unused. But when we look at healing as creating space for the stranger, it is clear that all Christians should be willing and able to offer this so much needed form of hospitality.

> While teaching at a professional school, I became overwhelmed by the great demand for counseling. Even if there were full-time counselors, they would be so loaded with work that they probably would soon ask for assistance or extra staff. But while living and working with the students for two years, I started to wonder more and more if the students themselves were not hiding their great interpersonal talents. During classroom conversations, at parties, and in the context of counseling itself, I started not only to see but also to experience compassion, openness, real interest, a willingness to listen and speak, and many other gifts which seldom became manifest in the student community itself. I suddenly realized that while many complained about loneliness, lack of community, or an impersonal atmosphere and expressed a great desire for friendship, support, and someone to share experiences with, only a few made their great healing talents visible and available to their fellow students. Fear or a lack of confidence in their own human gift caused many to hide their most precious talents.

We can do much more for each other than we often are aware of. One day Dr. Karl Menninger, the well-known psychiatrist, asked a class of psychiatric residents what the most important part of the treatment process of mental patients was. Some said the psychotherapeutic relationship with the doctor. Some said giving recommendations for future behavior. Others said the prescription of drugs. Others again said the continuing contact with the family after the treatment in the hospital has ended. And there were still different viewpoints.

But Karl Menninger did not accept any of these answers as the right one. His answer was "diagnosis." The first and most important task of any healer is making the right diagnosis. Without an accurate diagnosis, subsequent treatment has little effect. Or, to say it better, diagnosis is the beginning of treatment.

For Karl Menninger, speaking to a group of future psychiatrists, this obviously meant that the most attention should be paid to learning the diagnostic skills of the profession. But when we take the word "diagnosis" in its most original and profound meaning of knowing through and through (*gnosis* = knowledge; *dia* = through and through), we can see that the first and most important aspect of all healing is an interested effort to know the patients fully, in all their joys and pains, pleasures and sorrows, ups and downs, highs and lows, which have given shape and form to their lives and have led them through the years to their present situation. This is far from easy because not only our own but also other people's pains are hard to face. Just as we like to reach our own destination through bypasses, we also like to offer advice, counsel, and treatment to others without having really known fully the wounds that need healing.

But it is exactly in this willingness to know the other fully that we can reach out and become healers. Therefore, healing means, first of all, the creation of an empty but friendly space where those who suffer can tell their stories to someone who can listen with real attention. It is sad that often this listening is interpreted as technique. We say, "Give him a chance to talk it out. It will do him good." And we speak about the "cathartic" effect of listening, suggesting that "getting it out of your system" or "getting it out in the open" will in itself have a purging effect. But listening is an art that must be developed, not a technique that can be applied as a monkey wrench to nuts and bolts. It needs the full and real presence of people to each other. It is indeed one of the highest forms of hospitality.

Why is listening to know through and through such a healing service? Because it makes strangers familiar with the terrain they are traveling through and helps them to discover the way they want to go. Many of us have lost our sensitivity for our own history and experience our lives as capricious series of events over which we have no control. When all our attention is drawn away from ourselves and absorbed by what happens around us, we become strangers to ourselves, people without a story to tell or to follow up.

Healing means first of all allowing strangers to become sensitive and obedient to their own stories. Healers, therefore, become students who want to learn, and patients become teachers who want to teach. Just as teachers learn their course material best during the preparation and ordering of their ideas for presentation to students, so patients learn their own stories by telling them to healers who want to hear them. Healers are hosts who patiently and carefully listen to the stories of the suffering strangers. Patients are guests who rediscover their selves by telling their stories to the ones who offer them a place to stay. In the telling of their stories, strangers befriend not only their host but also their own past.

So healing is the receiving and full understanding of the story so that strangers can recognize in the eyes of their host their own unique way that leads them to the present and suggests the direction in which to go. The story can be hard to tell, full of disappointments and frustrations, full of deviations and stagnations, but it is the only story each stranger has, because it is her own and there will be no hope for the future when the past remains unconfessed, unreceived, and misunderstood. Quite often it is our fear of the hidden moments in our own histories that keeps us paralyzed.

As healers we have to receive the stories of our fellow human beings with compassionate hearts, hearts that do not judge or condemn but recognizes how the stranger's story connects with our own. We have to offer safe boundaries within which the often painful past can be revealed and the search for a new life can find a start.

Our most important question as healers is not "What can I say or do?" but "How can I develop enough inner space where the story can be received?" Healing is the humble but also very demanding task of creating and offering a friendly empty space where strangers can reflect on their pain and suffering without fear, and find the confidence that makes them look for new ways right in the center of their confusion.

This in no way means that professionally trained healers are less important. The opposite is true. A good host, a careful listener, is the first to recognize when professional help is needed. The many specialists will, in fact, be very grateful to those who have given a compassionate ear to their suffering neighbors, recognized that special care was needed, and referred them before their pains grew worse. On the other hand, a general atmosphere of careful attention by all the members of the Christian community can sometimes heal wounds before special care is demanded.

Receptivity and Confrontation

As parents and children, teachers and students, healers and patients, we all reach out to each other in different ways. But in all three types of relationships the concept of hospitality can help us to see that we are called not to own but to serve each other and to create the space where that is possible.

While we have been discussing the three types of relationships in the perspective of hospitality, the emphasis has been on receptivity. Indeed, strangers have to be received in a free and friendly space where they can reveal their gifts and become our friends. Reaching out to others without being receptive to them is more harmful than helpful and easily leads to manipulation and even to violence, violence in thoughts, words, and actions. Really honest receptivity means inviting strangers into our world on their terms, not on ours. When we say, "You can be my guest if you believe what I believe, think the way I think, and behave as I do," we offer love under a condition or for a price. This leads easily to exploitation, making hospitality into a business.

In our world, in which so many religious convictions, ideologies, and lifestyles come into increasing contact with each other, it is more important than ever to realize that it belongs to the essence of a Christian spirituality to receive our fellow human beings into our world without imposing our religious viewpoint, ideology, or way of doing things on them as a condition for love, friendship, and care.

We do not have to look far to find these different viewpoints and attitudes. Often our own children, students, or patients have become ideological strangers to us. Sometimes we feel guilty if we do not at least try to change their minds or bring them to our side, simply to find out that we only caused suspicion and anger and made it even more difficult to live together in peace.

But receptivity is just one side of hospitality. The other side, equally important, is confrontation. To be receptive to the stranger in no way implies that we have to become neutral "nobodies." Real receptivity asks for confrontation because space can only be a welcoming space when there are clear boundaries, and boundaries are limits between which we define our own position. Flexible limits, but limits nonetheless. Confrontation results from the articulate presence, the presence within boundaries, of the host to the guest by which the host offers her- or himself as a point of orientation and a frame of reference.

We are not hospitable when we leave our house to strangers and let them use it any way they want. An empty house is not a hospitable house. In fact, it quickly becomes a ghost house, making strangers feel uncomfortable. Instead of losing fears, guests become anxious, suspicious of any noise coming from the attic or the cellar. When we want to be really hospitable we have not only to receive strangers but also to confront them by an unambiguous presence, not hiding ourselves behind neutrality but showing our ideas, opinions, and lifestyle clearly and distinctly. No real dialogue is possible between a somebody and a nobody. We can enter into communication with the other only when our own life choices, attitudes, and viewpoints offer the boundaries that challenge strangers to become aware of their own positions and to explore them critically.

As a reaction to a very aggressive, manipulative, and often degrading type of evangelization, we sometimes have become hesitant to make our own religious convictions known, thereby losing our sense of witness. Although at times it seems better to deepen our own commitments than to evangelize others, it belongs to the core of Christian spirituality to reach out to the other with good news and to speak without embarrassment about what we "have heard[,] . . . seen with our own eyes, . . . watched and touched with our own hands" (1 Jn 1:1).

Receptivity and confrontation are the two inseparable sides of Christian witness. They have to remain in careful balance. Receptivity without confrontation leads to a bland neutrality that serves nobody. Confrontation without receptivity leads to an oppressive aggression which hurts everybody. This balance between receptivity and confrontation is found at different points, depending upon our individual positions in life. But in every life situation we have not only to receive but also to confront.

It might be worthwhile to stress at this point that confrontation is much more than "speaking up." Words are seldom the most important form of confrontation. We often have communicated many things long before we speak a word.

> I am always fascinated to see how newcomers in my room look around, make comments about the furniture, the paintings, and most of all the books on the shelves. Someone notices the cross on the wall, another makes a remark about an Indian mask; others ask how Freud, Marx, and the Bible can be together in one bookcase. But everyone tries to get a feel of the place just as I do when I enter for the first time someone else's space.

When we have lived awhile the walls of our lives have become marked by many events—world events, family events, personal events—as well as by our responses to them. These marks speak their own language and often lead to a dialogue, sometimes limited to the heart but occasionally expressed in words and gestures. It is in these situations that we reach out to each other and that parents, children, teachers, students, healers, patients, and all people meet on their way through life and start speaking to each other and discovering each other as part of a larger community with a common destination.

6

HOSPITALITY
AND THE HOST

■

At Home in Our Own House

THE MOVEMENT FROM HOSTILITY to hospitality cannot be thought of without a constant inner connection with the movement from loneliness to solitude. As long as we are lonely, we cannot be hospitable because as lonely people we cannot create free space. Our own need to still our inner cravings of loneliness makes us cling to others instead of creating space for them.

> I vividly remember the story of a student who was invited to stay with a family while studying at a university. After a few weeks he realized how unfree he felt, and slowly he became aware that he was becoming the victim of the crying loneliness of his hosts. Husband and wife had become strangers to each other and used their guest to satisfy their great need for affection. The hosts clung to the stranger who had entered their house in the hope that he could offer them the love and intimacy they were unable to give to each other. So the student became entangled in a complex net of unfulfilled needs and desires, and felt caught between the walls of loneliness. He felt the painful tension of having to choose between two lonely partners and was being pulled apart by the cruel questions: Are you for him or for me? Are you on her side or on mine? He no longer felt free to go and come when he wanted; he found himself gradually unable to concentrate on his studies while at the same time powerless to offer the help his hosts were begging for. He had even lost the inner freedom to leave.

This story illustrates how difficult it is to create free space for a stranger when there is no solitude in our lives. When we think back to the places

241

where we felt most at home, we quickly see that they were where our hosts gave us the precious freedom to come and go on our own terms and did not claim us for their own needs. Only in a free space can re-creation take place and new life be found. The real host is the one who offers that space where we do not have to be afraid and where we can listen to our own inner voices and find our own personal ways of being human. But to be such hosts we have first of all to be at home in our own houses.

Poverty Makes a Good Host

To the degree to which our loneliness is converted into solitude we can move from hostility to hospitality. There obviously is no question of chronology. The complex and subtle movements of the inner life cannot be neatly divided. But it remains true that loneliness often leads to hostile behavior and that solitude is the climate of hospitality. When we feel lonely we have such a need to be liked and loved that we are hypersensitive to the many signals in our environment and easily become hostile toward anyone whom we perceive as rejecting us. But once we have found the center of our lives in our own hearts and have accepted our aloneness, not as a fate but as a vocation, we are able to offer freedom to others. Once we have given up our desire to be fully fulfilled, we can offer emptiness to others. Once we have become poor, we can be good hosts.

It is indeed the paradox of hospitality that poverty makes a good host. Poverty is the inner disposition that allows us to take away our defenses and convert our enemies into friends. We can only perceive the stranger as an enemy as long as we have something to defend. But when we say, "Please enter—my house is your house, my joy is your joy, my sadness is your sadness, and my life is your life," we have nothing to defend, since we have nothing to lose but all to give.

Turning the other cheek means showing our enemies that they can only be our enemies while supposing that we are anxiously clinging to our private property, whatever it is: our knowledge, our good name, our land, our money, or the many objects we have collected around us. But who will be our robber when everything he or she wants to steal from us becomes our gift? Who can lie to us, when only the truth will serve? Who wants to sneak into our back door, when our front door is wide open?

Poverty makes a good host. This paradoxical statement needs some more explanation. In order to be able to reach out to the other in freedom, two forms of poverty are very important, the poverty of mind and the poverty of heart.

The Poverty of Mind

Someone who is filled with ideas, concepts, opinions, and convictions cannot be a good host. There is no inner space to listen, no openness to discover the gift of the other. It is not difficult to see how those who "know it all" can kill a conversation and prevent an interchange of ideas. Poverty of mind as a spiritual attitude is a growing willingness to recognize the incomprehensibility of the mystery of life. The more mature we become the more we will be able to give up our inclination to grasp, catch, and comprehend the fullness of life and the more we will be ready to let life enter into us.

Preparation for the ministry can offer a good example. To prepare ourselves for service we have to prepare for an articulate not-knowing, a *docta ignorantia,* a learned ignorance. This is very difficult to accept for people whose whole attitude is toward mastering the world. We all want to be educated so that we can be in control of the situation and make things work according to our own needs. But education to ministry is an education not to master God but to be mastered by God.

> I remember the educational story of a thirty-year-old Methodist minister from South Africa. When this man felt called to the ministry and was accepted by the church, he was sent as an assistant pastor to work in a parish without any formal theological training. But he was so convinced of his insights and experience, and his enthusiasm and fervor were so great that he had no problem in giving long sermons and strong lectures. But then, after two years, he was called back and sent to the seminary for theological education. Reflecting on his time in the seminary, he said, "During those years I read the works of many theologians, philosophers, and novelists. Whereas before everything seemed so clear-cut and self-evident to me, I now lost my certainties, developed many questions, and became much less certain of myself and my truth." In a sense, his years of formation were more years of unlearning than of learning and when he returned to the ministry he had less to say but much more to listen to.

This story illustrates that well-educated ministers are not individuals who can tell you exactly who God is, where good and evil are, and how to travel from this world to the next but people whose articulate not-knowing makes them free to listen to the voice of God in the words of the people, in the events of the day, and in the books containing the life experiences of men and women from other places and other times. In short, learned ignorance makes one able to receive the Word from others and the Other with great attention. That is the poverty of mind. It demands the continuing refusal to identify God with any concept, theory, document, or event, thus preventing people from becoming fanatic sectarians or enthusiasts while allowing for an ongoing growth in gentleness and receptivity.

What is true for the ministry is also true for other forms of human service. When we look at the daily life and work of psychiatrists, psychologists, social workers, and counselors, we can see how much of their skill consists of a careful listening, with or without instruments, and a continuing concern for not being in the way of their patients. A voluntary poverty of mind makes professionals open to receive constantly new knowledge and insight from those who ask their help. This in no way denies the importance of very concrete and visible help, or the urgency of new structures to alleviate the hunger, thirst, and lack of clothes or shelter of millions of people. The contrary is true. When we can work for the poor in a spirit of receptivity and gratitude our help can be accepted without shame. Many people in physical, mental, or spiritual need are making it increasingly clear that it is better to refuse help and maintain self-respect than to accept it while being reduced to the status of a beggar or a slave.

The Poverty of Heart

A good host has to be not only poor in mind but also poor in heart. When our hearts are filled with prejudices, worries, jealousies, there is little room for a stranger. In a fearful environment it is not easy to keep our hearts open to the wide range of human experiences. Real hospitality, however, is not exclusive but inclusive and creates space for a large variety of human experiences.

Also here the ministry can serve as an example of the value of this form of poverty. There are many people who claim to have had a religious experience which showed them the way to God. Frequently, the experience is of such an intensity that it is no longer possible for such people to realize that their way is not necessarily *the* way. Just as God cannot be "caught" or "comprehended" in any specific idea, concept, opinion, or conviction, God cannot be defined by any specific feeling or emotion either. God cannot be identified with a good, affectionate feeling toward our neighbor, or with a sweet emotion of the heart, or with ecstasies, movements of the body, or handling of snakes. God is not just our good inclinations, our fervor, our generosity, or our love. All these experiences of the heart may remind us of God's presence, but their absence does not prove God's absence. God is not only greater than our minds but also greater than our hearts, and just as we have to avoid the temptation of adapting God to our small concepts we have to avoid adapting God to our small feelings.

Not only in the ministry but in all other helping professions as well we have to remind ourselves constantly that an inflated heart is just as dangerous as an inflated mind. An inflated heart can make us very intolerant. But when we are willing to detach ourselves from making our own limited experience the criterion for our approach to others, we may be able to see that life is greater than our lives, history is greater than our histories, experience greater than our experience, and God greater than our God. That is the poverty of heart that makes a good host. With poverty of heart we can receive the experiences of others as a gift to us. Their histories can creatively connect with ours, their lives give new meaning to ours, and their God speak to ours in mutual revelation.

Johannes Metz described this disposition well when he wrote:

> We must forget ourselves in order to let the other person approach us. We must be able to open up to him to let his distinctive personality unfold—even though it often frightens and repels us. We often keep the other person down, and only see what we want to see; then we never really encounter the mysterious secret of his being, only ourselves. Failing to risk the poverty of encounter, we indulge in a new form of self-assertion and pay the price for it: loneliness. Because we did not risk the poverty of openness (Matthew 10:39), our lives are not graced with the warm fullness of human existence. We are left with only a shadow of our real self.[1]

Poverty of heart creates community since it is not in self-sufficiency but in a creative interdependency that the mystery of life unfolds itself to us.

Boasting of Our Weakness

So hospitality requires poverty, the poverty of mind and the poverty of heart. This might help us to understand the importance of a "training" for hospitality. There are many programs to prepare people for service in its different forms. But seldom do we look at these programs as training toward a voluntary poverty. Instead we want to become better equipped and more skillful. We want to acquire the "tools of the trade." But real training for service asks for a hard and often painful process of self-emptying.

The main problem of service is to be the way without being "in the way." And if there are any tools, techniques, and skills to be learned they are primarily to plow the field, to cut the weeds, and to clip the branches, that is, to take away the obstacles to real growth and development. Training for service is a training not to become rich but to become voluntarily poor; not to fulfill ourselves but to empty ourselves; not to conquer God but to surrender to God's saving power.

All this is very hard to accept in our contemporary world, which tells us about the necessity of power and influence. But it is important that in this world there remain a few voices crying out that if there is anything to boast of, we should boast of our weakness. Our fulfillment is in offering emptiness, our usefulness in becoming useless, our power in becoming powerless. It indeed belongs to the core of the Christian message that God did not reveal God's Self to us as the powerful other, unapproachable in omniscience, omnipotence, and omnipresence. Instead God came to us in Jesus Christ, who "did not count equality with God something to be grasped. But he emptied himself . . . becoming as human beings are; and being in every way like a human being, he was humbler yet, even to accepting death, death on a cross" (Phil 2:6–8). It is God who reveals to us the movement of our spiritual life. It is not the movement from weakness to power, but the movement in which we become less and less fearful and defensive and more and more open to other people and their worlds, even when it leads to suffering and death.

While the movement from loneliness to solitude makes us reach out to our innermost self, the movement from hostility to hospitality makes us reach out to others. The term "hospitality" was used only to come to a better insight into the nature of a mature Christian relationship to our fellow human beings. Words such as "creating space," "receptivity and confrontation," "poverty of mind and heart" were used to show that the spirituality of the Christian not only is rooted in the reality of everyday life but also transcends it by relying on the gift of God. To help, to serve, to care, to guide, to heal, these words were all used to express a reaching out toward our neighbor whereby we perceive life as a gift not to possess but to share.

This finally leads to the most important and difficult aspect of spiritual life, our relationship to the One who gives. God has been mentioned already, in fact more and more as we moved from loneliness to solitude and from hostility to hospitality. The emphasis until now, however, was on the question: How can we reach out to our innermost self and to our fellow human beings? But can we reach out to God, the source and giver of our own and our neighbors' lives? If the answer is no, then solitude and hospitality remain vague ideals, good to speak about but unreal in daily life. The movement from illusion to prayer, therefore, is the most crucial movement of the spiritual life, undergirding all that has been said thus far.

REACHING OUT
TO OUR GOD

■

The Third Movement:
From Illusion to Prayer

7

PRAYER AND MORTALITY

•

A Reality Hard to Touch

ALTHOUGH LONELINESS and hostility are more easily understandable in light of our day-to-day experiences than the awareness of the illusory quality of many of our strivings, it is only in the lasting effort to unmask the illusions of our existence that a real spiritual life is possible. In order to convert our crying loneliness into a silent solitude and to create a fearless place where strangers can feel at home, we need the willingness and courage to reach out far beyond the limitations of our fragile and finite existence toward our loving God, in whom all life is anchored. The silence of solitude is nothing but dead silence when it does not make us alert to a new voice sounding from beyond all human chatter. Hospitality leads only to a congested home when nobody is traveling anywhere.

Solitude and hospitality can bear lasting fruits only when they are embedded in a broader, deeper, and higher reality from which they receive their vitality. This reality has been presupposed and here and there touched upon in the description of the first two movements of the spiritual life. But these movements are "first" only in the sense that they are more quickly recognizable and easier to identify with. Not because they are more important. In fact, they could only be described and reflected upon because they are rooted in the most basic movement of the spiritual life, which is the movement from illusion to prayer. It is through this movement that we reach out to God, our God, the One who is eternally real and from whom all reality comes forth. Therefore, the movement from illusion to prayer undergirds and makes possible the movements from loneliness to solitude and from hostility to hospitality and leads us to the core of the spiritual life.

This "first and final" movement is so central to our spiritual life that it is very hard to come in touch with it, to get hold of it—or even to put a finger on it. Not because this movement is vague or unreal but because it is so close that it hardly allows the distance needed for articulation and understanding. Maybe this is the reason why the most profound realities of life are the easiest victims of trivialization.

Newspaper interviews with monks who have given their lives to prayer in silence and solitude, out of a burning love for God, usually boil down to silly stories about changes in regulations and seemingly strange customs. Questions about the "why" of love, marriage, the priesthood, or any basic life decision usually lead to meaningless platitudes, a lot of stuttering, and shrugging of shoulders. Not that these questions are unimportant, but their answers are too deep and too close to our innermost being to be caught in human words.

> Maybe we can learn something in this regard from the tightrope walker Philippe Petit! After being arrested by the police for walking on a rope, which he and his friends had shot from one of the towers of New York's World Trade Center to the other, he was taken to the city hospital for psychiatric examination. When they found him perfectly sane and in good spirits, they asked: "But why . . . why do you want to walk on a tightrope between the highest towers of the city and risk your life?" Philippe Petit, at first somewhat puzzled by the question, said: "Well . . . if I see three oranges, I have to juggle, and if I see two towers, I have to walk."[1]
>
> That answer says it all. What is most obvious, most close, doesn't need an explanation. Who asks a child why she plays with a ball; who asks a tightrope walker why he walks on his rope—and who asks lovers why they love?

What is closest to our person is most difficult to express and explain. This is true not just for lovers, artists, and tightrope walkers but also for those who pray. While prayer is the expression of a most intimate relationship, it also is the most difficult matter to speak about and becomes easily the subject of trivialities and platitudes. While it is the most human of all human acts, it is also easily perceived as the most superfluous and superstitious activity.

Still, we have to keep speaking about prayer as we keep speaking about love, lovers, art, and artists. Because when we do not stay in touch with that center of our spiritual life called prayer, we lose touch with all that grows from it. When we do not enter into that inner field of tension where the movement from illusion to prayer takes place, our solitude and our hospitality easily lose their depth. And then, instead of being essential to our spiritual life, they become pious ornaments of a morally respectable existence.

The Illusion of Immortality

The greatest obstacle to our entering into that profound dimension of life where our prayer takes place is our all-pervasive illusion of immortality. At first it seems unlikely or simply untrue that we have such an illusion, since on many levels we are quite aware of our mortality. Who thinks that she or he is immortal? But the first two movements of our spiritual life have already revealed to us that things are not quite that simple. Every time we search anxiously for another human being who can break the chains of our loneliness, and every time we build new defenses to protect our lives as inalienable property, we find ourselves caught in that tenacious illusion of immortality. Although we keep telling each other and ourselves that we will not live forever and that we are going to die soon, our daily actions, thoughts, and concerns keep revealing to us how hard it is to fully accept the reality of our own statements.

Small, seemingly innocent events keep telling us how easily we eternalize ourselves and our world. It takes only a hostile word to make us feel sad and lonely. It takes only a rejecting gesture to plunge us into self-complaint. It takes only a substantial failure in our work to lead us into a self-destructive depression. Although we have learned from parents, teachers, friends, and many books, sacred as well as profane, that we are worth more than what the world makes us, we keep giving an eternal value to the things we own, the people we know, the plans we have, and the successes we "collect."

Indeed, it takes only a small disruption to lay our illusion of immortality bare and to reveal how much we have become victimized by our surrounding world suggesting to us that we are "in control." Aren't the many feelings of sadness, heaviness of heart, and even dark despair often intimately connected with the exaggerated seriousness with which we have clothed the people we know, the ideas to which we are exposed, and the events we are part of? This lack of distance, which excludes the humor in life, can create a suffocating depression, which prevents us from lifting our heads above the horizon of our own limited existence.

Sentimentality and Violence

To come a little closer to our great illusion, it might be helpful to show two of its most visible symptoms: sentimentality and violence. Seemingly quite different forms of behavior, both can be understood, within the perspective of spirituality, as being anchored in the human illusion of immortality.

Sentimentality appears often where intimate relationships become "dead heavy" and people cling to each other with a nearly suicidal seriousness. When we load our fellow human beings with immortal expectations, separation or the threat of it can release uncontrollable sentiments.

> In Holland, during a yearly peace march in which 3,000 high school students walk and talk together for three days, the leaders were startled by the renewed sentimentality that characterized the interaction between the marchers. For these usually quite reserved Dutchmen, holding hands was the most important experience, and the hour of farewell saw a railway station filled with hugging and crying boys and girls. In their reflection after the march, some marchers even wondered how they could ever live happily again after such an experience of communion. While they felt distant from the religious words and gestures of the church which had called them to march, their unique experience of togetherness stirred up powerful and frightening sentiments.

This event illustrates how sentimentality can manifest itself as the result of false expectations of intimate human relationships. This intimacy can lead to depression and despair when it is masked with immortality. When we are not able to look beyond the boundaries of human togetherness and anchor our lives in God, the source of all intimacy, it is hard to cast off the illusion of immortality and be together without being drowned in a pool of sentimentality.

But sentimentality is only one side of the illusion of immortality. Violence is the other. It indeed is not so strange that sentimentality and cruelty are often found in the same people. The image of Hitler moved to tears by a small child stands in the memory of many who witnessed his merciless cruelties. The same illusion which in one situation can lead to tears can lead to torture in another. The following story shows this in all its consequences.

> During the Second World War, a Lutheran bishop, imprisoned in a German concentration camp, was tortured by an S.S. officer who wanted to force him to a confession. In a small room, the two men were facing each other, one afflicting the other with increasing pain. The bishop, who had a remarkable tolerance for pain, did not respond to the torture. His silence, however, enraged the officer to such a degree that he hit his victim harder and harder until he finally exploded and shouted at his

victim, "But don't you know that I can kill you?" The bishop looked in
the eyes of his torturer and said slowly, "Yes, I know—do what you
want—but I have already died—." At that moment the S.S. officer could
no longer raise his arm and lost power over his victim. It was as if he
were paralyzed, no longer able to touch him. All his cruelties had been
based on the supposition that this man would hold on to his own life as
to his most valuable property, and would be quite willing to give his
confession in exchange for his life. But with the grounds for his violence
gone, torture had become a ridiculous and futile activity.

This story makes it clear that not only sentimentality but also violence is
a symptom of the illusion that our lives belong to us. Our human relationships easily become subject to violence and destruction when we treat our
own and other people's lives as properties to be defended or conquered and
not as gifts to be received. We often see in the center of an intimate relationship the seeds of violence. The borders between kissing and biting, caressing
and slapping, hearing and overhearing, looking with tenderness and looking
with suspicion are very fragile indeed.

When the hidden illusion of immortality becomes dominant in our intimate relationship, it does not take much to turn our desire to be loved into
a lustful violence. When our unfulfilled needs lead us to demand from our
fellow human beings what they cannot give, we make them into idols and
ourselves into devils. By asking for more than a human response we are
tempted to behave as less than human. By acting on the illusion that the
world belongs to us as private property which nobody ever can take away
from us, we become a threat to each other and make intimacy impossible.

To reach a really nonviolent intimacy, we have to unmask our illusion of
immortality, fully accept death as our human destiny, and reach out beyond
the limits of our existence to our God, out of whose intimacy we are born.

The Idolatry of Our Dreams

But illusions are stronger than we might want them to be. Although we
can say in our waking hours that everything is mortal, that we cannot hold
anything forever, and although we can even develop a deep inner sense of
the preciousness of life, our night dreams and daydreams keep creating
immortal images. When we feel like small children during the day, our
frustrated minds are all too willing to make us into tall and great heroes in
our dreaming moments: into victorious heroes admired by all those who
do not take us so seriously when we are awake, or into tragic heroes recognized too late by those who criticized us during our lives.

In our dreams, we can become like the first Joseph generously forgiving his brother in Egypt or like the second one, carefully carrying his persecuted child to the same land. In our dreams, we can freely erect statues to honor our own martyrdom and burn incense for our wounded selves. These images with which we often fill our unfulfilled desires remind us how quickly we substitute one idol for another. Unmasking illusions twenty-four hours a day is harder than we might think.

It would be unwise to try to change our dreams directly or to start worrying about the unexpected images that appear during our nights. The idols of our dreams, however, are humbling reminders that we still have a long way to go before we are ready to meet our God, not the God created by our own hands or minds but the uncreated God, out of whose loving hands we are born. Idolatry, which is the worshiping of false gods, is a temptation much greater than we tend to believe. It will take much faithfulness and patience to allow not only our conscious but also our unconscious lives to move from illusion to prayer.

> St. Basil, father of monasticism in the Eastern Orthodox Church, living in the fourth century, was quite clear about the fact that even our dreams cannot be excluded from our spiritual life. When the question was raised to him: "What is the source of those unbecoming nocturnal phantasies?" he said: "They arise out of the disordered movements of the soul that occur during the day. But if a man should occupy himself with the judgments of God and so purify his soul and concern himself constantly with good matters and things pleasing to God, then these things will fill his dreams (instead)."[2]

Although the illusions of our dreams cannot be addressed directly, it indeed is our vocation to reach out to God, not only in our waking hours but in our dreams as well. Patiently but persistently we must slowly unmask the illusions of our immortality, dispelling even the feeble creations of our frustrated minds, and stretch out our arms to the deep sea and the high heaven in a never-ending prayer. When we move from illusion to prayer, we move from the human shelter to the house of God. It is there that our solitude as well as our hospitality can be sustained.

The Hard Questions

This leads to difficult questions: Can we reach out to God as our God? Is intimacy with God possible? Can we develop a loving relationship with the

One who transcends all our understanding? Is the movement from illusion to prayer anything more than a movement into a vague cloudiness?

These questions are not totally new. They were already present from the moment the first lines of a spiritual life were drawn. Reaching out to our innermost self was not just a reaching out to more of ourselves, to more detailed understanding of our inner complexities. No, it was indeed a reaching to a center where a new encounter could take place, where we could reach beyond our selves to the One who speaks in our solitude. Reaching out to strangers was not just a reaching out to the long row of people who are so obviously needy—in need of food, clothing, and many forms of care—but also a reaching out to the promises they are bringing with them as gifts to their host. All that has been said about solitude and hospitality points to someone higher than our thoughts can reach, someone deeper than our hearts can feel and wider than our arms can embrace, someone under whose wings we can find refuge (Ps 90) and in whose love we can rest, someone we call our God.

But although the questions about our relationship to God, our God, are not totally new, now they are raised more directly, more confrontingly, more drastically. At some point we all feel that solitude and hospitality are good things to strive for and reflect upon. They have some obvious human value, and few people will deny that they are elements of a mature existence, certainly when they are kept in balance. But prayer? The claim that prayer as a loving intimacy with God is the ground in which solitude and hospitality are rooted, that claim tends to lead to embarrassment. Many will say, "Well—I could follow you so far, but here you are on your own." And why should they feel differently? Don't we use the word "prayer" mostly when we feel that our human limits are reached? Isn't "prayer" more a word to indicate powerlessness rather than a creative contact with the source of all life?

It is important to say that these feelings, experiences, questions, and irritations about prayer are very real and often the result of concrete and painful events. Still, a spiritual life without prayer is like the Gospel without Christ. Instead of proving or defending anything, it might be worthwhile simply to bring all the doubtful and anxious questions together in this one question: "If prayer, understood as an intimate relationship with God, is indeed the basis of all relationships—to ourselves as well as to others—how then can we learn to pray and really experience prayer as the axis of our existence?" By focusing on this question, it becomes possible to explore the importance of prayer in our own lives and in the lives of those we have met through personal encounters or through stories and books.

The Paradox of Prayer

The paradox of prayer is that we have to learn how to pray while we can only receive prayer as a gift. It is exactly this paradox that clarifies why prayer is the subject of so many seemingly contrasting statements.

All the great saints in history and all the spiritual directors worth their salt say that we have to learn to pray, since prayer is our first obligation as well as our highest calling. Libraries have been written about the question of how to pray. Many men and women have tried to articulate the different forms and levels of their impressive experiences, and have encouraged their readers to follow their roads. They remind us repeatedly of St. Paul's words: "Pray constantly" (1 Thes 5:17), and often give elaborate instructions on how to develop an intimate relationship with God.

Theophan the Recluse, a nineteenth-century Russian mystic, offered a beautiful example of an instruction in prayer when he wrote:

> Make yourself a rule always to be with the Lord, keeping your mind in your heart and do not let your thoughts wander; as often as they stray, turn them back again and keep them at home in the closet of your heart and delight in converse with the Lord.[3]

There is no doubt that Theophan, and with him all great spiritual writers, considered a serious discipline essential to arriving at an intimate relationship with God. For them, prayer without a continuous and arduous effort is not worth talking about. In fact, some spiritual writers have written down their efforts to pray in such concrete and vivid details that they often leave the reader with the erroneous impression that you can reach any level of prayer by just hard work and stern perseverance. This impression has created many disillusions since many felt, after long years of strenuous "prayer work," that they were farther away from God than when they started.

But the same saints and spiritual guides who speak about the discipline of prayer also keep reminding us that prayer is a gift of God. They say that we cannot truly pray by ourselves, but that it is God's spirit who prays in us. St. Paul put it very clearly: "Nobody is able to say, 'Jesus is Lord' except in the Holy Spirit" (1 Cor 12:3). We cannot force God into a relationship. God takes the initiative to come to us, and no discipline, effort, or ascetic practice can make God come.

All mystics stress with an impressive unanimity that prayer is "grace," that is, a free gift from God, to which we can only respond with gratitude. But they hasten to add that this precious gift indeed is within our reach. In

Jesus Christ, God has entered into our lives in the most intimate way, so that we could enter into God's life through the Spirit. That is the meaning of the powerful words Jesus spoke to his Apostles on the evening before his death: "I am telling you the truth: it is for your own good that I am going, because unless I go, the Paraclete [=the Spirit] will not come to you; but if I go, I will send him to you" (Jn 16:7).

In Jesus, God became one of us to lead us through Jesus into the intimacy of divine life. Jesus came to us to become as we are and left us to allow us to become as he is. By giving us his Spirit, his breath, he became closer to us than we are to ourselves. It is through this breath of God that we can call God "Abba, Father" and can become part of the mysterious divine relationship between Father and Son. Praying in the Spirit of Jesus Christ, therefore, means participating in the intimate life of God.

Thomas Merton writes:

> The union of the Christian with Christ . . . is a mystical union in which Christ Himself becomes the source and principle of life in me. Christ Himself . . . "breathes" in me divinely in giving me His Spirit.[4]

There is probably no image that expresses so well the intimacy with God in prayer as the image of God's breath. We are like asthmatic people who are cured of their anxiety. The Spirit has taken away our narrowness (the Latin word for anxiety is *angustia* = narrowness) and made everything new for us. We receive a new breath, a new freedom, a new life. This new life is the divine life of God. Prayer, therefore, is God's breathing in us, by which we become part of the intimacy of God's inner life, and by which we are born anew.

So, the paradox of prayer is that it asks for a serious effort while it can only be received as a gift. We cannot plan, organize, or manipulate God; but without a careful discipline, we cannot receive God either. This paradox of prayer forces us to look beyond the limits of our mortal existence. To the degree that we have been able to dispel our illusion of immortality and have come to the full realization of our fragile mortal condition, we can reach out in freedom to the creator and re-creator of life and respond to God's gifts with gratitude.

Prayer is often considered a weakness, a support system, which is used when we can no longer help ourselves. But this is only true when the God of our prayers is created in our own image and adapted to our own needs and concerns. When, however, prayer makes us reach out to God, not on our own but on God's terms, then prayer pulls us away from self-preoccupations, encourages us to leave familiar ground, and challenges us to enter into a new world which cannot be contained within the narrow boundaries of our minds or hearts. Prayer, therefore, is a great adventure because the God with whom we enter into a new relationship is greater than we are and defies all our calculations and predictions. The movement from illusion to prayer is hard to make since it leads us from false certainties to true uncertainties, from an easy support system to a risky surrender, and from the many "safe" gods to the God whose love has no limits.

The Absence and Presence of God

God is "beyond," beyond our hearts and minds, beyond our feelings and thoughts, beyond our expectations and desires, and beyond all the events and experiences that make up our lives. Still God is in the center of all of it. Here we touch the heart of prayer since here it becomes manifest that in prayer the distinction between God's presence and God's absence no longer really distinguishes. In prayer, God's presence is never separated from God's absence and God's absence is never separated from God's presence. The presence of God is so much beyond the human experience of being together that it quite easily is perceived as absence. The absence of God, on the other hand, is often so deeply felt that it leads on to a new sense of God's presence. This is powerfully expressed in Psalm 22:1–5:

> My God, my God, why have you forsaken me?
> The words of my groaning do nothing to save me.
> My God, I call by day, but you do not answer,
> at night, but I find no respite.
> Yet you, the Holy One,
> who make your home in the praises of Israel,
> in you our ancestors put their trust,
> they trusted and you set them free.
> To you they called for help and were delivered;
> in you they trusted and were not put to shame.

This prayer is not only the expression of the experience of the people of Israel but also the culmination of the Christian experience. When Jesus spoke these words on the Cross, total aloneness and full acceptance touched each other. In that moment of complete emptiness all was fulfilled. In that hour of darkness new light was seen. While death was witnessed, life was affirmed. Where God's absence was most loudly expressed, God's presence was most profoundly revealed.

When God became part of our most painful experience of God's absence, God became most present to us. It is into this mystery that we enter when we pray. The intimacy with God in our earthly existence will always remain an intimacy that transcends human intimacy and is experienced in a faithful waiting on the One who came but is still to come. Although at exceptional moments we may be overwhelmed by a deep sense of God's presence in the center of our solitude and in the midst of the space we create for others, more often than not we are left with the painful sense of emptiness and can only experience God as the absent God.

The French author Simone Weil writes in her notebooks: "Waiting patiently in expectation is the foundation of the spiritual life."[5] With these words she expresses powerfully how absence and presence are never separated when we reach out to God in prayer. The spiritual life is, first of all, a patient waiting, that is, a waiting in suffering (*patior* = to suffer), during which the many experiences of unfulfillment remind us of God's absence. But it also is a waiting in expectation which allows us to recognize the first signs of the coming God in the center of our pains.

The mystery of God's presence, therefore, can be touched only by a deep awareness of God's absence. It is in the center of our longing for the absent God that we discover the footprints of the Divine One, and realize that our desire to love God is born out of the love with which God has touched us. In the patient waiting for the loved one, we discover how much he or she has filled our lives already. Just as the love of a mother for her son can grow deeper when he is far away, just as children can learn to appreciate their parents more when they have left the home, just as lovers can rediscover each other during long periods of absence, so our intimate relationship with God can become deeper and more mature by the purifying experience of absence.

By listening to our longings, we hear God as their creator. By touching the center of our solitude, we sense that we have been touched by loving hands. By watching carefully our endless desire to love, we come to the growing awareness that we can love only because we have been loved first, and that we can offer intimacy only because we are born out of the very inner intimacy of God.

In our violent times, in which destruction of life is so rampant and the raw wounds of humanity so visible, it is very hard to tolerate the experience of God as a purifying absence, and to keep our hearts open so as to patiently and reverently prepare God's way. We are tempted to grasp rapid solutions instead of inquiring about the validity of the questions. Our inclination to put faith in any suggestion that promises quick healing is so great that it is not surprising that spiritual experiences are mushrooming all over the place and have become highly sought after commercial items. Many people flock to places and persons who promise intensive experiences of togetherness, cathartic emotions of exhilaration and sweetness, and liberating sensations of rapture and ecstasy. In our desperate need for fulfillment and our restless search for the experience of divine intimacy, we are all too prone to construct our own spiritual events. In our impatient culture, it has indeed become extremely difficult to see much salvation in waiting.

But still . . . the God who saves is not made by human hands. God transcends our psychological distinctions between "already" and "not yet," absence and presence, leaving and returning. Only in a patient waiting in expectation can we slowly break away from our illusions and pray as the Psalmist prayed:

> God, you are my God, I pine for you,
> my heart thirsts for you,
> my body longs for you,
> as a land parched, dreary and waterless.
> Thus I have gazed on you in the sanctuary,
> seeing your power and your glory.
>
> Better your faithful love than life itself;
> my lips will praise you.
> Thus I will bless you all my life,
> in your name lift up my hands.
> All my longings fulfilled as with fat and rich foods,
> a song of joy on my lips and praise in my mouth.
>
> On my bed when I think of you,
> I muse on you in the watches of the night,
> for you have always been my help;
> In the shadow of your wings I rejoice;
> my heart clings close to you,
> your right hand supports me.
> (Ps 63:1–8)

Converting Protest into Prayer

When we can cast off our illusions of immortality we create the open-ended space in which we can stretch out our arms to our God, who transcends all our expectations, dreams, and desires. We will probably never be fully free from illusions, just as we will never be fully free from loneliness and hostility. But when we recognize our illusions as illusions, we also will recognize the first outlines of prayer. We are always on the move between the two poles of illusion and prayer. There are times when our daily work absorbs us so fully that the word "prayer" only evokes irritation. There also are times when prayer seems easy, obvious, and nearly another word for living. But usually we find ourselves somewhere in-between; praying while holding on with at least one hand to our cherished belongings, only vaguely aware of their illusory quality.

At some times, however, we are forced again to awaken from this half-asleep-half-awake state. When in a crisis of war, sudden poverty, illness, or death we are confronted with the "absurdities of life," we can no longer remain neutral and are asked to respond. Often our first and most visible response is a protest bursting forth from our bewilderment. It is at these crucial moments of life that we are reminded again of our illusions and asked to convert our protest into prayer. This is a very hard task, but a task leading us not away from reality but closer to it.

> Recently a student who had just finished his long studies for the ministry and was ready to start in his first church suddenly died after a fatal fall from his bike. Those who knew him well felt a strong, angry protest arising from their hearts. Why him, a very noble man who could have done so much for so many? Why now, just when his long, costly education could start bearing fruit? Why in this way, so unprepared and unheroic? There were no answers to all these reasonable questions. A strong, angry protest seemed the only human response.

But such a protest is the continuation of our illusion that we know what life is all about, that we rule it and determine its values as well as its goals. We do not and are challenged instead to convert our protest against the absurdities of the human existence into a prayer lifting us beyond the boundaries of our existence to the One who holds our lives with boundless love and mercy. In our attempts to accept this challenge, we are wise to say to ourselves with the words of the Psalmist:

> Children of men, how long will you be heavy of heart,
> why love what is vain and chase after illusions?
> Realize that Yahweh performs wonders for his faithful,
> Yahweh listens when I call to him.
> (Ps 4:2–3)

8

THE PRAYER
OF THE HEART

■

The Search for the Fitting Way

JUST AS THERE ARE MANY WAYS to be hospitable, there are many ways to pray. When we are serious about prayer and no longer consider it one of the many things people do in life but, rather, the basic receptive attitude out of which all of life can receive new vitality, we will, sooner or later, raise the question: "What is *my* way to pray, what is the prayer of my heart?" Just as artists search for the style that is most their own, so people who pray search for the prayer of their heart. What is most profound in life, and therefore most dear to us, always needs to be properly protected as well as expressed. It is, therefore, not surprising that prayer is often surrounded by carefully prescribed gestures and words, by detailed rituals and elaborate ceremonies.

A visit to a Trappist monastery can help us realize how those who have made themselves free for a life exclusively dedicated to prayer subject themselves to a very strict discipline. The Trappist monk lives his whole life, day and night, in obedience to St. Benedict's rule, the holy rule, which is safeguarded and interpreted with utmost consideration and discretion by the Abbot, the spiritual father of our community. The holy rule is for the prayer life of a Trappist monk like a golden setting for a precious stone. The rule makes the real beauty of prayer visible and allows it to be fully enjoyed. Neglect of the rule means neglect of prayer. The monk who wants to make his whole life, whatever he does, a continuing prayer knows that this is only possible in the context of a very concrete daily schedule that supports him in the realization of his goal. Therefore, we find that in a Trappist monastery, the celebration of the Eucharist, the communal psalmody, the individual meditation, study and manual work, eating and sleeping are all subject to careful regulation and conscientious observance. Anyone who participates in such a life, if only for a few days, can sense the great mystery of prayer that is hidden, as well as visible, in the deep rhythm of the contemplative day.

This little excursion to the Trappists serves to illustrate the fact that no one who seriously wants to live a life of prayer can persevere in that desire and realize it to some degree without a very concrete way. It may be necessary to make many changes in direction and to explore new ways as life develops, but without any way we won't arrive anywhere.

To come to an answer to the personal question: "What is the prayer of my heart?" we first of all have to know how to find this most personal prayer. Where do we look, what do we do, to whom do we go in order to discover how we as individual human beings—with our own histories, our own milieus, our own characters, our own insights, and our own freedom to act—are called to enter into intimacy with God? The question about the prayer of our heart is, in fact, the question about our own most personal vocation.

Words, Silence, and a Guide

It seems possible to establish a few guidelines. A careful look at the lives of people for whom prayer was indeed the only thing needed (see Lk 10:42) shows that three "rules" are always observed: a contemplative reading of the Word of God, a silent listening to the voice of God, and a trusting obedience to a spiritual guide. Without the Bible, without silent time, and without someone to direct us, finding our own way to God is very hard and practically impossible.

In the first place, we have to pay careful attention to the Word of God as it is written in the holy scriptures. St. Augustine was converted when he responded to the words of a child saying: "Take and read, take and read."[1] When he took the Bible and started reading the page on which he opened it, he felt that the words he read were directly spoken to him.

To take the holy scriptures and read them is the first thing we have to do to open ourselves to God's call. Reading the scriptures is not as easy as it seems since in our academic world we tend to make anything and everything we read subject to analysis and discussion. But the Word of God should lead us first of all to contemplation and meditation. Instead of taking the words apart, we should bring them together in our innermost being; instead of wondering if we agree or disagree, we should wonder which words are directly spoken to us and connect directly with our most personal story. Instead of thinking about the words as potential subjects for an interesting dialogue or paper, we should be willing to let them penetrate into the most hidden corners of our hearts, even to those places where no other word has yet found entrance. Then and only then can the Word bear fruit as seed sown in rich soil. Only then can we really "hear and understand" (Mt 13:23).

Second, we simply need quiet time in the presence of God. Although we want to make all our time time for God, we will never succeed if we do not reserve a minute, an hour, a morning, a day, a week, a month, or whatever period of time for God and God alone. This asks for much discipline and risk taking because we always seem to have something more urgent to do and "just sitting there" and "doing nothing" often disturbs us more than it helps. But there is no way around this. Being useless and silent in the presence of our God belongs to the core of all prayer. In the beginning we often hear our own unruly inner noises more loudly than God's voice. This is at times extremely hard to tolerate. But slowly, very slowly, we discover that the silent time makes us quiet and deepens our awareness of ourselves and God. Then, very soon, we start missing these moments when we are deprived of them, and before we are fully aware of it an inner momentum has developed that draws us more and more into silence and closer to that still point where God speaks to us.

Contemplative reading of the holy scriptures and silent time in the presence of God belong closely together. The Word of God draws us into silence; silence makes us attentive to God's Word. The Word of God penetrates through the thick of human verbosity to the silent center of the heart; silence opens in us the space where the Word can be heard. Without reading the Word, silence becomes stale, and without silence, the Word loses its re-creative power. The Word leads to silence and silence to the Word. The Word is born in silence, and silence is the deepest response to the Word.

But Word and silence both need guidance. How do we know that we are not deluding ourselves, that we are not selecting those words that best fit our passions, that we are not just listening to the voice of our own imagination? Many have quoted the scriptures and many have heard voices and seen visions in silence, but only few have found their way to God. Who can be the judge in her own case? Who can determine if his feelings and insights are leading him in the right direction?

Our God is greater than our own hearts and minds, and too easily we are tempted to make our hearts' desires and our minds' speculations into the will of God. Therefore, we need a guide, a director, a counselor who helps us to distinguish between the voice of God and all the other voices coming from our own confusion or from dark powers far beyond our control. We need someone who encourages us when we are tempted to give it all up, to just walk away in despair. We need someone who discourages us when we move too rashly in unclear directions or hurry proudly to a nebulous goal. We need someone who can suggest to us when to read and when to be silent, which words to reflect upon and what to do when silence creates much fear and little peace.

The first and nearly spontaneous reaction to the idea of a spiritual guide is: "Spiritual guides are hard to find." This might be true, but at least part of the reason for this lack of spiritual guides is that we ourselves do not appeal to our fellow human beings in such a way as to invite them to become our spiritual leaders. If there were no students constantly asking for good teachers, there would be no good teachers. The same is true for spiritual guides. There are many men and women with great spiritual sensitivity whose talents remain dormant because we do not make an appeal to them. Many would, in fact, become wise and holy for our sake if we would invite them to assist us in our search for the prayer of our heart. A spiritual director does not necessarily have to be more intelligent or more experienced than we are. It is important that he or she accepts our invitation to lead us closer to God and enters with us into the scriptures and the silence where God speaks to both of us.

When we really want to live a life of prayer and seriously ask ourselves what the prayer of our heart may be, we will also be able to express the type of guidance we need and find that someone is waiting to be asked to give it. Often we will discover that those whom we ask for help will indeed receive the gift to help us and grow with us toward prayer.

Thus, the Bible, silence, and a spiritual director are three important guides in our search for our most personal way to enter into an intimate relationship with God. When we contemplate the scriptures continuously, set some time aside to be silent in the presence of our God, and are willing to submit our experiences with Word and silence to a spiritual guide, we can keep ourselves from developing new illusions and open the way to the prayer of our heart.

The Wisdom of History

Although practically all Christians who want to reach out to their God with faithful perseverance will look at some point in their lives for someone who can be their guide, spiritual guidance is not limited to the one-to-one relationship. The spiritual wisdom of many Christians, who in the course of history have dedicated their lives to prayer, is preserved and relived in the different traditions, lifestyles, or spiritualities that remain visible in contemporary Christianity. In fact, our first and most influential guides are often the prayer customs, styles of worship, and modes of speaking about God that pervade our different milieus.

Each spiritual milieu has its own emphasis. Here silence is stressed, there study of the scriptures; here individual meditation is central, there communal worship; here poverty is the unifying concept, there it is obedience; here the great mystical experiences are suggested as the way to perfection, there the little way of common daily life. Much of the emphasis depends on the time in which a new spirituality found its beginning, on the personal character of the man or woman who was or is its main inspiration, and on the particular needs to which it responds.

The fact that these spiritualities are mostly related to influential historical personalities with great visibility helps us to use them as real guides in the search for our own personal way. Benedict, Francis, Dominic, Juliana of Norwich, Ignatius of Loyola, Teresa of Avila, Jacob Boehme, Francis de Sales, George Fox, John Wesley, Henry Martyn, John Henry Newman, Sören Kierkegaard, Charles de Foucauld, Dag Hammarskjöld, Martin Luther King, Jr., Dorothy Day, Thomas Merton, and many, many others offer us, by their own lives and the lives of their disciples and faithful students, a frame of reference and a point of orientation in our attempts to find the prayer of our heart.

> I remember meeting one day a very shy, somewhat withdrawn man. Although he was very intelligent, it seemed as if the world was just too big for him. Any suggestion that he do something outstanding or special scared him. For him, the little way, the conscientious living of the small realities of everyday life, was the way of prayer. When he spoke about the little Thérèse of Lisieux, his spiritual guide, his eyes lit up and he looked full of joy. But his more passionate neighbor needed the example of Anthony of the Desert or Bernard of Clairvaux and other great spiritual athletes to help him in his search for an authentic spiritual life.

Without such inspiring guides, it is very difficult to remain faithful to the desire to find our own way. It is a hard and often lonely search, and we constantly need new insights, support, and comfort to persevere. The really great saints of history don't ask for imitation. Their way was unique and cannot be repeated. But they invite us into their lives and offer a hospitable space for our own search. Some turn us off and make us feel uneasy; others even irritate us, but among the many great spiritual men and women in history we may find a few, or maybe just one or two, who speak the language of our heart and give us courage. These are our guides. Not to be imitated but to help us live our lives just as authentically as they lived theirs. When we have found such guides we have good reason to be grateful and even better reasons to listen attentively to what they have to say.

The Way of a Pilgrim

Among the many spiritualities, styles of prayer, and ways to God, there is one way that is relatively unknown but might prove to have special relevance in our contemporary spiritual climate. That is the spirituality of Hesychasm, one of the oldest spiritual traditions in the Eastern Orthodox Church, which lately received new attention in the West through the publication of an English edition of *The Way of a Pilgrim*.[2] Rather than giving short descriptions of different spiritual ways, it seems more valuable to discuss in some detail just one way: the way of the Hesychasts. This is valuable not only because Hesychasm illustrates much that has been said but also because what it says has a remarkably modern ring to it.

While all of us are called to search with diligence and perseverance for the prayer of our own heart—i.e., the prayer that is most our own and that forms our unique way of reaching out to our God—Hesychasm makes the prayer of the heart its central concept, gives it a very concrete content, and offers explicit guidelines to realize it.

What, then, is Hesychasm? Hesychasm (from the Greek word *hēsychia* = repose) is a spiritual tradition that found its beginnings in the fifth century, developed in the monasteries on Mount Sinai and later on Mount Athos, was found very much alive during the spiritual renewal in nineteenth-century Russia, and is gradually being discovered by the West as one of the most valuable "schools" of prayer. The prayer in which the hesychastic tradition finds its deepest expression is the Jesus prayer, consisting of the simple words: "Lord Jesus Christ, have mercy upon me." Timothy Ware says concerning the Jesus prayer:

> Around these few words many Orthodox over the centuries have built their spiritual life and through this one prayer they have entered into the deepest mysteries of Christian knowledge.[3]

There is probably no simpler nor livelier way to understand the richness of Hesychasm and the Jesus prayer than by listening to the remarkable story of an anonymous Russian peasant who wandered through his vast country discovering with growing amazement and inner joy the marvelous fruits of the Jesus prayer. In *The Way of a Pilgrim* his story is written down, most probably by a Russian monk whom he met on his journey.

> A few years ago I spent three days in retreat with two close friends. Most of the time we kept silence but after dinner we read to each other the story of the pilgrim. To our own surprise this pleasant and charming spiritual book had a profound influence on us and opened for us a new and very simple way to pray in the midst of our very restless and hectic lives. We still talk about those days as "the days with the pilgrim."

In *The Way of a Pilgrim* the Russian peasant tells us how he goes from town to town, church to church, and monk to monk to find out how to pray without ceasing (see 1 Thes 5:17). After having heard many sermons and consulted many people in vain, he finds a holy starets (monk) who teaches him the Jesus prayer. The starets first reads to him the following words of Simeon the New Theologian:

> Sit down alone and in silence. Lower your head, shut your eyes, breathe out gently and imagine yourself looking into your own heart. Carry your mind, i.e., your thoughts, from your head to your heart. As you breathe out say: "Lord Jesus Christ, have mercy on me." Say it moving your lips gently, or say it in your mind. Try to put all other thought aside. Be calm, be patient and repeat the process very frequently.[4]

After having read this to his visitor, the starets instructs him to say the Jesus prayer three thousand times each day, then six thousand times, then twelve thousand times, and finally—as often as he wants. The pilgrim is very happy to have found a master and follows carefully his instructions. He says:

> Under this guidance I spent the whole summer in ceaseless oral prayer to Jesus Christ, and I felt absolute peace in my soul. During sleep I often dreamed that I was saying the Prayer. And during the day, if I happened to meet anyone, all men without exception were as dear to me as if they had been my nearest relations. . . . I thought of nothing whatever but

my Prayer, my mind tended to listen to it, and my heart began of itself to feel at times a certain warmth and pleasure.[5]

After the death of his holy starets, the peasant wanders from town to town with his prayer. The prayer has given him new strength to deal with all the adversities of the pilgrim life and turns all pains into joy:

> At times I do as much as forty-three or -four miles a day, and do not feel that I am walking at all. I am aware only of the fact that I am saying my Prayer. When the bitter cold pierces me, I begin to say my Prayer more earnestly and I quickly get warm all over. When hunger begins to overcome me, I call more often on the Name of Jesus and I forget my wish for food. When I fall ill and get rheumatism in my back and legs, I fix my thoughts on the Prayer and do not notice the pain. If anyone harms me, I have only to think, "How sweet is the Prayer of Jesus!" and the injury and the anger alike pass away and I forget it all.[6]

The pilgrim, however, has no illusions. He realizes that, notwithstanding these events, his prayer has not yet become the prayer of the heart in the fullest sense. The starets had told him that all these experiences are part of "an artificial state which follows quite naturally upon routine."[7] For the prayer of the heart, he says, "I await God's time." After many unsuccessful attempts to find work and a place to stay, he decides to go to the tomb of St. Innocent of Irkutsk in Siberia.

> My idea was that in the forests and steppes of Siberia I should travel in greater silence and therefore in a way that was better for prayer and reading. And this journey I undertook, all the while saying my oral Prayer without stopping.[8]

It is on this journey that the pilgrim experiences the prayer of the heart for the first time. In very lively, simple, and direct words he tells us how it came about and how it led him into the most intimate relationship with Jesus.

> After no great lapse of time I had the feeling that the Prayer had, so to speak, by its own action passed from my lips to my heart. That is to say, it seemed as though my heart in its ordinary beating began to say the words of the Prayer within at each beat. . . . I gave up saying the Prayer with my lips. I simply listened carefully to what my heart was saying. It

seemed as though my eyes looked right down into it; . . . Then I felt
something like a pain in my heart, and in my thoughts so great a love
for Jesus Christ that I pictured myself, if only I could see Him, throwing
myself at His feet and not letting them go from my embrace, kissing
them tenderly, and thanking Him with tears for having of His love and
grace allowed me to find so great a consolation in His Name, me, His
unworthy and sinful creature! Further there came into my heart a gracious
warmth which spread through my whole breast.[9]

The prayer of the heart gives the pilgrim an immense joy and an unspeak-
able experience of God's presence. Wherever he goes and with whomever
he speaks from here on, he cannot resist speaking about God who dwells
in him. Although he never tries to convert people or change their behavior
but always looks for silence and solitude, he nevertheless finds that the
people he meets respond deeply to him and his words and rediscover God
in their own lives. Thus, the pilgrim, who by his confession of sin and
unceasing supplication for mercy recognizes his distance from God, finds
himself traveling through the world in God's most intimate company and
inviting others to share in it.

With the Mind in the Heart

If we should not move beyond the charming story of the Russian peasant
and are only enamored by the appeal of its nineteenth-century romanticism,
it might lead us no farther than it did Franny and Zooey in J. D. Salinger's
novel, that is, to mental confusion.[10]

The pilgrim's story, however, is just one ripple of the deep mystical
stream of Russian Hesychasm in the nineteenth century. How deep and
powerful this stream really was is revealed in *The Art of Prayer*. This book,
which was one of Thomas Merton's favorites, is an orthodox anthology on
the prayer of the heart, collected by Chariton of Valams, and contains ex-
cerpts of the works of nineteenth-century Russian spiritual writers, in particular, Bishop Theophan the Recluse. It is a rich record of mystical prayer
and shows us one of the most concrete ways to reach out to God from the
center of our innermost self. There we hear Theophan the Recluse say to
one of the many who asked his guidance:

I will remind you of only one thing: one must descend with the mind
into the heart, and there stand before the face of the Lord, ever present,

all seeing within you. The prayer takes a firm and steadfast hold, when a small fire begins to burn in the heart. Try not to quench this fire, and it will become established in such a way that the prayer repeats itself: and then you will have within you a small murmuring stream.[11]

To stand in the presence of God with our minds in our hearts, that is the essence of the prayer of the heart. Theophan expresses in a very succinct way that the prayer of the heart unifies our whole person and places us without any reservation, mind in heart, in the awesome and loving presence of our God.

If prayer were just an intelligent exercise of the mind, we would soon become stranded in fruitless and trivial inner debates with God. If, on the other hand, prayer involved only our hearts, we might soon think that good prayers consist in good feelings. But the prayer of the heart in the most profound sense unites mind and heart in the intimacy of the divine love.

It is about this prayer that the pilgrim speaks, thereby expressing in his own charming, naïve style the profound wisdom of the spiritual forebears of his time. In the expression "Lord Jesus Christ, have mercy upon me," we find a powerful summary of all prayer. It directs itself to Jesus, the son of God, who lived, died, and was raised for us; it declares him to be the Christ, the anointed one, the Messiah, the one we have been waiting for; it calls him our Lord, the Lord of our whole being: body, mind, and spirit, thought, emotions, and actions; and it professes our deepest relationship to him by a confession of our sinfulness and by a humble plea for his forgiveness, mercy, compassion, love, and tenderness.[12]

The prayer of the heart can be a special guide to present-day Christians searching for our own personal way to an intimate relationship to God. More than ever we feel like wandering strangers in a fast-changing world. But we do not want to escape this world. Instead, we want to be fully part of it without drowning in its stormy waters. We want to be alert and receptive to all that happens around us without being paralyzed by inner fragmentation. We want to travel with open eyes through this valley of tears without losing contact with the One who calls us to a new land. We want to respond with compassion to all those whom we meet on our way and ask for a hospitable place to stay while remaining solidly rooted in the intimate love of our God.

The prayer of the heart shows us one possible way. It is indeed like a murmuring stream that continues underneath the many waves of every day and opens the possibility of living in the world without being of it and of reaching out to our God from the center of our solitude.

At Home While Still on the Way

The prayer of the heart requires first of all that we make God our only thought. That means that we must dispel all distractions, concerns, worries, and preoccupations, and fill the mind with God alone. The Jesus prayer, or any other prayer form, is meant to be a help to gently empty our minds from all that is not God, and offer all the room to God alone. But there is more. Our prayer becomes a prayer of the heart when we have localized in the center of our inner being the empty space in which our God-filled mind can descend and vanish, and where the distinctions between thinking and feeling, knowing and experiencing, ideas and emotions are transcended, and where God can become our host.

"The Kingdom of God is among you," Jesus said (Lk 17:21). The prayer of the heart takes these words seriously. When we empty our minds of all thoughts and our hearts of all experiences, we can prepare in the center of our innermost being the home for the God who wants to dwell in us. Then we can say with St. Paul, "It is no longer I, but Christ living in me" (Gal 2:20). Then we can affirm Luther's words, "Grace is the experience of being delivered from experience." And then we can realize that it is not we who pray but the spirit of God who prays in us.

> One of the early Fathers said: "When thieves approach a house in order to creep up to it and steal, and hear someone inside talking, they do not dare to climb in; in the same way, when our enemies try to steal into the soul and take possession of it they creep all round but fear to enter when they hear that . . . prayer welling out.[13]

When our hearts belong to God, the world and its powers cannot steal them from us. When God has become the Ruler of our hearts, our basic alienation is overcome and we can pray with the Psalmist:

> You created my inmost self,
> knit me together in my mother's womb.
> For so many marvels I thank you;
> a wonder am I, and all your works are wonders.
> (Ps 139:13–14)

When God has become our shepherd, our refuge, our fortress, then we can reach out to God in the midst of a broken world and feel at home while still on the way. When God dwells in us, we can enter a wordless dialogue with God while still waiting on the day that we will be led into the house where a place has been prepared for us (Jn 14:2). Then we can wait while we have already arrived and ask while we have already received. Then, indeed, we can comfort each other with the words of Paul.

> Never worry about anything; but tell God all your desires of every kind in prayer and petition shot through with gratitude, and the peace of God which is beyond our understanding will guard your hearts and your thoughts in Christ Jesus. (Phil 4:6–7)

9

COMMUNITY
AND PRAYER

∎

Tabor and Gethsemane

THE MOVEMENT from illusion to prayer requires a gradual detachment from all false ties and an increasing surrender to the One from whom all good things come. It takes courage to move away from the safe place into the unknown, even when we know that the safe place offers false safety and the unknown promises us a saving intimacy with God. We realize quite well that giving up the familiar and reaching out with open arms toward the One who transcends all our mental grasping and clinging makes us very vulnerable. Somewhere we sense that although holding on to our illusions might lead to a truncated life, the surrender in love leads to the Cross. Jesus' way was the way of love but also the way of suffering. To Peter he said:

> When you were young
> you put on your own belt
> and walked where you liked;
> but when you grow old
> you will stretch out your hands,
> and somebody else will put a belt round you
> and take you where you would rather not go.
> (Jn 21:18)

It is a sign of spiritual maturity when we can give up our illusory self-control and stretch out our hands to God. But it would be just another illusion to believe that reaching out to God will free us from pain and suffering. Often, indeed, it will take us where we would rather not go. But

274

we know that without going there we will not find our lives. "Anyone who loses his life . . . will find it" (Mt 16:25), Jesus says, reminding us that love is purified in pain.

Prayer, therefore, is far from sweet and easy. Being the expression of our greatest love, it does not keep pain away from us. Instead, it makes us suffer more since our love for God is a love for a suffering God and our entering into God's intimacy is an entering into the intimacy where all of human suffering is embraced in divine compassion. To the degree that our prayer has become the prayer of our hearts we will love more and suffer more, we will see more light and more darkness, more grace and more sin, more of God and more of humanity. To the degree that we have descended into our hearts and reached out to God from there, solitude can speak to solitude, deep to deep, and heart to heart. It is there where love and pain are found together.

On two occasions, Jesus invited his closest friends, Peter, John, and James, to share in his most intimate prayer. The first time he took them to the top of Mount Tabor, and there they saw his face shining like the sun and his clothes white as light (Mt 17:2). The second time he took them to the garden of Gethsemane, and there they saw his face in anguish and his sweat falling "to the ground like great drops of blood" (Lk 22:44). The prayer of our hearts brings us to both Tabor and Gethsemane. When we have seen God in glory we will also see God in misery, and when we have felt the ugliness of God's humiliation we also will experience the beauty of the transfiguration.

The Hesychasts have always been very much aware of these two inseparable aspects of prayer. While they usually stress detachment in prayer, they do not hesitate to compare the height of prayer with the illumination of Moses on Mount Sinai and with the transfiguration of Jesus on Mount Tabor. Theophan the Recluse writes:

> He who has repented travels towards the Lord. The way to God is an inner journey accomplished in the mind and heart. It is necessary so to attune the thoughts of the mind and the disposition of the heart that the spirit of man will always be with the Lord, as if joined with Him. He who is thus attuned is constantly enlightened by inner light, and receives in himself the rays of spiritual radiance . . . like Moses, whose face was glorified on the Mount because he was illumined by God.[1]

While waiting patiently in expectation is the foundation of the spiritual life, we also know that this waiting is full of joy since in prayer we already see the glory of the One we are waiting for.

The Community of Faith

Much that has been said about prayer thus far might create the false impression that prayer is a private, individualistic, and nearly secret affair, so personal and so deeply hidden in our inner life that it can hardly be talked about, even less shared. The opposite is true. Just because prayer is so personal and arises from the center of our life, it is to be shared with others. Just because prayer is the most precious expression of being human, it needs the constant support and protection of the community to grow and flower. Just because prayer is our highest vocation needing careful attention and faithful perseverance, we cannot allow it to be a private affair. Just because prayer asks for a patient waiting in expectation, it should never become the most individualistic expression of the most individualistic emotion but should always remain embedded in the life of the community of which we are part.

Prayer as a hopeful and joyful waiting for God is a really unhuman or superhuman task unless we realize that we do not have to wait alone. In the community of faith we can find the climate and the support to sustain and deepen our prayer and we are enabled to constantly look forward beyond our immediate and often narrowing private needs. The community of faith offers the protective boundaries within which we can listen to our deepest longings, not to indulge in morbid introspection but to find our God, to whom they point. In the community of faith we can listen to our feelings of loneliness, to our desires for an embrace or a kiss, to our sexual urges, to our cravings for sympathy, compassion, or just a good word; also to our search for insight and to our hope for companionship and friendship. In the community of faith we can listen to all these longings and find the courage not to avoid them or cover them up but to confront them in order to discern God's presence in their midst. There we can affirm each other in our waiting and also in the realization that in the center of our waiting the first intimacy with God is found. There we can be patiently together and let the suffering of each day convert our illusions into the prayer of a contrite people. The community of faith is indeed the climate and source of all prayer.

A People Fashioned by God

The word "community" usually refers to a way of being together that gives us a sense of belonging. Often students complain that they do not experience much community in their schools; ministers and priests wonder how they can create better communities in their parishes; and social workers, overwhelmed by the alienating influences of modern life, try hard to form communities in the neighborhoods they are working in. In all these situations the word "community" points to a way of togetherness in which people can experience themselves as a meaningful part of a larger group.

Although we can say the same about the Christian community, it is important to remember that the Christian community is a waiting community, that is, a community which creates not only a sense of belonging but also a sense of estrangement. In the Christian community we say to each other, "We are together, but we cannot fulfill each other . . . we help each other, but we also have to remind each other that our destiny is beyond our togetherness." The support of the Christian community is a support in common expectation. That requires a constant criticism of anyone who makes the community into a safe shelter or a cozy clique, and a constant encouragement to look forward to what is to come.

The basis of the Christian community is not the family tie, or social or economic equality, or shared oppression or complaint, or mutual attraction . . . but the divine call. The Christian community is not the result of human efforts. God has made us into chosen people by calling us out of "Egypt" to the "New Land," out of the desert to fertile ground, out of slavery to freedom, out of our sin to salvation, out of captivity to liberation. All these words and images give expression to the fact that the initiative belongs to God and that God is the source of our new life together. By our common call to the New Jerusalem, we recognize each other on the road as brothers and sisters. Therefore, as the people of God, we are called *ekklesia* (from the Greek *kaleo* = call; and *ek* = out), the community called out of the old world into the new.

Since our desire to break the chains of our alienation is very strong today, it is of special importance to remind each other that, as members of the Christian community, we are primarily not for each other but for God. Our eyes should not remain fixed on each other but be directed forward to what is dawning on the horizon of our existence. We discover each other by following the same vocation and by supporting each other in the same search. Therefore, the Christian community is not a closed circle of people embracing each other but a forward-moving group of companions bound together by the same voice asking for their attention.

It is quite understandable that in our large, anonymous cities we look for people on our "wavelength" to form small communities. Prayer groups, Bible-study clubs, and house-churches all are ways of restoring or deepening our awareness of belonging to the people of God. But sometimes a false type of like-mindedness can narrow our sense of community. We all should have the mind of Jesus Christ, but we do not all have to have the mind of a schoolteacher, a carpenter, a bank director, a congressional representative, or whatever socioeconomic or political group.

There is a great wisdom hidden in the old bell tower calling people with very different backgrounds away from their homes to form one body in Jesus Christ. It is precisely by transcending the many individual differences that we can become witnesses of God, who allows divine light to shine upon poor and rich, healthy and sick alike. But it is also in this encounter on the way to God that we become aware of our neighbor's needs and begin to heal each other's wounds.

> During the last few years I was part of a small group of students who regularly celebrated the Eucharist together. We felt very comfortable with each other and had found "our own way." The songs we sang, the words we used, the greetings we exchanged all seemed quite natural and spontaneous. But when a few new students joined us, we discovered that we expected them to follow our way and go along with "the way we do things here." We had to face the fact that we had become clannish, substituting our minds for the mind of Jesus Christ. Then we found out how hard it is to give up familiar ways and create space for the strangers, to make a new common prayer possible.

Not without reason the Church is called a "pilgrim church," always moving forward. The temptation to settle in a comfortable oasis, however, has often been too great to resist, and frequently the divine call is forgotten and unity broken. At those times not just individuals but whole groups are caught in the illusion of safety, and prayer is shriveled into a partisan affair.

This explains why ideas, concepts, and techniques developed and used in contemporary groups cannot be transposed without careful consideration to the Christian community. When we describe the ideal Christian community as a "happy family" or as a "group of very sensitive people" or as an "action or pressure group," we speak about only a secondary and often temporary trait. Although it might be helpful to incorporate into the life of the Christian community behavior patterns and techniques which are derived from other forms of group life, we will have to relativize these attempts by making them subservient to the self-understanding of the Christian community as a people fashioned by God.

Many interpersonal processes, leadership patterns, and strategies that have been identified by psychological and sociological studies of groups can indeed offer new insight in understanding the life of the Christian community.

But the unique nature of the Christian community requires a constant awareness of the limited applicability of these findings. While living between the
first and second coming of Jesus Christ, the Christian community finds its
meaning in a patient waiting in expectation for the time when God will be
all in all. The community of faith always points beyond itself and speaks
its own unique language, which is the language of prayer.

The Language of the Community

Prayer is the language of the Christian community. In prayer the nature of
the community becomes visible because in prayer we direct ourselves to the
One who forms the community. We do not pray to each other, but together
we pray to God, who calls us and makes us into a new people. Praying is
not one of the many things the community does. Rather, it is its very being.
Many discussions about prayer do not take this very seriously. Sometimes
it seems as if the Christian community is "so busy" with its projects and
plans that there is neither the time nor the mood to pray. But when prayer
is no longer its primary concern, and when its many activities are no longer
seen and experienced as part of prayer itself, the community quickly degenerates into a club with a common cause but no common vocation.

By prayer, community is created as well as expressed. Prayer is first of
all the realization of God's presence in the midst of God's people and, therefore, the realization of the community itself. Most clear and most noticeable
are the words, the gestures, and the silence through which the community
is formed. When we listen to the Word, we not only receive insight into
God's saving work but also experience a new mutual bond. When we stand
around the altar, eat bread and drink wine, kneel in meditation, or walk in
procession we not only remember God's work in human history but also
become aware of God's creative presence here and now. When we sit together in silent prayer, we create a space where we sense that the One we
are waiting for is already touching us, as that One touched Elijah standing
in front of the cave (1 Kgs 19:13).

But the same words, gestures, and silence are also the ways in which the
community reaches out to the One it is waiting for. The words we use are
words of longing. The little piece of bread we eat and the little portion of
wine we drink make us aware of our most profound hunger and thirst, and
the silence deepens our sensitivity to the calling voice of God. Therefore,
the prayer of the community is also the expression of its unfulfillment and
desire to reach the house of God. Thus the praying community celebrates

God's presence while waiting and affirms God's absence while recognizing that God is already in its midst. Thus God's presence becomes a sign of hope and God's absence a call for penance.

Prayer as the language of the community is like our original tongue. Just as children learn to speak from their parents, brothers, sisters, and friends but still develop their own unique ways of expressing themselves, so our individual prayer life develops by the care of the praying community. Sometimes it is hard to point to any specific organizational structure which we can call "our community." Our community is often a very intangible reality made up of people living as well as dead, present as well as absent, close as well as distant, old as well as young. But without some form of community individual prayer cannot be born or developed. Communal and individual prayer belong together as two folded hands. Without community, individual prayer easily degenerates into egocentric and eccentric behavior, but without individual prayer, the prayer of the community quickly becomes a meaningless routine.

Individual and community prayer cannot be separated without harm. This explains why spiritual leaders tend to be very critical of those who want to isolate themselves and why they stress the importance of continuing ties with a larger community where individual prayer can be guided. This also explains why the same leaders have always encouraged the individual members of their communities to spend time and energy in personal prayer, realizing as they do that community alone can never fulfill the desire for the most unique intimate relationship between a human being and his or her God.

Until the Last Day

The prayer of the heart can grow strong and deep within the boundaries of the community of faith. The community of faith, strengthened in love by our individual prayers, can lift them up as a sign of hope in common praise and thanksgiving. Together we reach out to God beyond our many individual limitations while offering each other the space for our own most personal searches. We may be very different people with different nationalities, colors, histories, characters, and aspirations, but God has called all of us away from the darkness of our illusions into the light of divine glory. This common call transforms our world into the place where Gethsemane and Tabor both can exist, our time into the time of patient but joyful waiting for the last day, and ourselves into each other's brothers and sisters. St. Paul encourages us to be faithful to this common call when he writes:

> You are well aware in any case that the Day of the Lord is going to come like a thief in the night. . . . But you . . . do not live in the dark, that the Day should take you unawares like a thief. No, you are all children of light and children of the day: we do not belong to the night or to darkness, so we should not go on sleeping, as everyone else does, but stay wide awake and sober. . . . Let us put on faith and love for a breast-plate, and the hope of salvation for a helmet. God . . . destined us . . . to win salvation through our Lord Jesus Christ, who died for us so that, awake or asleep, we should still live united to him. So give encouragement to each other, and keep strengthening one another." (1 Thes 5:2–11)

When we reach out to God individually as well as in community, constantly casting off the illusions that keep us captive, we can enter into this intimate union while still waiting for the day of Christ's final return. Then the words of the old pilgrim song become our words:

> I lift my eyes to the mountains;
> where is my help to come from?
> My help comes from Yahweh
> who made heaven and earth.
>
> May he save your foot from stumbling;
> may he, your guardian, not fall asleep!
> You see—he neither sleeps nor slumbers,
> the guardian of Israel.
>
> Yahweh is your guardian, your shade,
> Yahweh, at your right hand.
> By day the sun will not strike you,
> nor the moon by night.
>
> Yahweh guards you from all harm
> Yahweh guards your life,
> Yahweh guards your comings and goings,
> henceforth and for ever.
> (Ps 121)

CONCLUSION

∎

ON THE NIGHT before his death, Jesus said to his Apostles:

> In a short time you will no longer see me,
> and then a short time later you will see me again. . . .
> In all truth I tell you,
> you will be weeping and wailing
> while the world will rejoice;
> you will be sorrowful,
> but your sorrow will turn to joy. . . .
> you are sad now,
> but I shall see you again, and your hearts will be full of joy,
> and that joy no one shall take from you.
> (Jn 16:16–22)

We are living in this short time, a time, indeed, full of sadness and sorrow. To live this short time in the spirit of Jesus Christ means to reach out from the midst of our pains and to let them be turned into joy by the love of the One who came within our reach. We do not have to deny or avoid our loneliness, our hostilities and illusions. To the contrary: When we have the courage to let these realities come to our full attention, understand them, and confess them, then they can slowly be converted into solitude, hospitality, and prayer.

This does not imply that a mature spiritual life is a life in which our old lonely, hostile selves with all their illusions simply disappear and we live in complete serenity with peaceful minds and pure hearts. Just as our adulthood shows the marks of the struggles of our youth, so our solitude bears the signs of lonely hours, our care for others reflects at times angry feelings, and our prayer sometimes reveals the memory and the presence of many illusions. Transformed in love, however, these painful signs become signs of hope, as the wounds of Jesus did for the doubting Thomas.

Once we have been touched in the midst of our struggles and had created in us the burning desire to be forever united with God, we will find the courage and the confidence to prepare the way of the Lord and to invite all who share our lives to wait with us during this short time for the day of complete joy. With this new courage and new confidence we can strengthen each other with the hopeful words of Paul to Titus:

> God's grace has been revealed to save the whole human race; it has taught us that we should give up everything contrary to true religion and all our worldly passions; we must be self-restrained and live upright and religious lives in this present world, waiting in hope for the blessing which will come with the appearing of the glory of our great God and Saviour Christ Jesus. (Ti 2:11–13)

NOTES

Preface

1. Dante Alighieri, *The Divine Comedy,* "Inferno," Canto I.
2. John Climacus, *The Ladder of Divine Ascent,* trans. by Lazarus Moore (New York: Harper & Row, 1959), p. 203.

1. A Suffocating Loneliness

1. *Newsweek,* Jan. 15, 1973.
2. Henry David Thoreau, *Walden and Other Writings* (New York: Modern Library, 1950), pp. 723–24.
3. Kahlil Gilbran, *The Prophet* (New York: Alfred A. Knopf, 1951), pp. 15–16.
4. *Zen Flesh, Zen Bones,* comp. by Paul Reps (Garden City, N.Y.): Doubleday, Anchor Books, 1961), pp. 30–31.

2. A Receptive Solitude

1. Rainer Maria Rilke, *Letters to a Young Poet,* trans. by M. D. Herter (New York: W. W. Norton, 1954), pp. 18–19.
2. Ibid., pp. 34–35.
3. Ibid., pp. 46–47.
4. Anne Morrow Lindbergh, *Gift from the Sea* (New York: Pantheon Books, 1955), p. 40.
5. Thomas Merton, *The Sign of Jonas* (Garden City, N.Y.: Doubleday, Image Books, 1956), p. 261.
6. Thomas Merton, *Conjectures of a Guilty Bystander* (Garden City, N.Y.: Doubleday, Image Books, 1968), pp. 157–58.
7. Rilke, *Letters to a Young Poet,* p. 59.
8. Lindbergh, *Gift from the Sea,* p. 40.

9. Gilbran, *The Prophet,* p. 50.

3. A Creative Response

1. Merton, *The Sign of Jonas,* p. 323.
2. Thomas Merton, *Contemplation in a World of Action* (Garden City, N.Y.: Doubleday, Image Books, 1973), p. 161.
3. Ibid., p. 165.

4. Creating Space for Strangers

1. Thoreau, *Walden,* p. 65.
2. See Carlos Castaneda, *A Separate Reality* (New York: Simon & Schuster, 1971), especially pp. 218–19.
3. *Zen Flesh, Zen Bones,* p. 5.

6. Hospitality and the Host

1. Johannes Metz, *Poverty of Spirit,* trans. by John Drury (New York: Newman Press, 1960), p. 45.

7. Prayer and Mortality

1. *New York Times,* Aug. 11, 1974, sec. 4, p. 18.
2. Regulae Breviter Tractatae, 296, II, 2.742C. See J. E. Bamberger, "MNHMH—DIATHESIS, The Psychic Dynamism in the Ascetical Theology of St. Basil," *Orientalia Christiana Periodica,* vol. 34, fasc. 2, 1968.
3. *The Art of Prayer,* comp. by Khariton (London: Faber & Faber, 1966), p. 119.
4. Thomas Merton, *New Seeds of Contemplation* (New York: New Directions, 1961), p. 159.
5. Simone Weil, *First and Last Notebooks,* trans. by Richard Rees (New York: Oxford University Press, 1970), p. 99.

8. The Prayer of the Heart

1. *Confessions of St. Augustine,* trans. by F. J. Sheed (New York: Sheed & Ward, 1943), p. 178.
2. *The Way of a Pilgrim,* trans. by R. M. French (New York: Seabury Press, 1965).
3. Introduction, *The Art of Prayer,* p. 9.
4. *The Way of a Pilgrim,* p. 10.
5. Ibid., p. 16.
6. Ibid., pp. 17–18.
7. Ibid., p. 18.
8. Ibid., p. 19.
9. Ibid., pp. 19–20.

10. J. D. Salinger, *Franny and Zooey* (Boston: Little, Brown, 1961).

11. *The Art of Prayer,* p. 110.

12. See Anthony Bloom, *Living Prayer* (Springfield, Ill.: Templegate, 1966); *Beginning to Pray* (New York: Paulist Press, 1970); *Courage to Pray* (New York: Paulist Press, 1973).

13. *The Art of Prayer,* p. 110.

9. Community and Prayer

1. *The Art of Prayer,* p. 73.